Coordenação Científica da Colecção Ciências e Culturas
João Rui Pita e Ana Leonor Pereira

Os originais enviados são sujeitos a apreciação científica por *referees*

Coordenação Editorial
Maria João Padez Ferreira de Castro

Edição
Imprensa da Universidade de Coimbra
Email: imprensa@uc.pt
URL: http://www.uc.pt/imprensa_uc

Design
António Barros

Pré-Impressão
Imprensa da Universidade de Coimbra

Capa
© 2009 Neno - Portugal • I have a lepidoptera in my face. Cortesia Museu da
Ciência da Universidade de Coimbra • Mail-Art: A (R)evolução de Darwin

Print By
CreateSpace

ISBN
978-989-26-0137-3

ISBN Digital
978-989-26-0342-1

DOI
https://doi.org/10.14195/978-989-26-0342-1

Depósito Legal
336324/11

Os volumes desta coleção encontram-se indexados e catalogados
na Basedados da Web of Science.

© Dezembro 2011, Imprensa da Universidade de Coimbra

Ana Leonor Pereira
João Rui Pita
Pedro Ricardo
Fonseca
(eds.)

Darwin,
Evolution,
Evolutionisms

I
IMPRENSA DA UNIVERSIDADE DE COIMBRA
COIMBRA UNIVERSITY PRESS
U

• COIMBRA 2011

SUMMARY

ANA LEONOR PEREIRA; JOÃO RUI PITA; PEDRO RICARDO FONSECA
INTRODUCTION 9

ANA LEONOR PEREIRA
THE DARWINIAN REVOLUTION IN THE SCIENCES
OF LIFE AND MAN 11

JOÃO RUI PITA; ANA LEONOR PEREIRA; PEDRO RICADO FONSECA
DARWIN, EVOLUTION, EVOLUTIONISMS:
A SELECTIVE CHRONOLOGY (1809-2009) 19

ANTONIO GONZÁLEZ BUENO
FROM LINNÉ TO DARWIN:
THE THEORIES ON THE ORIGIN OF SPECIES 23

JORGE PAIVA
DARWIN, PLANTS AND PORTUGAL 39

LEONEL PEREIRA
CORALLINES AND OTHER MACRO-ALGAE COLLECTED
DURING THE *BEAGLE* VOYAGE 53

ANNA CAROLINA K. P. REGNER
THE 'INTERPLAY OF THE ACTUAL AND THE POSSIBLE'
IN *THE ORIGIN OF SPECIES* 63

JACINTA MARIA MATOS
DARWIN'S *VOYAGE OF THE BEAGLE* AS SCIENTIFIC TRAVEL WRITING:
THE ORIGINS AND EVOLUTION OF A GENRE 69

PALMIRA FONTES DA COSTA
THE MEANING OF MONSTROSITIES IN CHARLES DARWIN'S UNDERSTANDING
ON THE ORIGIN OF SPECIES 75

MARIA MANUELA ALVAREZ
THE CONTRIBUTION OF GENETICS TO THE
EVOLUTION OF EVOLUTION 85

PEDRO RICARDO FONSECA
A DISCIPLE OF RONALD AYLMER FISHER IN PORTUGAL:
WILFRED LESLIE STEVENS IN THE ANTHROPOLOGICAL SCHOOL
OF COIMBRA DURING THE EARLY 1940's.................................... 91

RICARDO S. REIS DOS SANTOS; FRANCISCO CARRAPIÇO
DARWIN AND MERESCHKOWSKY: TWO IMAGES,
TWO EVOLUTIONARY CONCEPTS... 95

GÖKHAN AKBAY
FUNCTION, NATURAL SELECTION AND INFORMATION.................... 101

RITA SERRA
DARWIN, EVOLUTION AND PROGRESS 107

RICARDO S. REIS DOS SANTOS
EVOLUTION, PROGRESS AND THE CONFUSION OF THINGS...................... 113

SUSANA A.M. VARELA
SEXUAL SELECTION AND THE CULTURAL INHERITANCE
OF FEMALE MATING PREFERENCES...................................... 121

JOÃO ARRISCADO NUNES
THE STAKES OF DIVERSITY AND SEXUAL SELECTION:
ON NORMATIVE COMMITMENTS IN EVOLUTIONARY BIOLOGY 127

MARIA HELENA SANTANA
LITERATURE AND DARWINISM: AN INCURSION IN
PORTUGUESE NOVELS FROM THE END OF THE 19TH CENTURY................ 133

ALVES JANA
DARWINISTS, BUT NOT MUCH 141

DANIEL RODRIGUES
EDUCATION, SCIENCE AND SOCIAL DARWINISM IN
NAZI GERMANY: FORMATION OF A SOCIETY BASED ON
THE MYTH OF BLOOD AND SUPERIORITY OF THE ARIAN RACE 145

JOÃO PAULO AVELÃS NUNES
NEO-DARWINISM AND POLITICO-IDEOLOGICAL CONCEPTIONS IN PORTUGAL
DURING THE FIRST HALF OF THE 20TH CENTURY 151

SÉRGIO NETO
FROM THE ARIAN MYTH TO THE LUSO-TROPICALISM:
ECHOES OF SOCIAL DARWINISM IN PORTUGUESE FOREIGN PRESS 157

CONCEIÇÃO TAVARES
DYNAMICS AND SINGULARITIES OF SCIENTIFIC APPROPRIATION:
DARWINISM IN THE AZORES 163

JOSÉ FONFRÍA DÍAZ; ALFREDO BARATAS DÍAZ
DARWINISM IN *LA REVISTA EUROPEA* 169

JOSÉ MORGADO PEREIRA
THE INFLUENCES OF DARWIN'S THOUGHT AND
DARWINISM IN PORTUGUESE PSYCHIATRY 175

Introduction

Darwin, Evolution, Evolutionisms

One hundred and fifty years ago, more precisely on the 24th of November of 1859, Darwin introduced a new paradigm in natural history with the publication of *On the origin of species by means of natural selection, or the preservation of favoured races in the struggle for life*. As epistemology has already acknowledged, the *Darwinian theory of descent with modification* or *theory of natural selection* took around twenty years to be formulated, roughly between 1837 and 1859. The history of Darwinism and of evolution clearly illustrates the fertility of the *theory of natural selection,* in the field of the sciences of life and of man, as in the cultural field. Like almost everywhere else across the globe, Portugal's reception of Darwin began in the 1860's, featuring surprising novelties, especially if we take into account the country's level of development at the time.

The meeting "Darwin, Darwinisms and evolution" took place in Coimbra between the 22nd and the 23rd of September 2009. This meeting's main purpose was to provide a space of open discussion to all of those interested in the issue, both on the national and the international level. The meeting had, therefore, an international dimension, with the participation of researchers from different countries.

A CD-ROM incorporating some of the papers presented at the meeting has been edited under the title *Darwin, darwinismos, evolução (1859-2009)*. Many of the papers were reviewed and extended. The present work gathers together the reviewed and extended papers in English, in order to gain greater visibility among the international scientific community.

Ana Leonor Pereira
João Rui Pita
Pedro Ricardo Fonseca
(Editors)

Ana Leonor Pereira

Faculdade de Letras; CEIS20-Grupo de História e Sociologia da Ciência,
Universidade de Coimbra, Portugal

THE DARWINIAN REVOLUTION IN THE SCIENCES OF LIFE AND MAN[1]

In 1859, with the publication of *On the origin of species by means of natural selection,
or the preservation of favoured races in the struggle for life,* Darwin inaugurated a new
understanding of the historicity and the diversity of living organisms, including
the human species. This new understanding is called *descent with modification by
natural selection.* According to Darwinian theory, plant and animal species, including
the human species, reproduce at such a fast rate and so abundantly that the struggle
for life becomes inevitable: the struggle among individuals of the same species, the
struggle among individuals of different species, the struggle with the physical conditions
of life; the struggle for food, the struggle for descent, the struggle for territory. Species
multiplication is the force that initiates the struggle from which the survival of
the fittest and the elimination of the least fit will take place, i. e., the natural selection
of the advantageous variations and, consequently, adaptive evolution. Although the
struggle is fundamental, not-less important is the raw material upon which natural
selection operates: variation. Natural selection is more than a mechanism solely
devoted to the preservation and elimination of (respectively) favourable and harmful
individual variations in the adaptation process; it is also a "creative" agency, albeit
without any sort of *a priori* project – a feature well illustrated by Charles Darwins'
diagram of the tree of life.

Alluding to François Jacob's book *The Possible and the Actual* – that is urging a new
Portuguese edition –, we will state that variations are integrated and disposed "in adaptive
coherent sets, adjusted during millions and millions of generations, in response to the
challenge of the environment. It is natural selection that [...] slowly, progressively,
elaborates more complex structures, new organs, new species".[2] In the "*bricolage* of
evolution" (Jacob: 57-97; our italics), the randomness of variations and the constant
interaction of organisms with the environment, intersected by *contingency*, structures
the history of life. Thus, the *theory of descent with modification by natural selection*
also distances itself from vitalistic theologisms, whether from previous transformist
theories, whether from the traditional essentialist fixism. According to François Jacob,
"the Darwinian conception has, therefore, a fatal consequence: the present living

---

[1] The contents of the present chapter have been addressed in greater detail in: PEREIRA, Ana Leonor,
Darwin em Portugal, Coimbra, Almedina, 2001.

[2] Translated into English from the Portuguese edition: JACOB, François. 1985. *O jogo dos possíveis.
Ensaio sobre a diversidade do mundo vivo.* Lisboa: Gradiva, p. 34.

world, as we perceive it, is only one amongst many other possible. (...) It could well have been different. It could even not exist at all" (*Idem*: 34-35).

Darwin verifies the struggle of living beings among themselves, for territory, for food, for descent, being the survival of the fittest (natural selection), i. e., the survival of those that present useful and advantageous variations, the keystone of the genealogical differentiation by divergence and isolation. According to the Darwinian paradigm, the living world does not bear the marks of *necessity* and of *perfecting harmony*, neither is it the only, or the best, of all possible worlds, as postulated by Lamarck's *transformism*. It bears the marks of *randomness,* of *contingency,* of *unpredictability,* of *imperfection* and *improvisation.* Half a century after Lamarck's *Philosophie Zoologique* (1809), the Darwinian paradigm revolutionised both essentialist creationism and Lamarckian transformism.

Darwin's scientific revolution was possible thanks to a set of factors of diverse nature, among which, undoubtedly, we have to highlight the progresses achieved in the Earth and Life sciences, during the first half of the 19th century. It is the case of Charles Lyell's *Principles of Geology* (1830-1833), and his doctrine of *actual causes* or *actualism/uniformitarianism.* A good deal of knowledge on geology, biogeography, palaeontology, embryology and other fields, the voyage of the *Beagle,* Malthus' *Principle of Population,* the anxiety caused by the essay of the naturalist A. R. Wallace in 1858, the *genius* of Darwin – these are some of the factors usually invoked to explain the Darwinian revolution in the sciences of Life and Man. Like the scientific revolutions led by Newton in 1687, by Planck in 1900, by Einstein in 1905, Darwin also spent around twenty years (1839-1859) to elaborate and turn public the *theory of descent with modification by natural selection.* Darwin was thirty years old when he started to conceive the new theory and at the age of fifty he published his masterpiece *The Origin of Species* which spread all over the world, in eleven languages until his death in 1882, and in a total of twenty-nine languages by 1977. Around twelve years later, Charles Darwin explored the *"long argument"* of 1859 in more detail, particularly regarding the human species, in *The descent of man, and selection in relation to sex,* 1871 and *The expression of the emotions in man and animals,* 1872. From our point of view, in these two books, Charles Darwin, although recognising and stating his lack of knowledge on the laws of heredity, continued his enormous endeavour of arguing in favour of *the theory of descent with modification by natural selection,* commonly known as the theory of evolution. It is important to recall that Charles Darwin, during the voyage of the *Beagle* (1831-1836), read Charles Lyell's *Principles of Geology* (1830-1833), and that the British geologist was publicizing Lamarckian transformism under the name of the theory of evolution. Due to this reason, and others, Darwin obviously avoided the term evolution.

It is in 1871, in the first edition of the book *The descent of man,* that the noun evolution appears for the first time. Descent with modification becomes synonymous to gradual evolution. Later, in 1872, in the sixth edition of *The Origin of Species,* considered the definitive version, the term evolution appears five times. Evidently, the theory of gradual evolution, by natural selection of random variations, innovated the semantic charge of the term evolution, especially regarding the meaning that H. Spencer had generalised since 1852 in "The development hypothesis" (reproduced, for example, in *Essays: scientific, political, and speculative.* London, Williams and Norgate, 1868, vol. I, pp. 377-383). H. Spencer generalised the law of embryonic development (epigenesis) of Von Baer to build a universal philosophical formula: the evolutionary law of development from a simple, undifferentiated and incoherent homogeneity to a complex, differentiated and coherent heterogeneity.

In 1852, Spencer advanced the hypothesis of the evolution of species from the most simple monad (the homogeneity of a common egg, the only matrix of all living things), grounding his reflexion on embryologic development. The theory of evolution, "the Theory of Evolution" held by Herbert Spencer, since 1852, was much different from the theory of descent with modification published by Darwin in 1859. Darwin was perfectly aware that his *The Origin of Species* introduced a new evolutionary logic of life. This explains why, in the historical survey on the idea of the mutability of species before 1859 that Darwin included in the sixth edition of *The Origin of Species,* none of the thirty four authors mentioned are presented as pioneers of his evolutionary theory. Not even Lamarck or Herbert Spencer. Although Darwin's theory had given a new meaning to the term evolution, the misinterpretations were inevitable.

It has been acknowledged that Darwin linked natural selection to the Spencerian phrase "the survival of the fittest", and this linkage has functioned as a bridge to understand the lasting commitment between Darwinism and Spencerian Evolutionism in the history of international culture. Indeed, in the 5th edition of *The Origin of Species* (1869), Darwin introduced the Spencerian expression "the survival of the fittest", not only in the text, but also in the title of chapter IV ("natural selection; or the survival of the fittest"). Darwin justified his usage of the Spencerian expression "the survival of the fittest" as synonymous of natural selection, saying textually: "the expression often used by Mr. Herbert Spencer of the Survival of the Fittest is more accurate, and is sometimes equally convenient". However, it was Herbert Spencer in his *Principles of Biology* (1864-1867), who took the initiative to identify the principle of "the survival of the fittest" with Darwinian natural selection: "§ 165. This survival of the fittest, which I have here sought to express in mechanical terms, is that which Mr. Darwin has called natural selection, or the preservation of favoured races in the struggle for life", (*The principles of biology*, London, Williams and Norgate, 1880, vol. 1, pp. 444-445). Darwin limited himself to accept the identification, proposed by Herbert Spencer, between the latter's expression "the survival of the fittest", and his own "natural selection", which, although possibly causing some perplexity, leads us to admit the following: Darwin (who did not sympathise with Spencer) aimed to highlight that his theory had as domains the sciences of Life and Man, from psychology to history according to what he had written in 1859. He might also have aimed at opening some loophole in the Spencerian philosophical system or simply at broadening his audience. What is certain is that, since the end of the seventh decade of the 19th century, Darwin's theory circulated in local and global cultures almost always submissive to ideas of an illuminist nature (like the ideas of *progress* and *perfectibility)* and even dominated/forged by philosophical systems like H. Spencer's evolutionism or Ernst Hæckel's evolutionary monism.

Most interestingly, while presenting his work *The descent of man* (1871), Darwin distinguished and complimented Hæckel's work, among the various works on the animal ascendency of man, published after the 1st edition of *The origin of species,* in 1859. References were made to the results that had been published by Wallace, Th. Huxley, Lyell, Vogt, Lubbock, Büchner, Rolle, etc., but these did not exceed the normal procedure among peers of a scientific community. Very different were the words Darwin dedicated to Hæckel's work and particularly to his *Natürliche Schöpfungsgeschichte* (1868), which suggests a communion of ideas between the English naturalist and the German naturalist-philosopher. Darwin gives the idea that his work *The descent of man, and selection in relation to sex*, brings nothing innovative in regards to the Hæckelian *Natürliche Schöpfungsgeschichte*. Even regarding the theme of *sexual selection*, Darwin states in *The Descent of Man* that, after 1859, only the German zoologist understood it. But, symptomatically, Darwin says nothing about the monist-evolutionary determinism of the universe, of the earth, and of life, elaborated by Hæckel, or particularly about the philosophical and political value of the mechanicist naturalization of man and his history that Hæckel defended in his *Natürliche Schöpfungsgeschichte* (1868).

On the other hand, although Darwin's work of 1871 directs the reader to Hæckel's genealogic trees, it shows itself cautious regarding the *fundamental biogenetic law* and all the remaining laws of the German naturalist's authorship, as, for example, the law of evolution (divergence and progress), the laws of heredity and adaptation, etc. This means that, even in the field of scientific inferences and deductions, Darwin's work *The Descent of Man* is not that close to Hæckel's *Natürliche Schöpfungsgeschichte*. What distances Darwin from Hæckel is not only the philosophical and political intent of the German naturalist, but also the invincible distance between Darwin's original theory and Hæckel's idiosyncratic version of the same theory, even though, apparently, Hæckel did not question natural selection as the main mechanism of organic evolution.

The doctrinal nucleus that gives unity to Darwin's work and upholds his reading of the history of the human species, explained in 1871, in his book *The Descent of Man*, is the theory of evolution by natural selection, meaning the "preservation of favoured races" or the "survival of the fittest", in the struggle for life.

This statement, apparently peaceful, is far from consensual among darwinologists. The specialist Yvette Conry, namely in "Le statut de *La descendance de l'homme et la sélection sexuelle*", in *De Darwin au darwinisme: science et idéologie*, Paris, 1983, considers that the anthropo-historical and social theory of Darwin, presented in *The Descent of Man*, departs from the biological theory of 1859. In a few lines, the author argues that in *The Origin of Species*, Darwin operated a scientific revolution, whereas in 1871, the key concept of natural selection started to function as a law of progress, transfiguring the Darwinian evolution. Moreover, the latter covered itself with the ideological mantel of triumphant liberalism. According to Yvette Conry's perspective, the history of man is not presented in rigorously naturalistic moulds, since the book of 1871 conveys a set of ideological norms present in the works of Spencer, Bagehot, Galton and others, as, for example, the technological criteria to evaluate the degree of civilization, the colonising myths, the hierarchy of human races, the cultural universalism of an European matrix, the superiority of the European civilization, etc. For Yvette Conry, one of the best indicators of the non-scientific character of the book of 1871 is the lack of rigour in the distinction of the terms nation, race and population.

In our perspective it is undeniable that the book of 1871 bears profound marks of Darwin's socio-cultural background. However, Yvette Conry makes a radical distinction between science and ideology and believes that, departing from the scientific theory of 1859, Darwin could have elaborated, textually, "une bio-anthropologie de la différence, du pluralisme et de la contingence", i. e., a scientific bio-anthro-historical-social

Darwinism. To accomplish this, the English naturalist only had to remain faithful to the principles of 1859. As, according to Yvette Conry, *The Descent of Man* is an ideological work and not an extension of the 1859 text, she logically concluded that social Darwinism does not exist. What Darwin elaborated was an ideological theory of society and history that the author draws close to Herbert Spencer's social evolutionism and the like, whether individualists or holists. It is undeniable that Darwin's 1871 book reflects ethnocentric and classicist stereotypes (for example, the bio-moral superiority of the bourgeois), but what we point out as most relevant is that, like in the 1859 work, natural selection continues to be the creating power of evolution – a power that, in 1871, was reinforced by sexual selection.

Unlike Yvette Conry, the historian-epistemologist Patrick Tort advocates that Darwin always separated himself from the Darwinisms-Evolutionisms, whether Spencerian (reference-norm of individualist social Darwinism), or from the holists or racialists and the eugenicists. According to Patrick Tort's interpretation, the Darwinian theory is as much scientific in 1871 as it was in 1859 and has no relation with a series of *isms* that, since the end of the 19th century, maid claims for such a relation: neo-liberalism, racism, eugenicism, social selectism, etc.. In order to support his stance, Patrick Tort two-folded the Darwinian revolution. Thus, following a first scientific revolution in 1859, which inaugurated a new logic of the historicity of all living beings, Darwin operated *a second scientific revolution* in 1871 with his work *The descent of man, and selection in relation to sex*. In very synthetic terms, Tort argues that, in the 1871 book, Darwin founded an anthropology, a morality and a socio-politics of solidarities: *"une socio-politique des solidarités"*, absolutely distinct from Spencerian liberal evolutionism and all of the social and political doctrines based on competition in unequal conditions or in coercive selectionism.

The defence of the *second Darwinian revolution* is sustained by the so-called "reversive effect of evolution" ("L'effet réversif de l'évolution. Fondements de l'anthropologie darwinienne", in *Darwinisme et société*. Direction de Patrick Tort, Paris, Presses Universitaires de France, 1992). By this expression Patrick Tort means that, according to Darwin, in the course of human history, natural selection gives place to education and conflict is replaced by cooperation and the protection of the disfavoured, since these practices reveal themselves as advantages to the civilizational evolution of the human species. Thus, in human history, natural selection selects values and anti-selectionist social behaviours.

In our understanding, the Darwinian texts of 1859 and 1871 allow for a different interpretation of the summarized interpretations presented. In our perspective, natural selection is one and the same in 1859 and in 1871. The theory of the biological evolution of all living beings (1859) extends itself in the bio-anthropo-socio-historical theory of 1871 that Darwin had announced since 1859 with these very expressive words: *"light will be thrown on the origin of man and his history"*. And this idea is reinforced in the following editions: "Much light will be thrown on the origin of man and his history".

Indeed, in 1871, Darwin strived to demonstrate that man was descended from an inferior form, both physically and mentally, and that his genealogy is not punctuated by ruptures with sudden changes, but processed with slow, short and successive steps. *"Natura non facit saltum"*, according to the cannon defended in 1859 "as natural selection acts solely by accumulating slight, successive, favourable variations, it can produce no great or sudden modification; it can act only by very short and slow steps". The Darwinian originality lies, mainly, in the evolutionary mechanism defended, thus, the hypothesis according to which man is the modified descendent of a long series of ancestors, or better, the co-descendent of some ancient organic form, inferior and extinct, although implicit in *The Origin of Species*, was publically assumed by various naturalists between 1859 and 1871, namely Carl Vogt, Th. Huxley, Ch. Lyell, Ludwig Büchner and Ernst Hæckel, respectively in 1862-63, 1863, 1863, 1866 and 1868. However, the Darwinian work *The Descent of Man* was decisive in substantiating this scientific hypothesis.

When ending the book of 1871, Darwin highlighted that man still preserves marks of his lower origin: "Man still bears in his bodily frame the indelible stamp of his lowly origin". For example, some useless organs, like the rudimentary tail, but also in the psychological realm there is an abundance of evidence of man's ascendency from animal. In *The Origin of Species*, Darwin had already announced the complete naturalization of the mental, emotional and moral faculties of man: "Psychology will be based on a new foundation, that of the necessary acquirement of each mental power and capacity by gradation". A significant part of the book of 1871 deals precisely with the comparison of man's mental and moral faculties with those of the inferior animals and Darwin concludes that their nature is the same, although in man they have achieved a much higher level, what, in turn, was explained by the natural selection of useful variations, assisted by the action of sexual selection and the heredity effects of the use of the brain. The nerve cells of the brain of all vertebrates derive from the nerve cells of the common ancestor of the kingdom and, therefore, it is not surprising that, even the sense of the beautiful and the patterns of beauty of these animals "generally coincides with our own standard". In the book of 1872, *The Expression of the Emotions,* that completes *The Descent of Man,* Darwin argued in favour of the universality of body language of the various emotions, their gradual acquisition through the long series of ancestors of man and, therefore, their innate and instinctive character.

In summary: besides stating the common ascendance of man and of the other vertebrates, and the close physical and psychological kinship between superior mammals and human beings, Darwin remained faithful to the evolutionary mechanism presented in 1859. In fact, we agree with John Greene's perspective , namely his 1995 article entitled "La révolution darwinienne dans la science et la vision du monde": "sous tous ses aspects (physiques, mentaux, moraux, esthétiques, religieux), l'humanité devait être considérée comme le résultat de processus similaires — variation aléatoire, lutte pour l'existence, sélection naturelle secondée par la sélection sexuelle et les effets hérités de l'usage des facultés psychiques — à ceux qui avaient produit les autres êtres vivants". It was this light that illuminated the Darwinian understanding of the origin of man and his history. This means that the driving force of humanity's history is exactly that which enabled and determined all natural history, i. e., the mechanism of organic, mental and social evolution is one and the same: the natural selection of the fittest (races or individuals) in the struggle for existence.

The Darwinian version of historical and social Darwinism was synthesized by the English naturalist in the final paragraphs of his *The Descent of Man,* from where the following passage was drawn: "Man, like every other animal, has no doubt advanced to his present high condition through a struggle for existence consequent on his rapid multiplication; and if he is to advance still higher, it is to be feared that he must remain subject to a severe struggle. Otherwise he would sink into indolence, and the more gifted men would not be more successful in the battle of life than the less gifted (...) There should be open competition for all men". What elevated man to the condition of a civilized social being was the struggle for existence, which should not be neutralised, because, without competition, natural selection cannot act in the sense of preserving the most capable, "the fittest". This means, in the area of social engineering, that the states should avoid all measures that hinder the functioning of the natural mechanism of evolution. However, the power of human laws is not absolute. For Darwin, no protectionist measure of the weak, was, is, or will be, efficient and lasting enough to replace the laws of nature. In 1872, in a letter sent to Heinrich Fick, professor of Law at the University of Zurich, the English naturalist clearly expressed his selectionist optimism: "I fear that Cooperative Societies, which many look at as the main hope for the future, likewise exclude competition. This seems to me a great evil for the future progress of mankind. — Nevertheless under any system, temperate and frugal workmen will have an advantage and leave more offspring than the drunken and reckless". In this letter, Darwin reaffirms his faith in natural selection and speaks against the economic organisations and the levelling social conducts of all individuals, "the good and bad, the strong and weak".

The economic and social policy which better harmonizes with the laws of nature does not seem to be, as Patrick Tort intends, "une socio-politique des solidarities". Regarding social engineering, we think that Darwin is very close to Spencerian liberalism. With "the advancement of the welfare of mankind" in mind, it was most important to guarantee the success of the best ("the most able"; "the fittest"), which would happen on its own, as long as the imprudent-inferior man ("reckless-inferior") did not benefit from a public and private solidarity that would stimulate his multiplication and, therefore, increase his numeric superiority. Anyhow, Darwin does not fear that the larger number of disqualified may threaten the historic preservation of the elites. For this to be true, the access to the superior scientific, artistic, religious, moral, etc., cultures should not be solely the privilege of a few due to their economic and family tradition, but a conquest of those who are intellectually most gifted. This does not mean that Darwin supported the principle of equal conditions and opportunities for all individuals, for such equality was unsustainable in the light of his doctrinal nucleus: variation or inter-individual inequality, struggle and selection. In general, those who posses the most advantageous variations of a certain trait will end up victorious, because natural selection is the last judge, an unfaultable judge that rewards "the fittest".

In the end, what fuels Darwin's historic and social optimism is his faith in natural selection. It was not due to the grace of God or due to man's illusionary free will that some human races achieved high levels of civilization. In developing the topic "Natural selection as affecting Civilised Nations", Darwin argued that artificial selections practiced during the historic process (like the elimination of the best in war) did not supress the power of natural selection. It is, therefore, understandable that in the realm of social engineering, Darwin did not support any kind of eugenic fundamentalism, which does not mean that the English naturalist condemned positive eugenics, because he believed in its civilizational advantages.

In summary: *the Darwinian revolution in the sciences of Life and Man is one and the same revolution.* Since the 1860's, this scientific and cultural revolution has met as many variants as its students and interpreters, a reason that helps explain the longevity and projection of the Darwin Industry. And, this industry continues to prosper, through the ongoing of new studies about Darwinism and evolution, from country to country, and case to case, in the history of science and culture during the last 150 years.

João Rui Pita

Faculdade de Farmácia; CEIS20-Grupo de História e Sociologia da Ciência, Universidade de Coimbra, Portugal

Ana Leonor Pereira

Faculdade de Letras; CEIS20-Grupo de História e Sociologia da Ciência, Universidade de Coimbra, Portugal

Pedro Ricardo Fonseca

FCT; Faculdade de Letras; CEIS20-Grupo de História e Sociologia da Ciência, Universidade de Coimbra, Portugal

DARWIN, EVOLUTION, EVOLUTIONISMS: A SELECTIVE CHRONOLOGY (1809-2009)

1809	Birth of Charles Robert Darwin (1809-1882)
1809	*Philosophie zoologique* by Jean Baptiste Monet, chevalier de Lamarck (1744-1829)
1817	*Le règne animal distribué d'après son organisation, pour servir de base à l'histoire naturelle des animaux et d'introduction à l'anatomie comparée* by Georges Cuvier (1769-1832)
1830	Debate between Georges Cuvier and Geoffroy Saint-Hilaire (1772--1844) at the *Academie des Sciences*
1830-1833	*Principles of Geology* by Charles Lyell (1797-1875)
1831-1836	Voyage of *H. M. S. Beagle*
1835	Charles Darwin visits the Galapagos Islands
1838	Charles Darwin conceived his theory of natural selection
1839	*Journal of Researches into the Geology and Natural History of the Various Countries Visited by H.M.S. Beagle* by Charles Darwin
1843	Richard Owen (1804-1892) establishes the distinction between homology and analogy
1844	*Vestiges of the Natural History of Creation* by Robert Chambers (1802--1871), published anonymously
1856	Discovery of Neanderthal remains in Germany
1858	Charles Darwin receives an unpublished essay from Alfred Russel Wallace (1823-1913) that proposes a theory of natural selection very similar to his
1858	Joint presentation of extracts of Charles Darwin's earlier writings on natural selection and Alfred Wallace's unpublished essay to the *Linnean Society of London* by Charles Lyell and Joseph Dalton Hooker (1817-1911)
1859	*On the Origin of Species by Means of Natural Selection, or the Preservation of Favoured Races in the Struggle for Life* by Charles Darwin
1860	The first translations of *The Origin of Species* are published
1860	Debate between Bishop Samuel Wilberforce (1805-1873) and Thomas Henry Huxley (1825-1895) at the *British Association for the Advancement of Science*
1861	Discovery of *Archaeopteryx lithographica* remains in Germany

1862	William Thomson, Lord Kelvin (1824-1907), estimated that the age of the Earth was between 20 million and 400 million years
1863	*Evidence as to Man's Place in Nature* by Thomas Henry Huxley
1864-1867	*Principles of Biology* by Herbert Spencer (1820-1903)
1866	Gregor Mendel (1822-1884) publishes his work on the inheritance in pea plants
1868	*The Variation of Animals and Plants Under Domestication* by Charles Darwin
1868	*Natürliche Schöpfungsgeschichte* by Ernst Hæckel (1834-1919)
1871	*The Descent of Man, and Selection in Relation to Sex* by Charles Darwin
1872	*The Expression of the Emotions in Man and Animals* by Charles Darwin
1872	Sixth edition of *The Origin of Species*
1876	*Darwiniana* by Asa Gray (1810-1888)
1882	Death of Charles Darwin
1883	Francis Galton (1822-1911) coins the term "Eugenics"
1885	August Weismann (1834-1914) presents the Continuity of the Germ-plasm Theory
1887	*The life and letters of Charles Darwin, including an autobiographical chapter* edited by Francis Darwin (1848-1925)
1889	Francis Galton presents the Law of Ancestral Heredity
1891	Discovery of Java Man by Marie Eugene Dubois (1858-1940)
1894	*Materials for the Study of Variation* by William Bateson (1861-1926)
1896	James Mark Baldwin (1861-1934) presents the "Baldwin Effect"
1897	William Thomson, Lord Kelvin, advances with a new estimate on the age of the Earth: between 20 and 40 million years
1900	Mendel's laws are independently "rediscovered" by Hugo de Vries (1848-1935), Carl Correns (1864-1933) and Erich von Tschermak (1871-1962)
1901-1903	*Die Mutationslehre* by Hugo de Vries
1902	*Mutual Aid: A Factor of Evolution* by Peter Kropotkin (1842-1921)
1903	Wilhelm Ludwig Johannsen (1857-1927) introduces the distinction between genotype and phenotype
1904	Nelson Ernest Rutherford (1871-1937), based on the new knowledge of radioactivity, discredits Lord Kelvin's reduced estimates on the age of the Earth
1908	Establishment of the Hardy-Weinberg law
1909	Centenary of Charles Darwin's birth and the 50th anniversary of the first publication of *The Origin of Species*. Cambridge is the main stage of the celebrations, gathering scientists and dignitaries from many different countries
1909	Constantin Mereschkowsky (1855-1921) introduces the concept of Symbiogenesis
1909	Discovery of the Burgess Shale by Charles Walcott (1950-1927)
1911	Lucien Cuénot (1866-1951) introduces the concept of Pre-adaptation
1912	Alfred Wegener (1880-1930) presents the Theory of Continental Drift
1912	Discovery of the Piltdown Man

1915	*The Mechanism of Mendelian Heredity* by Thomas Hunt Morgan (1866-1945), Alfred H. Sturtevant (1891-1970), Calvin B. Bridges (1889-1938) and Herman Joseph Muller (1890-1967)
1919	*The Physical Basis of Heredity* by Thomas Hunt Morgan
1924	*The Origin of Life* (in Russian) by Alexander Ivanovich Oparin (1894-1980)
1925	Discovery of the Taung Baby by Raymond Dart (1893-1988)
1925	Scopes Monkey Trial in Dayton, Tennessee
1929	*The Origin of Life* by John Burdon Sanderson Haldane (1892-1964)
1929	Trofim Lysenko (1898-1976) rejects the validity of Mendelian Genetics and of chromosome theory
1930	*The Genetical Theory of Natural Selection* by Ronald Aylmer Fisher (1890-1962)
1932	"The roles of mutation, inbreeding, crossbreeding, and selection in evolution" by Sewall Wright (1889-1988)
1932	*The Causes of Evolution* by J. B. S. Haldane
1937	*Genetics and the Origin of Species* by Theodosius Dobzhansky (1900-1975)
1940	*The Material Basis of Evolution* by Richard B. Goldschmidt (1878-1958)
1942	*Evolution: The Modern Synthesis* by Julian Huxley (1887-1975)
1942	*Systematics and the Origin of Species* by Ernst Mayr (1904-2005)
1944	*Tempo and Mode in Evolution* by George Gaylord Simpson (1902-1984)
1950	*Variation and Evolution in Plants* by George Ledyard Stebbins (1906-2000)
1953	Discovery of the double helix by James Watson (b. 1928) and Francis Crick (1916-2004)
1954	New estimates indicate that the Earth is 5 or 6 billion years old
1955	Henry Bernard D. Kettlewell's (1907-1979) studies on predation in peppered moths demonstrated the effects of natural selection in the wild
1955	*Le phénomène humaine* by Pierre Teilhard de Chardin (1881-1955)
1959	Centenary of the *The Origin of Species* and the 150th anniversary of Charles Darwin's birth. Chicago is the centre of the major celebrations, gathering scientists and dignitaries from around the world
1964	"The Genetical Evolution of Social Behaviour" by William Donald Hamilton (1936-2000)
1968	Motoo Kimura (1924-1994) proposes the Neutral Theory of Molecular Evolution
1972	"Punctuated Equilibria: An Alternative to Phyletic Gradualism" by Niles Eldredge (b. 1943) and Stephen Jay Gould (1941-2002)
1974	Discovery of Lucy by Donald Johanson (b. 1943)
1975	*Sociobiology: The New Synthesis* by Edward Osborne Wilson (b. 1929)
1975	Beginning of the Sociobiology Debate
1976	*The Selfish Gene* by Richard Dawkins
1978	*On Human Nature* by Edward O. Wilson

1981	Arkansas Creation Trial
1982	Centenary of Charles Darwin's death
1996	Pope John Paul II accepts evolution, with the exception of the human soul
2005	Dover Intelligent Design Trial
2009	Several events take place all around the world celebrating the 150th anniversary of *The Origin of Species* and the bicentenary of Charles Darwin's birth

Bibliography

BOWLER, Peter J. – *Evolution: the history of an idea, 25th Anniversary Edition, With a New Preface.* 3rd edition, completely revised and expanded. Berkeley, Los Angeles and London: University of California Press, 2009.

FONSECA, P. R.; PEREIRA, A. L.; PITA, J. R. – "A história do evolucionismo no século XX: metodologias e perspectivas historiográficas", *Estudos do Século XX*, Coimbra, Nº 11, 2011, pp. 373-388.

GAYON, Jean – *Darwin et l' après Darwin: Une histoire de l'hypothèse de sélection naturelle.* Paris: Editions Kimé, 1992.

GOULD, Stephen Jay – *The stucture of evolutionary theory.* Cambridge, Mass. and London: The Belknap Press of Harvard University Press, (sixth printing) 2002.

HODGE, J.; RADICK, G. (eds.) – *The Cambridge Companion to Darwin.* New York: Cambridge University Press, 2003.

MAYR, Ernst – *The growth of biological thought: diversity, evolution and inheritance.* Cambridge, Mass.: The Belknap Press of Harvard University Press, 1982.

PEREIRA, Ana Leonor – *Darwin em Portugal. Filosofia. História. Engenharia Social – (1865-1914).* Coimbra: Livraria Almedina, 2001.

PEREIRA, A. L.; FONSECA, P. R. – "The Darwin centennial celebrations in Portugal". In: GLICK, T.; SHAFFER, E. (eds.), *The Reception of Charles Darwin in Europe*, vol. 3, London and New York: Continuum, (In Press). – Series on the Reception of British and Irish Authors in Europe.

RUSE, Michael – *The Evolution Wars: A Guide to the Debates.* 2nd ed. Millerton, NY: Grey House Publishing, 2nd ed., 2009.

SEGERSTRÅLE, Ullica – *Defenders of the truth: the battle for science in the sociobiology debate and beyond.* Oxford and New York: Oxford University Press, 2000.

TORT, Patrick (dir.) – *Dictionnaire du darwinisme et de l'évolution.* Paris: Presses Universitaires de France, 3 vols., 1996.

WYHE, John (ed.) – *The Complete Works of Charles Darwin Online*, 2002-. http://darwin-online.org.uk/

Antonio González Bueno

Faculdad de Farmácia, Universidade Complutense, Madrid, España

FROM LINNÉ TO DARWIN: THE THEORIES ON THE ORIGIN OF SPECIES

Between May and August of 1876, Charles Darwin recalled in the pages of his *Autobiography*:

> "One day, as we were walking together, he [Robert Edmond Grant (1793-1874)] burst out in great admiration for Lamarck and his views on evolution. I listened in silent amazement, without being affected in any way emotionally. I had read my grandfather's Zoonomy earlier, and it had contained similar views. Nevertheless, it is quite probable that the fact that I was exposed at an early age to such views and heard them being praised made it easier for me to uphold the same ideas in a different form in my Origin of Species...."[1]

Which were the prevailing theories about the natural world at the moment in which Charles Darwin carried out his classical works? In which way did these ideas intervene in his thesis formulation? It is to these questions that I want to dedicate the following lines.

From fixism to transformism

The theories on the origin of the species, which prevailed well into the 18th century, will maintain the immutability of the created forms: species are stable and unchangeable. In his *Philosophia botanica...* (Stockholmiae: apud G. Kiesewetter, 1751), Carl Linné (1707-1778) states: "Species tot sunt, qut diversas formas ab initio produxit infinitum ens"[2]. In this way, a creationist tradition, based on the literal interpretation of the Biblical Assumptions established in the Genesis is gathered.

The creationist idea of the natural world is even more clearly present in other works by Linné, especially in some geological essays and in his works about natural economy. Carl Linné outlined his concepts on the origin of the Earth in a short speech: *Oratio de telluris habitabilis incremento...* (Lugduni Batavorum: apud Cornelium Haak Leiden, 1743) in which, following the Biblical Doctrine, he imagined the existence of an Earthly Paradise

---

[1] Charles Darwin [José Luis Gil Aristu, trans.]. *Autobiografía*. [Pamplona]: Laetoli, 2008. Supplied text in Spanish on page 47.

[2] *Cf.* the aphorism 157 (page 99) in the Carl von Linné's edition *Philosophia botanica, in qua explicantur Fundamenta Botanica*. Stockholmiae: apud Godofr. Kiesewetter, 1751.

situated on an island in Ecuador, in which animals and plants, confronting the scarcity of water, had started a progressive expansion, colonising the rest of the Planet. This is a speech in which he clearly expresses his approaches and ideas about Nature's harmonic balance, in accordance with the perfect proportion established in the Holy Scriptures.

This concept about natural harmony acquires even greater dimensions in the academic dissertations defended by his disciples on his economic vision of Nature, such as *Oeconomia naturae...* (Upsaliae: [s.n.], [1749]) or *Politia naturae...* (Upsaliae: [s.n.], [1760]), which is conceived as an eternal cycle in which the death or birth of each living being occupies a specific place within a global model perfectly defined, clearly reflecting the Divine Plan of Creation.

The accumulation of materials, especially during the elaboration process of *Species Plantarum...* (Holmiae: impensis L. Salvii, 1753), will modify this fixist theory clearly defended in his first works coming closer to new concepts in which species are interpreted as entities formed after the moment of Creation, through hybridism: a hypothesis whose draft can be found in previous texts like his *Dissertatio botanica de Peloria...* (Upsaliae: [s.n.], [1744]) in which he described a monstrous form of the *Linaria vulgaris* L., interpreted by him as a hybrid between a specimen of *Linaria* L. and a completely different plant. These and other observations led him to maintain that the development of new plant species through hybridism was possible, a theory developed in the *Plantae hybridae...* (Upsaliae: [s.n.], 1751). In other reports such as *Disquisitio de sexu plantarum...* (Petropoli: [s.n.], 1760) and *Fundamentum fructificaciones...* (Upsaliae: [s.n.], 1762) you can clearly find this new line of thought to which Carl Linné arrives at through his own observation. After broadening it, he sustained the risky hypothesis that all the plants of one same gender derived from a single species, the one created by Divine Decision, and that the remaining species of that gender have been formed through hybridism processes that have occurred between the primary species and others of different genders. This is a theory that develops similar principles to those defended by Andrea Cesalpino (1519-1603) to explain the variability of Nature. In the last years of his life, around 1760, Carl Linné magnified his hypothesis up to the point of maintaining that, at the moment of Creation, only one specimen for each order existed, generating the rest through hybridism processes implying the acceptance of a variation of Nature, in time as well as in space.

This was not a new idea; the botanist Jean Marchant (f. 1738) had already exposed a similar hypothesis in 1719, at the *Académie Royale des sciences* in Paris:

> "Through this observation [he writes referring to a pyloric mercurial], there are reasons to think that the Divine Omnipotence has created plant individuals as models for gender formed through imaginable structures and features, capable of reproducing like the model (...) or types of each gender, in order for them to perpetuate, have finally produced varieties, among which those that have stayed constant and permanent, form species. These species, with time, and in the same way, have given way to different productions with which Botany has increased in certain genders..."[3]

---

[3] Jean Marchant. "Observations sur la nature des plantes". *Mémoires de Mathématique et de Physique, tirez des registres de l'Académie Royale des Sciences de l'Année MDCCXIX*. Paris, 1721. About this author and his contributions to this area, *cf.* Henri Hus. "Jean Marchant; an Eighteenth century mutationist".

Thus, from the strictest fixist approaches there seems to be a particular accepted transformist hypothesis, limited to the permitted progress measured by the creation order.

This interest in the origin of the species is not only limited to the scientific circles. In 1745 Pierre Louis Moreau de Maupertuis (1698-1759) had his *Vénus Physique...* ([Paris: s.n.], 1745)[4] printed, a booklet halfway between scientific diffusion, literary gossip, experimentation, erotic fiction and philosophy, so common to that 'underground' literature of the Old Regime[5]. The small piece of work was an editorial success, for in 1751 it was already in its sixth edition leading the sarcastic Voltaire to state that Maupertuis' 'Venus' was in everyone's hands.[6]

If we bring this text into consideration, a story that takes place in the middle of one of the Parisian rooms, presided over by a woman with intellectual aspirations, a fact that emphasises the non-academic character of the story, it is because of the commentaries the author makes on the processes of production of new species in Nature. Referring to the case of albinism in the black race, the real generator of his article, he will write:

> "It's a four or five-year-old boy that has all the features of black people but who's very livid skin only increases his ugliness. His head is covered in a white, turning to red, wool. His light blue eyes seem to be hurt by the clearness of the day. His hands, thick and badly formed, look more like an animal's legs than the hands of a man. He was born, according to what has been assured, from an African father and mother, who were very black (...)
>
> These changes in colour are more frequent in animals than in men. The colour black is as inherent in vultures and blackbirds as it is to black people. However, I have sometimes seen white vultures and white blackbirds. In fact, these variations would form new species, if they were cultivated. I have seen regions in which the hens were white. The whiteness of their skin, ordinarily linked to the whiteness of their feathers, has caused the preference for these hens and not others and, from generation to generation it has lead to seeing only white hens (...).

The American Naturalist, 45(536): 493-506. Chicago, 1911, who translates into the English language Jean Marchant's booklet (*cf.* pages 501-506 and who we follow in the transcribed paragraph; page 506-).

[4] Previously partially published in an anonymous way, [Pierre Louis Moreau de Maupertuis]. *Dissertation physique a l'occasion du negre blanc*. Leiden: [s.i.], 1744. A detailed study about the biological ideas of this author in Michael H. Hoffheimer. "Maupertuis and the Eighteenth-Century Critique of Preexistence". *Journal of the History of Biology*, 15(1): 119-149. Boston, 1982.

[5] An analysis of Maupertuis' work, in which his scent for the 'subversive and clandestine literature' in Mary Terrall is discovered. "Salon, Academy, and Boudoir: Generation and Desire in Maupertuis's Science of Life". *Isis*, 87(2): 217-229. Chicago, 1996. On this type of literature *cf.* Robert Darnton. *The literature underground of the Old Regime*. Cambridge [Mass.]: Harvard University Press, 1982; *Ibid., The forbidden bestsellers of pre-revolutionary France*. New York: Norton, 1994.

[6] *Cf.* Nelson Papavero and Jorge Llorente-Bousquets, *Principia taxonómica: una introducción a los fundamentos lógicos, filosóficos y metodológicos de las escuelas de taxonomía biológica. 4. El sistema natural y otros sistemas, reglas, mapas de afinidades y el advenimiento del tiempo en las clasificaciones: Buffon, Adanson, Maupertuis, Lamarck y Cuvier*. [México]: Universidad Nacional Autónoma de México, Facultad de Ciencias, Coordinación de Servicios Editoriales, 1994. *cf.* page 51.

If there is a necessity to find out what occurs in plants in order to confirm what I say here, those who cultivate them would say that all plant and plumed small tree species which are admired in our gardens are due to different varieties which have become inherited. These can disappear if we forget to take care of them..."[7]

In Maupertuis' text we can see the presence of Nature's capacity to produce changes and to conserve them. He makes reference to 'unforeseeable productions' favoured by artificial selection and which can disappear through Nature but also know the way of forcing the process and are able to perpetuate these 'unforeseeable productions': those generations only have to repeat themselves several times and, in that way, man acts on the beings that he modifies in pursuit of a strange concept of beauty which borders the exotic or the abnormal.

A not so different attitude to this was the one defended by Georges Louis Leclerc, Comte de Buffon (1707-1788), member of the *Academie des Sciences* of Paris and head of the *Jardin du Roi*, the French institution *par excellence*, dedicated to Natural History. Buffon, not an advocate of the systematic theories defended by Carl Linné, understood the species as stable entities in which the features continue from generation to generation and among which there is a possibility of obtaining fertile descendents. However, his experience distanced him from the dominant creationist perspective. He was the first Christian European to publicly consider that the Earth's age was far older than the one established by the theory defended by the Ecclesiastic authorities of his time: the four thousand and four years Before Christ.

Comte de Buffon was the author of an extensive work, the *Histoire naturelle, générale et particuliére, avec la description du Cabinet du roy.* (Paris: Imprimerie royale, 1749-1804. 44 vols.), an effort to make accessible, in a synthesised manner, all the available scientific knowledge. We owe the term 'degeneration' to Comte de Buffon. According to his theory, presented in 1766 in volume XIV of his *Histoire naturelle...,* in the chapter dedicated to "De la dégénération des animaux", the related species have a common 'unity of type', from which they branch off. The concept of 'degeneration', using it in the sense given by Buffon, does not suppose the loss of the structural complexity, it supposes a common origin. Buffon admitted that the natural environment could cause an influence on living beings, causing forced variations of temperature or nutrition, but he also thought that these variations were not long-lasting and that, when the conditions that forced these varieties disappeared, the species would once again obtain their previous structure.

Buffon did not deny the Creator Principle but he did deny the direct intervention of the Maker in each of the species that form Nature. He would maintain that God is not personally in charge of the folding of each wing of a beetle. These are 'secondary causes' which he did not know how to specify but to which he attributed natural features, those that are in charge of organising these structures. Even though he examined some ideas, he never formalised a hypothesis about the origin and evolution of species, in the way in which Chevalier de Lamarck would do.

---

[7] Pierre Louis Moreau de Maupertuis. *Op. cit.* (*Cf.* Nelson Papavero and Jorge Llorente-Bousquets, *op. cit.*, pages 81-82 supplied text in Spanish).

Lamarckism

This capacity of the natural forms to transform themselves and to perpetuate the changes which they acquired is underlying in Jean Baptiste de Monet (1744-1829), Chevalier de Lamarck's thoughts. In his opinion, the species is only provisionally stable, with an innate availability to change, depending on the environment in which it is developed:

> "Those who have observed and consulted the great collections ended up convincing themselves that, the same as the circumstances of habitat, exposure, climate, food, habit of living, etc., (…) the characteristics of size, form, proportion of parts, colour, consistency, agility and industry in animals proportionally change…"[8]

In this way, the environmental changes cause transformations in living beings, transformations that eternalize to the extent in which the changes of its habitat conditions are stabilised.

> "It is not the organs: nature and the form of the parts of an animal's body which have given place to their habits and their particular features, but on the contrary, the habits, the way of living and the circumstances in which the individuals they come from have lived, are what, with time, have constituted the form of their body, the number and state of an organ and the capabilities, which they enjoy…"[9]

The book *Philosophie zoologique…* (Paris: chez Dentu, 1809), in which these postulates show their most radiant expression, is full of examples. Let us recall the most classical ones:

> "In relation to habits it is curious to observe the product in the particular form and height of the giraffe. It is known that this animal, the tallest of the mammals, lives in the interior of Africa, in which the arid region without prairies makes them browse among the trees. Of this habit, maintained after much time in all the individuals of its race, we have the result that its front legs have become longer than its back legs and its neck has elongated in such a way that the animal, without rising on his back legs, raises its head and reaches about six metres high"[10].
>
> "The bird, to which the necessity attracts towards the water to find in it the prey which will feed it, separates the fingers of their legs when it wants to strike the water and move on its surface. The skin that links its fingers in the base contracts and, due

---

[8] Jean Baptista de Monet [Lamarck]. *Philosophie zoologique…* Paris: chez Dentu, 1809. [Spanish edition from José González Llama, printed in Valencia: Editorial Sempere, 1910] *cf.* page 170, supplied text in Spanish.

[9] *Cf.* page 177 from the Spanish edition from Jean Baptista de Monet [Lamarck] *cit. ut supra*, an idea that, as the own author recognises, is already present in *Recherches sur l'organisation des corps vivants, et particulièrement sur son origine, sur la cause de son développement et des progrès de sa composition… Précédé du discours d'ouverture du cours de Zoologie donné dans le Muséum d'histoire naturelle…* Paris: chez l'auteur [Maillard], l'an X de la République [1801-1802]

[10] *Cf.* page 187-188 of the Spanish edition from Jean Baptista de Monet [Lamarck] *cit. ut supra*.

to such non-stop and repeated deviations, the habit of extending itself. That's why, with time, they have formed broad membranes that link the fingers of ducks, geese, etc."[11].

"Is there any example more surprising than the one that the kangaroo offers? This animal, which takes its breeding in the bag that it has under its abdomen, has acquired the custom of standing up, only on its back legs and on the tail, and walk jumping maintaining a straight attitude in order not to hurt its siblings. Here, the result: its front legs, very sporadically used, have not acquired a proportionate development in relation to the rest of its parts, becoming very small, very weak and almost without any strength. On the contrary, the back legs, almost always in action, have achieved a considerable development, being very big and strong. Lastly, the tail, which the animal uses to carry out its main movements, has acquired a considerable strength and thickness in its base. These very well known facts are very appropriate to demonstrate what animals undertake through the use of any organ…"[12].

The examples can be multiplied, but I think that these extensively prove the reasoning exposed by Chevalier de Lamarck in order to sustain his hypothesis which, even though signalled by Charles Darwin as one of his precedents[13], had, in his time, a scarce scientific and social reception.

Lamarck's theory comes from a basic premise: Nature's progressive complexity. In Lamarck's opinion, the simplest forms of life are born by spontaneous generation and an internal fluid system (which acts over and is the origin of the different organs, which are more and more complex). In this process of the 'path towards complexity', we can see that the environmental conditions are capable of modifying the habits of the living beings and, with that, their organs' activities, developed or atrophied, according to the use and which then perpetuate through reproduction.

"If it is common to the individuals that in fertilisation come together to the reproduction of its specie, all change obtained in an organ produced by its continuous habit of having it in action is immediately conserved by the next generation. In sum, this change advances and passes on to all the individuals which follow and find themselves submitted to the same circumstances, without having seen themselves in the obligation to acquire them through the way in which it had really been created"[14].

---

[11] *Cf.* page 183 of the Spanish edition from Jean Baptista de Monet [Lamarck] *cit. ut supra.*

[12] *Cf.* page 188-189 of the Spanish edition from Jean Baptista de Monet [Lamarck] *cit. ut supra.*

[13] Charles Darwin valued Chevalier de Lamarck's works in the historic preface that, since the April 1861 edition, has preceded *On the Origin of Species…*: "Lamarck was the first whose conclusions on this point caused great attention (…). In relation to the modification forms, he attributed some part to the direct action of the physical conditions of life, some on the growth of already existing forms and a lot to the use and disuse, this is, the effects of the habit (…). Besides this, he also believed in the progressive development law: and as all the forms of life tend to progress, in order to explain the existence of simple production in the present days, he maintains that these are spontaneously generated…" (*cf.* page 2 [text in Spanish] of the Charles Darwin edition [Enrique Godínez, trans.]. *Origen de las especies por medio de la selección natural ó la conservación de las razas favorecidas en la lucha por la existencia…* Madrid / París: Biblioteca Perojo, 1877).

[14] *Cf.* page 190 of the Spanish edition from Jean Baptista de Monet [Lamarck] *cit. ut supra.*

In his *Système des animaux sans vertèbres...* (Paris: chez l'auteur, 1801), considered by some authors as the 'birth certificate' of Lamarckism[15], Chevalier de Lamarck argued that the existence of life on Earth went back several thousand of millions of years, thus solving an apparent contradiction: we do not see a variation in the species and, however, they do have it; a variation that is very slow in relation to the humans' perception scale but which can be perceived in the scale of geological time.

Of course, Charles Darwin's mention of Lamarckist assumptions is more rhetoric than real. In a letter to his cherished friend Joseph Dalton Hooker (1817-1911), dated as early as January 11th 1844, he wrote:

> "Besides a general interest about the Southern lands, I have been now ever since my return engaged in a very presumptuous work & which I know no one individual who wd not say a very foolish one.
>
> I was so struck with distribution of Galapagos organisms &c &c & with the character of the American fossil mammifers, &c &c that I determined to collect blindly every sort of fact, which cd bear any way on what are species.
>
> I have read heaps of agricultural & horticultural books, & have never ceased collecting facts.
>
> At last gleams of light have come, & I am almost convinced (quite contrary to opinion I started with) that species are not (it is like confessing a murder) immutable. Heaven forfend me from Lamarck nonsense of a 'tendency to progression' 'adaptations from the slow willing of animals' &c, – but the conclusions I am led to are not widely different from his – though the means of change are wholly so – I think I have found out (here's presumption!) the simple way by which species become exquisitely adapted to various ends.
>
> You will now groan, & think to yourself 'on what a man have I been wasting my time in writing to.' – I shᵈ, five years ago, have thought so..."[16].

And, in a letter to the same correspondent on November 10th 1844, he would not vacillate at the moment of writing:

> "With respect to Books on this subject, I do not know of any systematical ones, except Lamarck's, which is veritable rubbish..."[17].

The contributions of Comparative Anatomy

In Napoleonic France, in the beginning of the 19th century, the re-founded *Muséum d'Histoire Naturelle* would see the birth of a discipline which would

---

[15] *Cf.* Franck Bourdier. "Lamarck et Geoffroy Saint-Hilaire face au problème de l'évolution biologique". *Revue d'Histoire des Sciences*, 25(4): 311-325. Paris, 1972.

[16] *Cf.* letter 729 in *Darwin correspondence project.* [http://www.darwinproject.ac.uk/] [consulted on IV-2008].

[17] *Cf.* letter 789 in *Darwin correspondence project.* [http://www.darwinproject.ac.uk/] [consulted on IV-2008].

bring new light to the dark mystery of the origin of species: we are speaking of Comparative Anatomy.

The abundant studies which on the similarities between animal skeletons were quite old. Pierre Belon (1517-1564) had already established, in 1555, the concordance between human and bird skeletons, but the academic maturity of this discipline would only take place in the beginning of the 19th century by Georges Cuvier, (1769-1832), thanks to his ability to summarise the contributions of taxonomy and palaeontology.

In Cuvier's thoughts, the functional disposition of the animal's organs responds to its life's conditions. Carnivores, who need to locate, catch and tear its prey, need visual keenness, limbs suitable to run and jaw bones and teeth suitable to tear. On the contrary, herbivores do not have any claws in their limbs and these are substituted by hooves, and their jaws and teeth are adapted, the same as their stomach, to the food which they are to ingest and digest. These ideas, which he theoretically organised in his 'principle of parts correlation', are linked to a 'principle of function dependence', in which he establishes a hierarchic structure of the functions which will develop the organism, in contrast to those that form the functions of the nervous system.

In his classificatory model, Cuvier states that the weight of the feature is determined by its functional importance and in that way establishes an order in the animal kingdom in four great morphological types: vertebrates, articulated, mollusks and radiates, among which there are no intermediate forms. The establishment of these four great organisation plans, isolated among each other, supposes a rupture against the conceptions of a 'Natural chain' defended by Lamarck and other naturalists, in which all living beings share a common model from which their development begins.

In Cuvier's discourse, the study of an American fossil, the *Megatherium*, has a special impact: the comparative works about structure which internalised the South American sloths along with other fossil rests of Siberian mammoths, compared to the actual elephants, led him to maintain that the extinction of these beings was due to conditions that he considered as abrupt changes in Nature. This is a contradictory attitude to what Chevalier de Lamarck defended: slow adaptation. The living beings plastically modelled by environmental conditions, as Lamarck had described, turn into stabilised structures, with firmly fixed features, which only great environmental catastrophes, such as the Flood, can wipe off the face of the Earth.

Chevalier de Lamarck and Baron Cuvier shared the same space, but not the same ideas[18], in the *Muséum d'Histore Naturelle* in Paris. Along with them, Etienne Geoffroy, also known as Geoffroy Saint-Hilaire (1772-1844) was in charge of, after the transformation occurred in the *Jardin des Plantes* in June 1793, of the official chair of the zoology of vertebrates.

Geoffroy's works on Comparative Anatomy go in a different direction than that maintained by Cuvier, closer to the traditional line defended by Comte de Buffon, inspired on the search of a prototype, of a single composition plan, aside from form or organ functionality. In his analysis on the similarity and homology among organs, he called upon the study of embryonic forms which appears in *Philosophie*

---

[18] The lecture of the "Éloge de Lamarck" done by George Cuvier is very illustrative in relation to this topic (*Recueil des Éloges Historiques*: 179-210. Paris: Didot, [1832], 1861).

anatomique... (Paris: Méquignon-Marvis, 1818). For example, the similarity among the number of pieces in bird and fish skulls and among these and human embryos. The results lead him to formulate an 'economic principle of nature' according to which the development of an animal structure leads to the atrophy of another[19]. His latest works on the exoskeleton of insects and vertebral columns, published in 1820, intensify this formulation of structural unity, until then restricted to animals with vertebras[20].

This idea of searching for the prototype has a strong connection with the German *Naturphilosophie*. In *Versuch die Metamorphose der Pflanzen zu erklären* (Gotha: bey Carl Wilhelm Ettinger, 1790) Johann Wolfgang von Goethe (1749-1832) argued that the different parts of the vegetables could be considered as modifications of a unique utopian base structure which he considered an 'ideal leaf'.

But let us return to Paris, at the beginning of the 19th century, in order to attend the public debate between Cuvier and Geoffroy in March 1830; a debate which left a lively impression on Goethe, up to the point of making him go back to his works on Comparative Anatomy[21]. There, in the *Academie des Sciencies*, Cuvier mentioned the necessity of having to comply with the facts and avoid hypothetical theoretic constructions like the 'Natural Chain' defended by Lamarck or the 'composition unity' defended by Geoffroy. In his formulation there was a strong religious content making pressure: Creation could not constrain to a single organisation plan. On his side, Geoffroy argued the naturalist's liberty to formulate general theories and interpret the observations according to his own beliefs. The debate reached the press and the omnipotent and elder Cuvier had to count on the support of the most conservative publications to confront the liberal newspapers that showed his opponent, Geoffroy, as a warlord of the liberty of thought, opposed to the rigid structure defended by the academic stalls[22].

The studies on Comparative Anatomy in Great Britain have their maximum representation in the works of the powerful Richard Owen (1804-1892), who Charles

---

[19] Théophile Cahn has taken care of the relation between Etienne Geoffroy's studies and the evolution theory. "L'oeuvre d'Etienne Geoffroy Saint-Hilaire dans une perspectiva de l'evolution de la pensée scientifique". *Revue d'Histoire des Sciences*, 25(4): 301-310. Paris, 1972. The 'understanding' among the theories maintained by Etienne Geoffroy on animal structures, by Valentin Haüy on minerals and Agustin De Candolle on vegetables, has been analysed by F. Dagognet. "Valentin Haüy, Etienne Geofroy Saint--Hilaire, Agustin P. de Candolle: Une conception d'ensemble mais aussi un ensemble de conceptions". *Revue d'Histoire des Sciences*, 25(4): 327-336. Paris, 1972

[20] Etienne Geoffroy Saint-Hilaire. "Sur un squelette chez les insectes, dont toutes les pièces, identiques entre elles dans les divers ordres du système entomologique, correspondent à chacun des os du squelette dans les classes supérieures, Lu à l'Académie des Sciences, le 3 janvier 1820". *Annales générales des sciences physiques* 5: 96-132. Paris, 1820.

[21] "At the end of this year [1831] and beginning of the next [1832], Goethe started once again to fully dedicate himself to his favourite studies, Natural Science (...) especially due to his interest on the debate between Cuvier and St. Hilaire on different topics related to plant metamorphosis and the animal world..." (*Cf.* Johann Peter Eckermann [Rosa Sala Rose, ed.]. *Conversaciones con Goethe en los últimos años de su vida*. Barcelona: Acantilado, 2005; quote from pages 578-579 [text in Spanish]; the controversy will be analysed again on page 801).

[22] Jean Piveteau. "Le débat entre Cuvier et Geoffroy Saint-Hilaire sur l'unité de plan et de composition". *Revue d'Histoire des Sciences*, 3(4): 343-363. Paris, 1950; Toby A. Appel. *The Cuvier-Geoffroy debate, french biology in the decades before Darwin*. New York: Oxford University Press, 1987.

Darwin met and even visited with certain frequency during his years as a Londoner and who would even make him suffer with his critics[23]. Richard Owen's *Lectures on the comparative anatomy and physiology of the vertebrate animals* (London: Longman, Brown, Green & Longmans, 1843) and his contemporary presentation of the vertebrates' prototype[24], accepting the scheme defended by Cuvier, represent the theoretical base that prevailed at the moment of the publication of *The Origin of Species...*

From the 'geological flood' to actualism

During the last years of the 18th century, the history of the Earth and the history of living beings, up to then travelling through different pathways, converged in their courses. The connecting link were the fossils. The triumph of Georges Cuvier's catastrophic theories over the transformist conceptions of Chevalier de Lamarck's ideas was due, mostly, to the increase of the fossil record. Against the abundant invertebrates, particularly molluscs, of the records near Paris, that turned out to be very useful at the time of completing the series established by Lamarck, the emergence of the remains of vertebrates which were hard to locate on the scale of Nature backed up the catastrophic hypothesis. However, all the theories had their audiences.

Towards the central years of the 19th century, Isidore Geoffroy Saint-Hilaire (1805-1861), son of Étienne Geoffroy, through the study of animal breeding in domestication and of the acclimatisation of species, reformulated his father's and Chevalier de Lamarck's theories, favourable to selective variation. On their side, the supporters of Natural Theology, rebuking the perfection of the creational order, exposed the perfect adaptation of the organic forms to the environment, showing themselves contrary to any variation process. Robert Jameson (1774-1854), professor of Natural History in Edinburgh, published an adaptation of George Cuvier's texts under the title *Essay on the theory of the Earth...* (Edinburgh: printed for William Blackwood, John Murray & Robert Baldwin, 1813) in which the Biblical Flood catastrophes were identified. This work, along with the interpretation of the geological data under the light of the Scriptures carried out by William Buckland (1784-1856) in his *Vindiciae geologicae, or the connexión of Geology with Religión explained...* (Oxford: at the University Press for the author, 1820) are good indicators of the influence of these theories in Great Britain during the first half of the 19th century, whose structure was greatly influenced by the broad power of the Anglican Church's hierarchy in political and social life.

The counterpoint to this catastrophic 'geological flood' came from Charles Lyell's (1797-1875) work. In 1830 he started the publication of his influential

---

[23] Charles Darwin himself recalls it in his biography: "While I lived in London I often met with Owen, for I felt a great admiration but I was never able to understand his character and I never intimated with him. After the publication of *The Origin of Species* he became a very strong enemy. This was not due to any argument among us but, up to where I am able to judge, by the jealousy produced due to the success of the work..." (Charles Darwin [José Luis Gil Aristu, trans.]. *Autobiografía*. [Pamplona]: Laetoli, 2008; text on page 91 [supplied in Spanish]).

[24] Richard Owen. *On the Archetype and Homologies of the Vertebrate Skeleton*. London: J. Van Voorst, 1848.

Principles of Geology... (London: John Murray, 1830-1833), in which he maintains that the actual geological structure is due to changes caused by slow and constant processes which act during vast periods of time. These geological processes, such as the wear of the rocks by the action of water, the marine tides, the continuous action of the waves on the coast, the volcanic activity or erosion, transport and sedimentation caused by the rivers, perfectly observable nowadays, are, according to Lyell's theory of uniformitarianism, the same as those that help us explain the changes produced in the complete history of the Earth. In his opinion, the constant changes in the physical geography were linked to modifications in the environmental conditions, that provoked variations in the fauna and flora – and also in the fossils – of the different regions of the Globe[25]. In Lyell's theorizing, Biogeography obtains a special importance as an element capable of nourishing his hypothesis. The ideas mentioned by Charles Darwin would have even more importance. Charles Lyell, whose theories influenced Charles Darwin's thinking, fiercely defended the stability of species. However, after reading *The Origin of Species,...* he would accept evolutionism[26].

Between Nature and Economy: the 'struggle for existence'

The question about the dynamic balance of Nature was another of the topics discussed during the first decades of the 19th century. The cleric William Paley (1743- -1805) justified, in texts such as *Natural Theology or, evidences of the existence and attributes of the deity...* (London: printed for R. Faulder, Wilks and Taylor, 1802), the adaptation of the organisms to the environment and explained, as a result of this perfect harmony, the relations among hunters and their prey: only the weakest, those that cannot subsist anymore in an adequate manner, would fall in the power of their beater. William Paley's work was well known by Charles Darwin, for its lecture was mandatory in order to obtain a Degree in Arts by the University of Cambridge and, according to his commentaries, left a certain influence on his thoughts:

> "The logic of this book [referring to *Evidences of Christianity*] and maybe also, Paley's *Natural Theology* caused as much pleasure as Euclides. A careful study of his works, without trying to memorise none of its parts, was the only one of my academic degree which was minimally useful to educate my thoughts, as it seemed to me at that moment, and still believe. At that time I was not worried about Paley's assumption and since they were accepted without critic, I liked his argumentative line, and he convinced me..." [27].

---

[25] A biography of Charles Lyell in Carmina Virgili. *El fin de los mitos geológicos. Lyell.* Madrid: Nivola, 2003.

[26] A situation that even Charles Darwin comments: "He possessed a great and notable honesty and demonstrated it by changing to the theory evolution despite having obtained great fame by opposing Lamarck's theories. Even more, he did it at an elderly age..." (Charles Darwin [José Luis Gil Aristu, trans.]. *Autobiografía.* [Pamplona]: Laetoli, 2008; text – in Spanish – on page 88).

[27] Charles Darwin [José Luis Gil Aristu, trans.]. *Autobiografía.* [Pamplona]: Laetoli, 2008. Text – in Spanish – on page 55.

However, years later, after reflecting upon the origin of species, his opinions about William Paley's theories had changed substantially:

> "The old argument of Nature's design as exposed by Paley and that previously seemed to me so solid, failed after the discovery of the Natural Selection law. We cannot sustain anymore, for example, that the beautiful hinge of a bivalve shell should have been produced by an intelligent being, like the hinge of a door by a human. In the variability of the organic beings and in the effects of natural selection there seems to be no more indication than in the direction in which the wind blows..."[28]

The effect of the demographic pressure had had a doctrinal concretion in relation to human groups, in the formulations that Thomas Malthus (1766-1834) had carried out in 1798 when he published *Essay on the principle of population...* (London: printed for J. Johnson, 1798), in which he established the geometrical progression of human growth against the arithmetics of available nutritional resources in a way that the survival of the individuals was subordinated to social adaptation. The terms adaptation, development and progress were already related to the available literature of the time. The mechanisms which permitted to interpret this relation were still obscure when Charles Darwin started to work on the most classical of his works.

The origin of *On the Origin of Species*...

According to Charles Darwin himself he started to collect notes for *The Origin of Species*... shortly after he returned to England and strongly influenced by Charles Lyell's geological works (1797-1875):

> "I started my first notebook in July 1837. I started working with the authentic Baconian principles, dispensed any theory and compiled all types of data, especially in what refers to domesticated species. For this, I appealed to printed questionnaires, conversations with skilled stockmen and gardeners and a great number of readings. When I see the list of books I have read, including complete collections of magazines and annuals, I surprise myself with my hard work..."[29].

It did not take him long to find out that selection was the key to the success of artificial creation, but the way in which this principle could be applied to the natural world was a complete mystery for him.

In October 1838, fifteen months after having started his enquiries, he read (he maintains that "by casualty and to entertain myself") one of the books that shed new light on the problem, the *Essay on the principle of population...* (London, 1798) by Thomas Malthus (1766-1834).

---

[28] Charles Darwin [José Luis Gil Aristu, trans.]. *Autobiografía*. [Pamplona]: Laetoli, 2008. Text – in Spanish – on page 78.

[29] Charles Darwin [José Luis Gil Aristu, trans.]. *Autobiografía*. [Pamplona]: Laetoli, 2008. Text – in Spanish – on page 103-104.

"There I finally had a theory on which I could work but I was very worried about trying to avoid any type of prejudice and I decided not to write anything during a certain period of time, not even a minor draft. In June 1842 I permitted myself, for the first time, the satisfaction of putting on paper, with a pencil and on 35 pages, a very brief summary of my theory, which I expanded during the summer of 1844 to 230 pages which I then copied with a legible handwriting and still conserve..."[30]

One of the most fundamental elements of *On the Origin of Species...* is not present in any of these papers: the natural tendency of living beings to branch off in their features as they are modified. The problem, and its solution, was addressed by Darwin some years later:

"I can remember this beautiful place in the street in which I felt the happiness of having thought of a solution while I was in my carriage. It was much later after I had moved to Down. The solution is, from what I think, that in Nature's economy, the modified offspring of all the dominating and in expansion forms tend to adapt themselves to many and very diversified places" [31].

The main ideas that would form the central body of the work were already in his mind, the rest of the story is well known to us: spurred by Charles Lyell (1797-1875), Darwin started to write with great detail, "with an extension three or four times superior to the one that I maintained later in *The origin of Species...*", a compilation version of the cases on which he founded his hypothesis. In the summer of 1858, when he had hardly written half of the extensive discourse, he received Alfred Russel Wallace's (1823-1913) article *On the tendency of varieties to depart indefinitely from the original type....* An emergency solution was necessary in order to publish a short summary of Darwin's theory along with Wallace's papers and Darwin's famous letter to Asa Gray on September 5, 1857 in which he showed a draft of his theories, in the August 1858 *Journal of the Proceedings of the Linnean Society*. It was clearly a compromising solution:

"Nor the manuscript nor the letter to Asa Gray had been produced in order to be published and they were poorly written. On the other hand, Mr. Wallace's paper was wonderfully expressed and amazingly clearly written. However, our combined productions did not cause great attention and the only piece of news published about them that I can remember was that written by professor Haughton, from Dublin, whose verdict was that all the new things exposed in them were false and all the true things, old..."[32].

[30] Charles Darwin [José Luis Gil Aristu, trans.]. *Autobiografía*. [Pamplona]: Laetoli, 2008. Text – in Spanish – on page 104. The texts have been converted into Spanish by Joan Lluis Riera. Charles Darwin & Alfred Russell Wallace [Fernando Pardos, ed.]. *La teoría de la evolución de las especies*. Barcelona: Crítica, 2006.

[31] Charles Darwin [José Luis Gil Aristu, trans.]. *Autobiografía*. [Pamplona]: Laetoli, 2008. Text – in Spanish – on page 104-105.

[32] Charles Darwin [José Luis Gil Aristu, trans.]. *Autobiografía*. [Pamplona]: Laetoli, 2008. Text – in Spanish – on page 105.

In September 1858, practically forced by Charles Lyell (1797-1875) and Joseph Dalton Hooker (1817-1911), Charles Darwin recovered his old notes and elaborated them once again – at a time when his poor health had worsened, compelling him to visit Dr. Lane's hydropathical hospital once again. He elaborated them out according to the format they would appear in, in November 1859, under the title *On the origin of species...*, a text that the author considered to be "the main work of my life".

The book obtained an immediate commercial success: the first edition, with 1,250 copies, was sold the same day of its publication, and the second edition, with 3,000 copies, shortly after. Where does the key of his success dwell? Darwin offers some elements:

> "I think that the success of *Origin* can be ascribed in great measure to the fact that, long before, I had written two condensed drafts and I abridged a much longer manuscript which was already a summary of itself. This let me select the most striking data and conclusions. During many years I also followed a golden rule: to write immediately, and without delay, a note every time that I found myself with a new, or opposite to my general results, piece of published data, observation or thought..."[33]

He also refutes other interpretations:

> "It has been said many times that the success of *Origin* demonstrated that 'the topic floated in the environment', or that 'the human mind was prepared for it'. I do not think that this is completely true because, once in a while, I asked not few naturalists and I never found any one of them that doubted the permanence of the species. Not even Lyell nor Hooker seemed to agree with me, even if they used to hear me with interest. In one or two occasions I tried to explain capable people what I understood by Natural selection but I vigorously failed..."[34]

However, there is something in this refutation. On the one hand, the fact itself that such opinions were produced and, on the other hand, the heap of works, of one or other type, which come before Darwin's texts and which he himself mentioned in the 'Historical sketch' included in *The Origin of Species...* This sketch, that first appeared in the third edition, printed in April 1861, was orientated to comment both the progress of the acceptance of his theories and the acceptance of authors that, before him, had addressed the same problem. In it he pays special attention to an anonymous piece of work, *Vestiges of the Natural History of Creation...* (London: [s.n.], 1844), today attributed to Robert Chambers (1802-1871), a bookseller from Edinburgh. This work was another editorial success of the time[35]. In it we find a defence of the evolution of the organism based on modifications that take place during

---

[33] Charles Darwin [José Luis Gil Aristu, trans.]. *Autobiografía*. [Pamplona]: Laetoli, 2008. Text – in Spanish – on page 106.

[34] Charles Darwin [José Luis Gil Aristu, trans.]. *Autobiografía*. [Pamplona]: Laetoli, 2008. Text – in Spanish – on page 107.

[35] James A. Secord. *Victorian Sensation. The extraordinary publication, reception, and secret authorship of Vestiges of the Natural History of Creation.* Chicago: University of Chicago Press, 2001.

the embryonic period, abnormally outstretched by external situations, leading to more advanced stages in the natural scale, whose last result would be the human being.

Charles Darwin knew how to value Robert Chambers' contributions within their real meaning:

> "The work, because of its powerful and brilliant style, even though it shows little exact knowledge and a great lack of scientific concern in its first editions, had immediately produced a very extensive circulation. In my opinion, it has offered an excellent service to this country for having called the attention on this point, stirring worries and preparing the terrain for the reception of analogous opinions..."[36].

To create a state of opinion, that was Robert Chambers' main contribution, a bookseller who knew very well the business he worked in; and, in one way or another, the idea of evolution was already present in the feelings of many who were just waiting to find an adequate and well supported formulation with strong arguments.

The precedents that Charles Darwin presents in 'Historical sketch' are many more. In it he made reference to the Natural selection hypothesis exposed by William Charles Wells (1757-1817), in the second decade of the 19th century at the *Royal Society*[37]. He would also mention experiments on the cultivation of hyacinths carried out by William Herbert (1778-1847)[38] and the hypothesis on the improvement of the descendents drafted out by Robert Edmond Grant (1793-1874) in his studies on *Spongilla friabilis*[39]. Darwin would also make reference to the opinion of the geologist Leopold von Buch (1774-1853), of neptunism training, in his *Description physique des Isles Canaries...* (Paris: F.-G. Levrault, 1836)[40] and supported by the botanist Constantine Samuel Rafinesque-Schmaltz (1783-1840)[41], according to who the varieties achieve constant features, little by little, until they become species. Of

---

[36] Charles Darwin [Enrique Godínez, trans.]. *Origen de las especies por medio de la selección natural ó la conservación de las razas favorecidas en la lucha por la existencia...* Madrid / París: Biblioteca Perojo, 1877 (Quote – in Spanish – from page 6).

[37] William Charles Wells. *Two essays: on upon Single Vision with Two Eyes; the other on Dew. A Letter to... Lord Kenyon and an account of a female of the white race... part of whose skin resembles that of a negro... with a memoir of his life, written by himself.* London: A. Constable and Co., 1818. The second of these papers, in which Charles Darwin centred his interest, was read in 1813 but not published until 1818.

[38] William Herbert. *Amaryllidaceae*. London: J. Ridgeway and Sons, 1837.

[39] Robert E. Grant. "On the structure and nature of Spongilla friabilis". *Edinburgh Philosophical Journal*, 14: 270-284. Edinburgh, 1826.

[40] Leopold von Buch. *Description physique des îles Canaries, suivie d'une indication des principaux volcans du globe, par Léopold de Buch. Traduite de l'allemand par C. Boulanger,... revue et augmentée par l'auteur.* Paris: F.-G. Levrault, 1836. The original edition was published in German (*Physicalische Beschreibung der Canarischen Inseln.* Berlin: Koenigliche Akademie der Wissenschaften, 1825), but it was the French edition to which Charles Darwin made reference in his paper.

[41] Constantine Samuel Rafinesque-Schmaltz. *New flora and botany of North America or a supplemental flora, additional to all the botanical works on North America and the United States, containing 1.000 new or revised species. In four parts. I. Lexicon and Monographs. II. Neophyton &c. III. New Sylva &c. IV. Neobotanon &c. with introductions, sketches, notes, indexes, &c.* Philadelphia: [Printed for the author and publisher], 1836-1838. Charles Darwin mentions the first pages of the work (*cf.* pages 6, 18).

course, he also had to make reference to the opinions that preceeded from his own family environment: his grandfather, Erasmus Darwin (1731-1802), presented his *Zoonomy...* (London: J. Johnson, 1794-1796), during the final years of the 18th century, a pre-Lamarckist draft, that Charles Darwin read, first with admiration, and then with a certain disdain[42].

These are, among many others, the predecessors of the Theory of Natural Selection which Charles Darwin wanted to have remembered. His son, Francis Darwin (1848--1925), left us a very different opinion:

> "As a whole, I have the impression that the influence of the first evolutionists on his thoughts was priceless and in what refers to the story of *The Origin of Species*, has no particular importance, because (...) the theory of evolutionism did not thrive in his thought until he was notable to conceive the cause of the modification.
>
> I think that Mr. Huxley [Thomas Henry Huxley (1825-1895)] is right when he states that 'It is not exaggerated to say that the biggest part of Darwin's work is the result of the decided application of the main idea to biology and of the applied method to geology [of Charles Lyell] in *Principles...*"[43].

My opinion, and I think most of the Darwinists opinions, is totally favourable to the one issued by Francis Darwin who knew, maybe better than anyone, the birth of Charles Darwin's works.

---

[42] "...reading it for the second time, after a discontinuity of 10 or 15 years, I suffered a great disappointment: his speculations are proportionally more in quantity in comparison to the contributed data..." (Charles Darwin [José Luis Gil Aristu, trans.]. *Autobiografía*. [Pamplona]: Laetoli, 2008. Text – in Spanish – on page 47)

[43] Charles Darwin. *Autobiografía* [*Selección de Francis Darwin*]. Madrid: Alianza, 1977 (translation from Aarom Cohen and María Teresa de la Torre, introductory study from Luís García Ballester. The mentioned text – in Spanish – belongs to volume 2: 263-264).

Jorge Paiva

Centro de Ecologia Funcional, Universidade de Coimbra, Portugal

DARWIN, PLANTS AND PORTUGAL

Introduction

Charles Darwin's naturalist preparation started practically with his childhood education, roaming through the countryside, collecting insects, mineral shells and rocks. Still at a young age (16 years old), Darwin learned not only to observe and prepare plants as well as animals, when he went to the University of Edinburgh to study medicine. There he took the subject of Natural History taught by Robert Jameson and worked with the taxidermist John Edmonstone, a former slave, who taught him embalming. When, at the age of 18, he went to the University of Cambridge, the theoretical and practical preparation given to him by the professor of botany John Stevens Henslow, as well as the contacts he maintained throughout all his life with the botanists of the Royal Botanic Gardens of Kew, particularly with the respective Director, Joseph Dalton Hooker, were crucial for the botanical works he later developed.

Darwin did not simply collect plants during the voyage. He also herborised in Great Britain, so much so, that the oldest specimens collected by him are from August 1831, in Barmouth, Wales (Great Britain). It is a collection deposited in the Herberium of Christ's College [University of Cambridge (CGE)]

During the five year voyage, Darwin collected more than 2600 specimens of plants mounted on 950 herbarium sheets, arquived in the Herbarium of the University of Cambridge (CGE), not counting those collected in Great Britain and the small collections arquived in other Herbariums (BM; COL; E-GL; FI-W; GL; GOET; IH; K; MANCH; MO; NY; OXF; P and U). Many of those specimens are type specimens of the various new species he collected.

Darwin did not herborise in an indiscriminated manner, although he declares that he did so in the Galapagos ("*On the origin of species by means of natural selection, or the preservation of favoured races in the struggle for life*";1859), for his notebooks are filled with botanical commentaries, as well as the books he published, some (seven) exclusively on plants.

The books he wrote on plants were a result not only of his literary culture (reading and sharing of opinions he made, in writing and orally, with various botanists and collectors), as well as from observations and experiences he did at his propriety in Down (Kent, England). Thus, he selectively cultivated (Artificial Selection) around 54 varieties of gooseberries and many of bean plants, pea plants and cabbages; he carried out interesting experiences, particularly with insectivorous plants; wrote essays on polinization; he studied the heterostyly of flowers of some plants; he conducted research on movements and nastic movements of plants, etc.

There are many species of fossils, animals, funghi, algae and plants, whose scientific names have restrictives as a tribute to Charles Darwin. In a list of scientific names of plants (*sensu lato*) dedicated to Darwin we elaborated, there are 6 fungi (currently included in the Kingdom of *Mycota*); 4 of algae (currently included in the Kingdom of *Chromysta*) and 88 in the Kingdom of *Plantae* [12 red algae (*Rhodophyta*), 1 green algae (*Chlorophyta*), 1 hepatica (*Marchantiophyta*), 4 Pteridophytes (2 *Lycopodiophyta* and 2 *Polypodiophyta*) and 70 Spermatophyta (*Magnoliophyta*)].

Charles Darwin (1809-1882) was a "Counter-Current", as was Nicolaus Copernicus (1473-1543) and Galileo Galilei (1564-1642). Copernicus ended with Aristotle's geocentrism, which got him convicted for going against the "Holy Scriptures" (Joshua 10: 13). Basically one century later, Galileo aggreeing with the heliocentrism modelled by Copernicus ("Revolution of the celestial spheres"; 1543), was convicted, having been forced, in his seventies, to abjure on his knees in the Court of the Roman Holy Office (Inquisition); Darwin ended up renouncing criationism (fixism) and antropocentrism based on the Biblical Genesis. Science showed that any one of them was right. The basic principles of evolutionism or darwinism, as Alfred Russell Wallace (1823-1913) called it in 1889, are currently well-established by various fields of Science (Biology, Geology, Biochemistry, Anatomy, Embryology, Paleonthology, Biogeography, Climatology, etc.) Evolutionism is not a theory but a natural phenomenon. With Genetics, Biochemistry and Molecular Biology it was confirmed that natural selection, which does not act (fenotipically) on the characters acquired, but through variations and genetic mutations are also extremely relevant evolutionary factors, as genetic recombinations, differential migrations, genetic derivatives and diverse mechanisms of isolation (neo-darwinism). Nowadays, with a better knowledge of symbiotic organisms it is considered that evolution occurs not only through competitive processes, but also cooperative, as is symbiogenesis (post-neodarwinism).

When Charles Darwin started the long voyage of the Beagle, he was a fixist, but when it ended, he was already a "transformist"; in other words, an evolutionist, as the diagram testifies ("evolutionary tree") that he designed in 1837 (6 months after returning to England), maybe based on the ramified structure of a corallinacea (*Rhodophyta*, red algae), probably *Amphiroa orbignyana* Decn. = *Bossiella orbignyana* (Decn.) P.C. Silva, he collected on the coasts of South America. It took many years to publish the first edition of *The Origin of Species*, not because of a fear of criticism and consequences, as it has been written and said many times, but because he wanted to be sure that he had confirmatory data that scientifically explained the "transmutations" (designation he attributed to specific variations). Natural Selection was the essence of all of his arguments.

Darwin was a researcher and tireless naturalist, without mentioning that, during the Beagle voyage, he collected 1529 species conserved in liquid, 3907 labelled and dry skins, as well as bones, fossils and about 2600 specimens of plants. Darwin was a scientist of great merit (he wrote more than a dozen books and more than two hundred articles), very cultured, having been careful not only to keep up to date with what he published on Earth Sciences, but also maintaining a constant dialogue and correspondence (he wrote around 14500 letters) with many contemporary scientists.

As Darwin himself said, he was lucky to be a wealthy person, not needing to work to support his family, which gave him a lot of time for his investigations, as well as not losing time in meetings and activities of life in society, because he was always ill and rarely left home.

This is how Charles Darwin became an important figure, not only scientifically but also philosophically, having received many honours and awards during his lifetime, such as the doctorate *Honoris Causa* by the University of Cambridge, Honorary Professor of the Instituto Libre de Enseñanza Universitaria (Spain) and honorary member of 75 British and foreign Scientific Societies. Many statues were erected in his honour and his name was given to a city (Australia), an Institution for Scientific Research (Galapagos), a Botanical Institute (Argentina), a Natural Park (Australia), a Museum (Darwin Centre, Natural History Museum, London), geomorphological formations (Galapagos, South America and Tropical Africa), a scientific magazine (Darwiniana) and scientific epithet to many species and varieties of animals, plants and fossils. He was buried in Westminster Abbey, a few metres from Newton's grave.

The plants

Charles Darwin's naturalist preparation started practically with his childhood education, roaming through the countryside, collecting insects, mineral shells and rocks. Still at a young age (16 years old), Darwin learned not only to observe and prepare plants as well as animals, when he went to the University of Edinburgh to study medicine. There he took the subject of Natural History taught by Robert Jameson (1774-1854) and worked with the taxidermist John Edmonstone, a former slave, who taught him embalming (1825-1827). When, at the age of 18, he went to the University of Cambridge, the theoretical and practical preparation given to him by the professor of botany John Stevens Henslow (1796-1861), was crucial for the botanical works he later developed. John Henslow not only granted him the practice for harvesting plants still in Cambridge, but also advised him during the Beagle voyage, in writing (letter 13.01.1833), not to collect fragments, but specimens which were the most complete ("perfect") as possible (roots, leaves and flowers). During the mentioned voyage, Darwin had an assistant (Syms Covington) not only for harvesting (collected birds and mammals, after 1833), but also for helping him in the last months of the expedition to prepare the lists of numbered plant specimens, ordered by taxonomic groups, to later distribute among the respective specialists. Finally, the constant contacts he maintained during his lifetime with botanists of the Royal Botanic Gardens of Kew, particularly with Joseph Dalton Hooker (1817-1911, director of Kew 1865-1885), the scientist to whom he first exposed in writing (letter dated 14th of July 1844) that he was convinced that the species were not fixed and that he had found the explanation for the process on how species adapted to the respective environments (here he did not use the term "Natural Selection"). This botanist studied a great part of the plants collected by Darwin during the Beagle voyage. Elucidatory of those contacts is what Darwin refers to in *The Origin of Species* ("*On the origin of species by means of natural selection, or the preservation of favoured races in the struggle for life*"; 1859) on the similarities that Joseph Hooker detected among the flora of the Kerguelen Island (located between South

Africa and Australia) and New Zealand and Tierra del Fuego, and not with Africa's, much closer than Tierra del Fuego. At that time, nothing was known on the shift of continental plates and that South America had been connected to Australia and New Zealand. Thus, Darwin admitted that seeds had been transported by "icebergs" from the Land of Fire to New Zealand, as Charles Lyell (1797-1875), professor of geology at Cambridge suggested, who's "*Principles of Geology*" (1830) Darwin had read during the voyage (27.XII.1831 – 2.X.1836).

Darwin did not only collect plants during the voyage. He also herborised in Great Britain, so much so that the oldest specimens collected by him are from August 1831, in Barmouth, Wales (Great Britain), during the expedition that took place there, led by his Professor of Geology, Adam Sedgwick (1785-1873), at the University of Cambridge. It is a collection deposited in the Herbarium of Christ's College [University of Cambridge (CGE)], belonging to *Matthiola sinuata* (L.) R.Br., one Cruciferae (family of cabbages).

During the five-year voyage, Darwin collected more than 2600 specimens of plants mounted on 950 herbarium sheets, in the Herbarium of the University of Cambridge (CGE), not counting those collected in Great Britain and the small collections in other Herbariums (BM; COL; E-GL; FI-W; GL; GOET; IH; K; MANCH; MO; NY; OXF; P and U). Many of those specimens are taxonomical types of the various new species he collected.

Darwin did not herborise in an indiscriminated manner, although he declares he did so in the Galapagos ("*On the origin of species by means of natural selection, or the preservation of favoured races in the struggle for life*"; 1859), for his notebooks are filled with botanical commentaries, as well as the books he published, some exclusively on plants, such as "*On the contrivances by which British and foreign orchids are fertilised by insects*" (1862 and 1877, 2nd ed.); "*On the movements and habits of climbing plants*" (1865-1882); "*The variation of animals and plants under domestication*" (1868 and 1875, 2nd ed.); "*Insectivorous Plants*" (1875 and 1888, 2nd ed.); "*The effects of cross and self fertilisation in the vegetable kingdom*" (1876 and 1878, 2nd ed.); "*Different forms of flowers*" (1877); "*The power of movement in plants*" (1880).

The specimens of the herbarium of plants collected by Darwin in the Galapagos, form the first scientific plant collection of that archipelago. Although there were Scientific Expeditions to the Galapagos before the Beagle, in 1835 (Archibald Menzies, in 1795; David Douglas and John Scoulter, in 1825; James MacRae, in 1825; Hugh Cumming, in 1829), Darwin's collection was the largest and most representative. All these collections were studied by Joseph Hooker (he established 114 new *taxa* for science), except Archibald's collection, the first naturalist to visit the Archipelago. Some authors comment that the expedition of Malaspina, between 1789 and 1794 and sponsored by King Charles III of Spain, was the first scientific expedition to the Galapagos, but there are no confirmatory documents of that fact. Nowadays, around 500 native species are referenced in this Archipelago, of which 180 (240 *taxa*) are endemic, and about 900 introduced. Darwin collected 290 numbered specimens of plants in the Galapagos, which he sent to the professor that had taught him to collect and prepare plants for herbarium (John Stevens Henslow). Initially, he tried to study them, being actually the first known scientific name for a plant in the Galapagos (1837) of John Henslow's authorship (*Opuntia galapageia* Hensl.), having dedicated another to Darwin [*Opuntia darwinii* Hensl. = *Maihueniopsis darwinii* (Hensl.) F. Ritter].

Later on, Joseph Hooker, at that time Director of the Royal Botanic Gardens in Kew, was in charge of carrying out that study, having described, in 1843, his first species of the Galapagos. This botanist described 78 new taxa, from material collected by Darwin, and 8 species dedicated to him [*Abutilon darwinii* Hook. f.; *Chiliotrichum darwinii* Hook. f. = *Nardophyllym darwinii* (Hook. f.) A. Gray; *Eugenia darwinii* Hook. f. = *Pseudocaryophyllus darwinii* (Hook. f.) Burret; *Galapagoa darwinii* Hook. f. = *Tiquilia darwinii* (Hook. f.) A.T. Richardson; *Hymenophyllum darwinii* Hook. f.; *Pleuropetalum darwinii* Hook. f.; *Scalesia darwinii* Hook. f.; *Urtica darwinii* Hook. f.] and a variety of [*Conferva clavata* C.Agardh var. *darwinii* Hook. f. & Harv. = *Chaetomorpha coliformis* (Mont.) Kütz.].

William Jackson Hooker (1785-1865), father of Joseph Dalton Hooker, previous Director of the Royal Botanic Gardens in Kew (1841-1865), also studied some of the material collected by Darwin, and dedicated to him five species [*Baccharis darwinii* Hook. & Arn. = *Neomolina darwinii* (Hook. & Arn.) F. Hellweg; *Berberis darwinii* Hook.; *Neosparton darwinii* Benth. & Hook. = *Lippia darwinii* (Benth. & Hook.) Speg.; *Panargyrus darwinii* Hook. & Arn. = *Nassauvia darwinii* (Hook. & Arn.) O. Hoffm. & Dusé; *Senecio darwinii* Hook. & Arn.].

Darwin was a shrewd observer, as is notorious in any of his botanical works. His prediction on the type of butterfly that was the pollinator of the big white flowers of the orchid *Angraecum sesquipedale* Thouars, which James Bateman (1811-1897), a wealthy collector of orchids, had sent him in January 1862, is famous. This orchid is endemic to Madagascar (Darwin did not see this orchid on the island, as many authors mention, since the Beagle never docked in Madagascar). Darwin, in Chapter V of the mentioned book on fertilisation of orchids by insects (*On the contrivances by which British and foreign orchids are fertilised by insects*") predicted, not only that the butterfly that pollinated this species was nocturnal, but also that it had to have an extraordinarily long proboscis, since this flower has a spur of about 30 cm, at the end of which is the nectar. Thus he says "...The pollinia are collected by a big nocturnal butterfly, possessing a magnificently long proboscis...." Besides that, he predicted not only that the butterfly was also a Malagasy endemic, as well as an interdependency between the two species (co-evolution or "correlated variation", as he called it) "... the disappearence of *Angraecum* would probably be a loss of these lepidoptera." About 40 years later, in 1903, Lionel Rothschild and Karl Jordam discovered, in Madagascar, the mentioned pollinating butterfly of the *Angraecum sesquipedale* Thouars, with the long proboscis, which they scientifically baptised with the epithet referring to the Darwinian prediction: *Xanthopan morganii-praedicta* Rothsch. & Jord. As a matter of fact, the prediction made by Darwin was used by criationists to fight his evolutionist ideas. Thus, five years after Darwin made the mentioned prediction public, George Campbell published a book ("*The Reign of Law*"; 1867), in which it is said that a species like this, implicated having been raised by a supernatural being.

The books he wrote on plants were a result, not only of his literary culture (reading and sharing opinions he made, in writing and orally, with various botanists and collectors), but also from observations and experiences he prepared in his propriety in Down. Thus, he selectively cultivated (Artificial Selection) around 54 harvests of gooseberries (*Ribes* spp.) and many bean plants (*Phaseolus* spp.), pea plants (*Pisum* spp.) and cabbages (*Brassica* spp.). He performed interesting experiences, particularly with insectivorous plants, as he describes with **Drosera rotundifolia** L. ("*Insectivorous Plants*"), placing, among other products, small pieces of meat on the leaves: with the leaves as a trap on the **Dionaea muscipula** Ellis, whose leaves he considered caught insects just as mouse traps in "costilha" (backbreaker); with the leaves on the **Pinguicula lusitanica** L. (it exists not only in Portugal, but also in the British Isles, France and Spain, having Darwin obtained living plants on Cornwall, England), that roll to capture insects; he wrote essays on auto-polinization and crossed polinization such as the ones described with **Linaria vulgaris** Mill. ("*The effects of cross and self fertilisation...*), a Scrophulariaceae (family of the snapdragon) and with orchids ("*On the contrivances...*"); he studied heterostyly of the flowers of some plants, for example, the **Lythrum salicaria** L., purple loosestrife, and **Primula vulgaris** Huds., primrose ("*Different forms of flowers*"); he conducted research on understanding movements and nastic movements of plants ("*On the movements and habits of climbing plants*") and ("*The power of movement in plants*"); etc.

Darwin was concerned on studying vegetable activities with living plants, a topic that interested him. Thus, not only did he plant them in his farm in Down, where he even had greenhouses for plants that needed them, but he also tried, by every means, to find someone that could send him the living plants he wanted. He knew that in Portugal there existed an unusual insectivore plant, the **Drosophyllum lusitanicum** L. At that time it was thought that it was only found in Portugal, but today we know that this insectivore does not only exist in our country, but also in the Southwest of Spain and the Northwest of Africa. He asked Joseph Hooker, Director of the Royal Botanic Gardens in Kew, to ask for plants of that species from the Directors of the Botanical Gardens of Portugal [at that time there were two Gardens of that kind in our country: the Royal Garden of Ajuda and the Botanical Garden of Coimbra, whose Director was António José Rodrigues Vidal (1868-1872)], but Joseph Hooker never received an answer. However, on January 26th, 1869, Darwin received a letter from William Chester Tait (1844-1921), a British enologist and amateur botanist, resident and owner of a farm in Porto (Casa Tait, Quinta do Meio, currently propriety of the Town-hall of Porto), in which he questioned him on the heredity of dogs with docked tails (19.02.1869). Darwin, in his reply (24.02.1869), said that he was not interested in the issue of dog tail mutilation and respective transmission or not. However, he took the opportunity to ask William Tait if he could send him living plants of **Drosophyllum lusitanicum** L. William Tait sent him the first sample (02.03.1869), together with a piece of a fern leaf that he had seen at the location where he had collected the insectivore plant (Monte de Santa Justa, Valongo), so that Darwin could tell him what kind of fern it was (concluding that it would be **Culcita macrocarpa** K. Presl, a very robust fern, that is only seen in Portugal and is not cited in Flora Lusitanica de Brotero, that W. Tait possessed, as he mentions in that letter). Darwin answered him (12 and 16.03.1869), saying that he did not know the fern, confirming and thanking the reception of the **Drosophyllum lusitanicum** L. William Tait sent more samples (living and in containers) of the insectivore plant (they exchanged amongst themselves 18 letters each – between 19.02 and 29.09.1869), with some "curious" information, such as the fact that the local population put these plants in the balconies of houses to catch flies. He even said that the locals called it "erva-apanha-moscas" (fly-catching grass), common name which is not currently used for this species, which is known as Portuguese sundew or dewy pine.

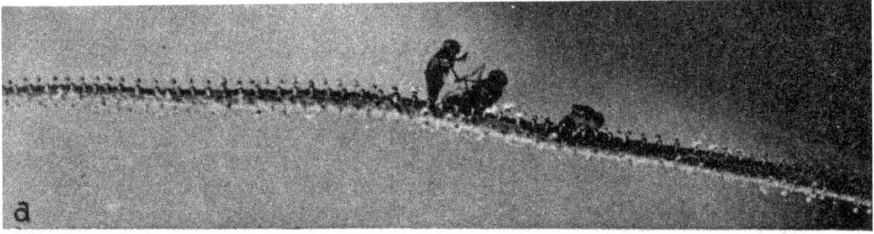

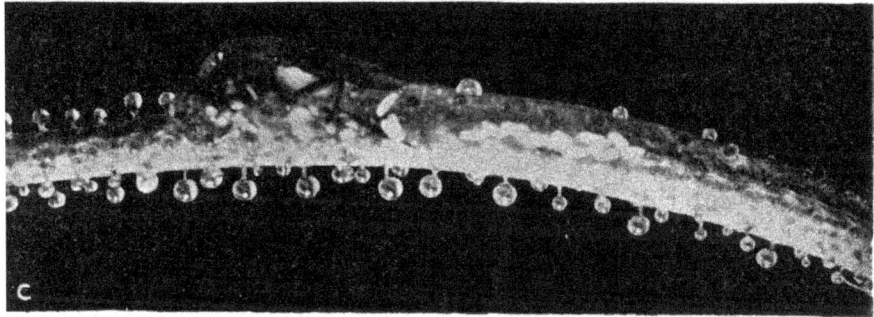

Flies caught in the leaves of *Drosophyllum lusitanicum*.
Foto in: Abílio Fernandes, 1941. Morfologia e Biologia das Plantas Carnívoras.Separata do
Anuário da Sociedade Broteriana, Anos VI e VII

In his publication on the Beagle voyage (*"Journal of researches into the natural history and geology of the countries visited during the voyage of H.M.S. Beagle round the world."*; 1839) there are incredible botanical observations, still valid nowadays, such as those referring to the endemic flora of the Galapagos: "If we take a look now at the flora we will discover that the aboriginal plants of the different islands are surprisingly different. I present the set of the following results having the support of the solid authority of my friend Dr J. Hooker. I have to anticipate that I indiscriminately collected all the flowers found in the different islands and that due to luck I kept my collections separate...However, my drawings show the amazing fact that in James Island, of the thirty eight Galapagan plants or those that cannot be found anywhere else in the world, thirty are exclusively confined to this island; and at Albemarle Island, of the twenty six aboriginal galapagan plants, twenty two are confined to it; this is, they are only known until today to be grown on other islands of the archipelago; and so forth...The *Scalesia*, an incredible arborescent genus of the Compositae, is confined to the Archipelago. It has six species; one of Chatham, one of Albemarle, one of Charles Island, two from James Island and a sixth of one of the last three islands...none of these six species is grown on two islands." Or yet its American origin: "Dr. Hooker lets me know that the flora has an undoubtedly American western character; in the same way, he does not detect any affinity with the Pacific flora." In reality, all that can be confirmed, being *Scalesia* Hook. f. a endemic genus of the Galapagos, with 6 species, 5 of Joseph Hooker's authorship (*S. affinis* Hook. f., *S. darwinii* Hook. f., *S. gummifera* Hook. f., *S. incisa* Hook. f. e *S. pedunculata* Hook. f.) and 1 of G. Arnott (*S. atractyloides* Arn.), all tipified by specimens collected by Darwin.

The research for a plausible explanation on the way plants colonized the oceanic islands was one of his concerns, as he notes in some publications, like *"Journal of researches into the natural history and geology of the countries visited during the voyage of H.M.S. Beagle around the world."* "Thus, the flora of Madeira resembles, to a certain degree, the tertiary flora extinct in Europe." and in some letters, like the answer sent to the Azorean Francisco Arruda Furtado, with dated 3rd of July 1881 "If it were possible, I would visit and collect in one or various of the furthest islands and would compare the plants and animals with the other islands...Samples should be collected from all plants and animals from the highest points of the mountains of all them... Is there a lighthouse in the Azores? If there is, probably there are sometimes birds that fly against the window and die. If so, it would be advisable to examine not only their feet and beaks searching for dirt, but also remove all the content from the food channels and observe the existence of seeds that might germinate. If that happens, let the plants grow and identify them..Does the sea usually drag trees with roots to the shore? If so, the roots should be separated and any trace of earth among them, should be washed and placed in burnt earth and moistened in pure sand, under a glass canopy, in order to observe if the earth has any living seeds... After very strong winds, it might be worth it to look among the rubbish thrown on the shore, seeds, insects, etc."

Darwin exchanged letters with only one Portuguese person, Francisco Arruda Furtado (1854-1887) and it was at the end of his life (1881). Francisco Arruda was a scribe from the Azores and an amateur malacologist, that decided to write (13.06.1881) to Darwin, after reading his famous work *"On the origin of species by means of natural selection, or the preservation of favoured races in the struggle for life"*

(1859) and knowing that Darwin had a special interest in the study of Mollusks. In his answer (03.07.1881), Darwin, besides other recommendations, such as reading Alfred Russel Wallace's work, advised him to collect plants from the mountains and all the vegetable testimonies (roots, trunks) that came upon the Azorean shores, because they could help understand how the colonization happened, for plants in the Archipelago. In the scarce correspondence they exchanged (10 letters), Francisco Arruda, in one of the letters (29.07.1881), announced that he was going to send him seeds of 3-4 species, collected from the coasts of the island, dragged by the Gulf Current, that fisherman used as table decorations and emptied the biggest which they called "favas--do-mar" (sea broad lean), to make snuff boxes. In August (17.08.1881), Francisco Arruda asked Darwin to who he sent two small herbariums of plants collected in the mountains [Serra Gorda and Pico da Cruz (Pico da Pedra)] and said that he could not buy Wallace's work, which Darwin had recommended (13.07.1881) to read, because it was too expensive. Darwin announced (02.09.1881) that he sent Wallace's work by post, a work which he offered him. A few days later (12.09.188), Darwin told Francisco Arruda that he should send the plants to J. Hooker (providing him the address), who appeared to be very interested and advised him to investigate the existence of big cypress trunks that were found buried in the soil of the Azorean mountains, because they were considered extinct. These trunks were, most probably, of *Juniperus brevifolia* (Seub.) Antoine, the cedar of the Azores, an endemic species of this Archipelago, currently rigorously protected. Darwin never accused the reception of the seeds, maybe because he did not have time to study them or because Francisco Arruda never sent them. According to Francisco Arruda's description, it is possible to identify them, since they are seeds of trees from the African Tropical coast, dispersed by the Warm Current of the Gulf which hit azorean shores. The ones Francisco Arruda said were being used by Azorean fishermen for snuff boxes are huge seeds of the Leguminosae species, of the group of Mimosoideae, belonging to the genus *Entada* Adans., which have pods that reach 1,80 metres long and seeds ("favas-do-mar") diameters of 4-5 cm. Due to the geographical position of the Azores, it probably would have been seeds of *Entada pursaetha* DC. or *Entada gigas* Fawc. & Rendel, two species which are found in the Western coast of Tropical Africa and the Eastern coast of Tropical America. Seeds of these species have recently appeared at the coast of Continental Portugal, from the South to Praia da Barra (Aveiro), which indicates the dislocation of the Warm Current of the Gulf further North, due to "Global Warming". The other seeds, much smaller (no longer than a broad bean), that Francisco Arruda said are used as decoration objects, are seeds of Leguminosae, also from the group of Mimosoideae, belonging to the genus *Dioclea* Kunth, equally trees of the tropical coast that are still used today as ornaments, particularly necklaces. For the reasons mentioned for the species of *Entada* Adans., probably seeds of *Dioclea reflexa* Hook. f. or *Dioclea megacarpa* Rolfe.

In a description like this, it is not possible to refer to all the observations and studies that Darwin did with plants, which were many, although he studied and published more, on geology and zoology.

There are many species of fossils, animals, funghi and plants, whose scientific names have specific restrictives or varieties as a tribute to Charles Darwin. As I am a botanist, I present a list of scientific names of plants dedicated do Darwin.

NAMES OF "PLANTS" DEDICATED TO DARWIN

Kingdom *MYCOTA* (Fungi)

Ascomycota

> **Cyttaria darwinii** Berk.
> **Darwiniella** Spegg.
> **Darwiniella antarctica** Spegg.
> **Darwiniella globulosa** (Cooke & Massee) Sacc.
> *Dothidea globulosa* Cooke & Massee
> **Darwiniella gracilis** (Spegg.) Spegg.
> *Dothidea gracilis* Spegg.
> **Darwiniella orbiculata** Syd.

Kingdom *CHROMISTA* (Algae)

Bacillariophyta

> **Asterolampra darwinii** (Ehrenb.) Grev.
> *Asteromphalus darwinii* Ehrenb.
> *Asteromphalus darwinii* Ehrenb. = **Asterolampra darwinii** (Ehrenb.) Grev.

Ochrophyta

> **Distephanopsis crux** (Ehrenb.) Dumitrica
> subsp. **darwinii** (Bukry) Desikachary & Prema
> *Distephanus crux* (Ehren.) Haeckel subsp. **darwinii** Bukry
> *Distephanus crux* (Ehren.) Haeckel
> subsp. **darwinii** Bukry = **Distephanopsis crux** (Ehrenb.) Dumitrica
> subsp. **darwinii** (Bukry) Desikachary & Prema

Kingdom *PLANTAE*

Algae

Rhodophyta

> *Amphiroa darwinii* Harv. = **Bossiella chiloensis** (Decne.) H.W. Johans.
> *Arthrocardia darwinii* (Harv.) Weber Bosse = **Bossiella chiloensis** (Decne.) H.W. Johans.

Amphiroa darwinii Harv.

Botryocladia darwinii C.W.Schneid. & C.E. Lane

Chaetomorpha darwinii (Hook. f. & Harv.) Kütz. = **Chaetomorpha coliformis** (Mont.) Kütz.

Conferva clavata C.Agardh var. *darwinii* Hook. f. & Harv.

Cheilosporum darwinii (Harv.) De Toni = **Bossiella chiloensis** (Decn.) H.W. Johans.

Amphiroa darwinii Harv.

Conferva clavata C.Agardh
var. *darwinii* Hook. f. & Harv. = **Chaetomorpha coliformis** (Mont.) Kütz.

Conferva darwinii (Hook. f. & Harv.) Harv. = **Chaetomorpha coliformis** (Mont.) Kütz.

Conferva clavata C.Agardh var. *darwinii* Hook. f. & Harv.

Goniolithon darwinii (Harv.) Foslie = **Lithothamnion darwinii** (Harv.) Foslie

Melobesia darwinii Harv

Lithophyllum darwinii (Harv.) Foslie = **Lithothamnion darwinii** (Harv.) Foslie

Melobesia darwinii Harv

Lychaete darwinii (Hook. f. & Harv.) Laing = **Chaetomorpha coliformis** (Mont.) Kütz.

Conferva clavata C.Agardh var. *darwinii* Hook. f. & Harv.

Lithothamnion darwinii (Harv.) Foslie

Melobesia darwinii Harv

Melobesia darwinii Harv. = **Lithothamnion darwinii** (Harv.) Foslie

Chlorophyta

Pediastrum darwinii Haeckel

Bryophyte (Non-vascular)

Marchantiophyta

Frullania darwinii Gradst. & Uribe

Cormophyta (Vascular)

Lycopodiophyta

Huperzia darwiniana (Herter ex Nessel) B. Ollg.

Urostachys darwinianus Herter ex Nessel

Urostachys darwinianus Herter ex Nessel = **Huperzia darwiniana** (Herter ex Nessel) B. Ollg.

Polypodiophyta

Hymenophyllum darwinii Hook. f.
Thelypteris darwinii L.D. Gómez

Magnoliophyta

Abutilon darwinii Hook. f. (*Malvaceae*)
Acmella darwinii (D.M. Porter) R.K. Jansen (*Asteraceae*)
Spilanthes darwinii D.M. Porter
Allochlamys darwinii Moq. = **Pleuropetalum darwinii** Hook. f. (*Amaranthaceae*)
Asteriscus vogelii (Webb) Walp.
   var. *darwinii* (Webb) Walp. = **Nauplius daltonii** (Webb) Wiklund *subsp. vogeliii*
(Webb) Wiklund (*Asteraceae*)
   Astragalus darwinianus Gómez-Sosa (*Fabaceae*)
Baccharis darwinii Hook. & Arn. = **Neomolina darwinii** (Hook. & Arn.) F.
Hellweg (*Asteraceae*)
   Berberis darwinii Hook. (*Berberidaceae*)
Bonatea darwinii Weale = **Bonatea cassidea** Sond. (*Orchidaceae*)
Calceolaria darwinii Benth. = **Calceolaria uniflora** Lam. (S*crophulariaceae*)
Fagelia darwinii (Benth.) Kuntze
   Carex darwinii Boott (*Cyperaceae*)
   Catasetum darwinianum Rolfe (*Orchidaceae*)
Chiliotrichum darwinii Hook. f. = **Nardophyllym darwinii** (Hook. f.) A. Gray
(*Asteraceae*)
   Clinopodium darwinii (Benth.) Kuntze (*Lamiaceae*)
Micromeria darwinii Benth.
Satureja darwinii (Benth.) Briq.
Coldenia darwinii (Hook. f.) A. Gray = **Tiquilia darwinii** (Hook. f.) A.T. Richardson
(*Boraginaceae*)
   Galapagoa darwinii Hook. f.
   Croton scouleri Hook. f.
   var. *darwinii* G.L. Webster (*Euphorbiaceae*)
Darwinia Raf. (1817) = **Sesbania** Scop. (*Fabaceae*)dedicated to his Grandfather,
Erasmus Darwin
   Darwinia Dennst. (1818) = **Litsea** Lam. (*Lauraceae*) dedicated to his Grandfather,
Erasmus Darwin
   Darwinia Rudge (1816) (*Myrtaceae*)dedicated to his Grandfather, Erasmus Darwin
Darwiniella Braas & Lückel = **Stellilabium** Schltr. (*Orchidaceae*)
Darwiniera Braas & Lückel (*Orchidaceae*)
Darwiniera bergoldii (Garay & Dunst.) Braas & Lückel (*Orchidaceae*)
Trichoceros bergoldii Garay & Dunst.
Darwiniothamnus Harling (*Asteraceae*)
Darwiniothamnus alternifolius Lawesson & Adsersen (*Asteraceae*)
Darwiniothamnus lancifolius (Hook. f.) Harling (*Asteraceae*)

Erigeron lancifolius Hook. f

Darwiniothamnus lancifolius (Hook. f.) Harling (*Asteraceae*)

Erigeron tenuifolius Hook. f.

Decalophium darwiniodes Turcz. = **Chamelaucium ciliatum** Desf. (*Myrtaceae*)

Drosera darwinensis Lowrie (*Droseraceae*)

Eucalyptus darwinensis D.J. Carr & S.G.M. Carr (*Myraceae*)

Eugenia darwinii Hook. f. = **Pseudocaryophyllus darwinii** (Hook. f.) Burret (*Myraceae*)

Eustephia darwinii Vargas (*Amaryllidaceae*)

Fagelia darwinii (Benth.) Kuntze = **Calceolaria uniflora** Lam. (*Scrophulariaceae*)

Galapagoa darwinii Hook. f. = **Tiquilia darwinii** (Hook. f.) A.T. Richardson (*Boraginaceae*)

Garcinia darwiniana Kesh. Murthy, Yogan. & Vasud. Nair (*Clusiaceae*)

Gossypium barbadense L.

Var. **darwinii** (Watt) J.B. Hutch. (*Malvaceae*)

Gossypium darwinii Watt

Gossypium darwinii Watt = **Gossypium barbadense** L. var. **darwinii** (Watt) J.B. Hutch. (*Malvaceae*)

Hebe darwiniana (Colenso) Wall. (*Scrophulariaceae*)

Veronica darwiniana Colenso

Homoranthus darwinioides (Maiden & Betche) Cheel = **Rylstonea darwinioides** (Maiden & Betche) R.T. Baker (*Myrtaceae*)

Verticordia darwinioides Maiden & Betche

Hoya darwinii Loher (*Asclepiadaceae*)

Laeliocatlleya x **darwiniana** Hort. (*Orchidaceae*)

Lagopsis darwiniana Pjak (*Lamiaceae*)

Lecocarpus darwinii Adersen (*Asteraceae*)

Lippia darwinii (Benth. & Hook.) Speg. (*Verbenaceae*)

Neosparton darwinii Benth. & Hook.

Maihueniopsis darwinii (Hensl.) F. Ritter (*Cactaceae*)

Opuntia darwinii Hensl.

Tephrocactus darwinii (Hensl.) Backeb.

Micromeria darwinii Benth.= **Clinopodium darwinii** (Benth.) Kuntze (*Lamiaceae*)

Myrtus darwinii Barnéoud (*Myrtaceae*)

Nardophyllym darwinii (Hook. f.) A. Gray (*Asteraceae*)

Chiliotrichum darwinii Hook. f.

Nassauvia darwinii (Hook. & Arn.) O. Hoffm. & Dusén (*Asteraceae*)

Panargyrus darwinii Hook. & Arn.

Neomolina darwinii (Hook. & Arn.) F. Hellweg (*Asteraceae*)

Baccharis darwinii Hook. & Arn.

Neosparton darwinii Benth. & Hook. = **Lippia darwinii** (Benth. & Hook.) Speg. (*Verbenaceae*)

Odontospermum vogelii Webb

var. *darwinii* Webb = **Nauplius daltonii** (Webb) Wiklund **subsp. vogeliii** (Webb) Wiklund (*Asteraceae*)

Opuntia darwinii Hensl. = **Maihueniopsis darwinii** (Hensl.) F. Ritter (*Cactaceae*)

Oxalis darwinii Ball (*Oxalidaceae*)

Panargyrus darwinii Hook. & Arn. = *Nassauvia darwinii* (Hook. & Arn.) O. Hoffm. & Dusé (*Asteraceae*)

Pandanus darwinensis H.St. John (*Pandanaceae*)

Pisonia darwinii Hemsl. (*Nyctaginaceae*)

Pleuropetalum darwinii Hook. f. (*Amaranthaceae*)

Poa darwiniana Parodi (*Poaceae*)

Polygala darwiniana A.W Benn. (*Polygalaceae*)

Pseudocaryophyllus darwinii (Hook. f.) Burret (*Myraceae*)

Eugenia darwinii Hook. f.

Rumex darwinianus Rchb. f. (*Polygonaceae*)

Rylstonea darwinioides (Maiden & Betche) R.T. Baker (*Myrtaceae*)

Verticordia darwinioides Maiden & Betche

Homoranthus darwinioides (Maiden & Betche) Cheel

Satureja darwinii (Benth.) Briq. = *Clinopodium darwinii* (Benth.) Kuntze (*Lamiaceae*)

Micromeria darwinii Benth.

Scalesia atractyloides Arn.

var. *darwinii* (Hook. f.) Eliason. = *Scalesia darwinii* Hook. f. (*Asteraceae*)

Scalesia darwinii Hook. f. (*Asteraceae*)

Senecio darwinii Hook. & Arn. (*Asteraceae*)

Siegfriedia darwinioides C.A. Gardner (*Rhamnaceae*)

Spilanthes darwinii D.M. Porter = *Acmella darwinii* (D.M. Porter) R.K. Jansen (*Asteraceae*)

Tephrocactus darwinii (Hensl.) Backeb. = *Maihueniopsis darwinii* (Hensl.) F. Ritter (*Cactaceae*)

Opuntia darwinii Hensl.

Tiquilia darwinii (Hook. f.) A.T. Richardson (*Boraginaceae*)

Galapagoa darwinii Hook. f.

Coldenia darwinii (**Hook. f.**) **A. Gray**

Urtica darwinii Hook. f. (*Urticaceae*)

Veronica darwiniana Colenso = *Hebe darwiniana* (Colenso) Wall. (*Scrophulariaceae*)

Verticordia darwinioides Maiden & Betche = *Rylstonea darwinioides* (Maiden & Betche) R.T. Baker (*Myrtaceae*)

Zinnia x *darwinii* Haage & Schmidt (*Asteraceae*)

Leonel Pereira

Departamento de Ciências da Vida, Faculdade de Ciências e Tecnologia, IMAR-CMA, Universidade de Coimbra, Portugal

CORALLINES AND OTHER MACROALGAE
COLLECTED DURING THE *BEAGLE* VOYAGE

Introduction

The *Beagle* voyage lasted four years and nine months, two thirds of which Darwin was on shore (Keynes, 2000). He studied a great diversity of geological characteristics, fossils, living organisms (animals and plants) and met various people, among natives and colonists, during the voyage. Darwin collected methodically a great number of specimens, many of which new to science, characteristic which gave him the reputation of naturalist. His detailed annotations showed his gift for theorization and were at the base of his previous works, giving his descriptive, social, political and anthropological points of view of the regions he visited.

Charles Darwin is not usually remembered as a "botanist" although he had published various books about different aspects of vegetable life, based partly on his personal experience. In his autobiography (Barlow, 1958), Darwin wrote: "my appreciation for natural history, in particular the gathering and collecting of living organisms was well developed during my life. I tried to name the plants and collected various types of objects: shells, stamps, coins and minerals. The passion for collecting is the reason a man is a systematic naturalist, a virtuoso or a scrooge, it was very strong in me and clearly innate, as none of my brothers or sisters ever had". This "passion for collecting" was more evident during the expedition aboard the *Beagle*. After the voyage, Darwin traded his passion for collecting specimens to collecting information (Porter, 1987).

By publishing "Darwin's coralline algae collected on the voyage of the *Beagle*", the Irish botanist William Henry Harvey (1811- 66, Curator of the Herbarium, "Trinity College", Dublin) cites various excerpts of handwritten notes of Darwin about his collected material and thanks Darwin for the donation to his Herbarium of coralline which he had collected during his voyage around the world, on board the *Beagle* and for the permission to freely use his handwritten notes. However, the transcribed excerpts by Harvey differ, in some cases, from the "field notes" of Darwin included in *Zoological Diary* (Porter, 1987).

Darwin wrote in his autobiography (Barlow, 1958) that "... on the *Beagle* another of my occupations was to collect animals and plants of various classes, writing a brief description and dissecting many of the marine organisms collected. However, due to my lack of skill for drawing and an absence of profound knowledge of the anatomy of some of the beings collected, a great pile of marine organisms mounted in my cabin and much of what I did during the voyage revealed itself almost useless. Thus, I lost much of my time, with exception of that which I spent acquiring some knowledge of Crustaceans, knowledge which allowed me to later on write a monograph on the infraclass Cirripedia". Despite of what Darwin wrote in his autobiography on these notes and drawings in 1876, today researchers (Porter, 1987) consider all this information (written and iconographic) of extreme usefulness to understand Darwin's evolution of thought and his transformation from naturalist to scientist.

The specimens collected by Darwin and described in this work can be found, in their great majority, in the herbariums of "Botany School, Trinity College", in Dublin and in the "Cryptogamic Herbarium" of the British Museum of Natural History. Many of these specimens are the types of names published by Harvey.

The Voyage

Santiago, Cape Verde Archipelago

The Voyage of the Beagle is the title generally given to the book written by Darwin and published in 1839 as *Journal and remarks*. The title refers to the second expedition of topographical survey of the *Beagle*, which sailed from Plymouth Sound on December 27th 1831 under the command of Captain Robert FitzRoy. It passed Madeira Island, then went to Tenerife, but was prohibited to disembark due to the cholera quarantine imposed on ships coming from England.

The first stop was made on the volcanic island of Santiago in the Cape Verde Archipelago, where Darwin's Journal had its first account. While precise readings were done to confirm the data on longitude, Darwin visited the beach, having stayed on the island from January 16th until February 8th. During this period he made several notes in his Journal (Barlow, 1933) regarding organisms collected from the coastline, including a specimen of *Jania micrarthrodia* J.V. Lamoroux (Corallinales, Rhodophyta), having been mounted on the same page along with nine other specimens, including a specimen entitled "close to *J. micrarthrodia* of King George Sound, in Western Australia" (Porter, 1987). The epilitic specimens are, apparently, less common than epiphyte specimens (see Figure 1A) (Womersley & Johansen, 1996).

During the return voyage to England, the *Beagle* was in the harbour of the city of Praia from August 31st until September 4th of 1836. Darwin collects a few more specimens of algae, mainly *Amphiroa beauvoisii* J.V. Lamouroux (Figure 1B) (Corallinales, Rhodophyta).

Archipelago of Fernando de Noronha, Brazil

On February 20th 1832, Darwin was at the archipelago of Fernando de Noronha, aboard the *Beagle*, where he did various studies of the place, leaving an important account of his observations on the archipelago. From his observations and notes there is *Caulerpa webbiana* Montagne algae (Caulerpaceae, Chlorophyta) (see Figure 1C).

Bahia, Brazil

After passing through various other islands, the *Beagle* arrived at Salvador da Baía (Brazil) on February 29th; Darwin was marvelled with the luxuriant rainforest (tropical forest). At this location he collected various specimens of *Melobesia mamillaris* Harvey (see Figure 1D), synonymous (basionym) of *Neogoniolithon mamillare* (Harvey) Setchell & L.R. Mason (Corallinaceae, Rhodophyta). The syntype locations of these species are: Bahia, Brazil; Tierra del Fuego; Cape Verdean Islands; Algoa Bay, Cape Province, South Africa (Silva, Basson & Moe 1996).

During the return voyage to England the *Beagle* docked in Bahia, in August 1836. Darwin logs in his Journal that *Melobesia mamillaris* Harvey synonymous *Neogoniolithon mamillare* (Harvey) Setchell & L.R. Mason) and the *Lithothamnion scabiosum* (Harvey) Foslie "are very common fouling species on the smooth surfaces of granite rocks, in tide pools."

Archipelago of Abrolhos, Bahia, Brazil

Abrolhos is an archipelago located in the Atlantic Ocean south of the coastline of the state of Bahia and composed of five islands situated six nautical miles (approximately seventy two kilometers) from the coast of Caravelas. The *Beagle* was near the Archipelago of Abrolhos from March 27th until March 30th 1832 (Porter, 1987). Darwin collected at this location various specimens of *Halimeda opuntia* (Linnaeus) J.V. Lamouroux (see Figure 1E), and, contrary to what was assumed then, these organisms are not coralline algae, but members of Halimedaceae (Chlorophyta) (Guiry & Guiry, 2009).

Cabo Frio, Rio de Janeiro, Brazil

Close to this location were collected samples of *Amphiroa variabilis* Harvey, synonymous (Basionym) of *Arthrocardia variabilis* (Harvey) Weber-van Bosse (Harvey, 1847; Weber-van Bosse, 1904. According to Darwin's Journal (Barlow, 1933), the *Beagle* was in the proximity of Cabo Frio from April 3rd until July 5th 1832, but does not explicit if the samples were collected during these dates. Most likely they were collected during his trip, on land, to the Macaé River, between April 8th and 22nd or were collected by someone that stayed aboard the *Beagle* (Porter, 1985).

Botafogo Bay, Rio de Janeiro, Brazil

Various specimen of *Amphiroa variabilis* were collected at Botafogo bay in June 1832. These specimens are, maybe, the ones mentioned in his Journal, dated June 8th: "...collecting some coralline on rocks surrounding part of Botafogo's bay...". There is a description of these specimens of a type of *Amphiroa* on page 56 of *Zoological Diary* (briefly paraphrased by Sloan, 1985): "...very flat branches, formed by arched layers, very fragile, calcareous, in the shape of parallel longitudinal fibres...". Besides these species, "in Spirits" specimens of *Amphiroa beauvoisii* J.V. Lamouroux (Figure 1B) (Corallinales, Rhodophyta) were also collected and preserved.

On page 63 of *Zoology Notes there are some general notes on the distribution of corallines and other organisms on Brazil's coastline:* "Roaming the coast: the rocks, as in Bahia and other tropical locations, are visited by... many species of *Pilumnus* (type of class Malacostraca, crabs) on specimens of the order Fucales: in the original. "Fuci" (Fucales, Phaeophyceae) ..."

Falkland Islands

Passing by the Falkland Islands, Darwin collected, on March 25th 1833 numerous samples of *Corallina officinalis* Linnaeus (see Figure 1F). From light pink to purple, calcified, articulated fronds with 60-70 (-120) mm in height, from cylindrical to long axles, always feather-like. Very polymorphic species, sometimes of reduced dimensions. In disfavouring habitats this algae presents a vestigial erect system and can exhibit an extensive basal part (Guiry & Guiry, 2009). According to Porter (1987) there were presumably collected samples of *Amphiroa exilis* Harvey, synonymous of *Amphiroa beauvoisii* J.V. Lamouroux (Corallinales, Rhodophyta).

Regarding *Macrocystis pyrifera,* although Darwin apparently did not collect these conspicuous brown algae, he wrote in *Zoolgical Diary,* due to its ecological importance: "...the immense quantity and number of species and organic beings which are intimately connected to "Kelp". This plant, *Fucus giganteus* (Figure 1G), is always anchored to the rocks. In fact, the algae is very common in this area of the globe and the name is synonymous to *Macrocystis pyrifera* (Linnaeus) C. Agardh (Laminariales, Phaeophyceae) (Porter, 1987; Guiry & Guiry, 2009).

Puerto Deseado, Patagonia, Argentina

At this location, in January 1834 there were samples collected from the species *Amphiroa orbigniana* Decaisne (see Figure 1H), synonymous (basionym) of *Bossiella orbigniana* (Decaisne) P.C. Silva (Corallinales, Rhodophyta),

Strait of Magellan

The Strait of Magellan is a navigable passage of approximately 600 km immediately south of South America, situated between the continent and Tierra del Fuego with Cape Horn south. The strait is the biggest and most important natural passage between the Atlantic and Pacific Oceans and, during its crossing, Darwin collected various specimen of *Polysiphonia berkeleyi* (Montagne) J.D. Hooker, synonymous of *Heterosiphonia berkeleyi* Montagne (Ceramiales, Rhodophyta) (Montagne, 1842).

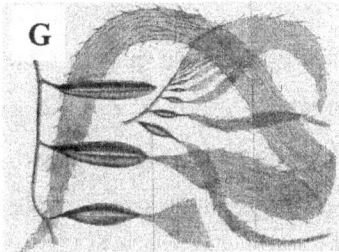

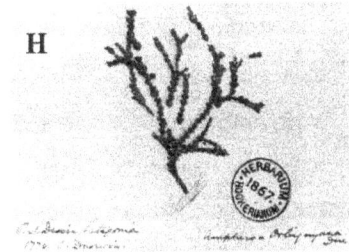

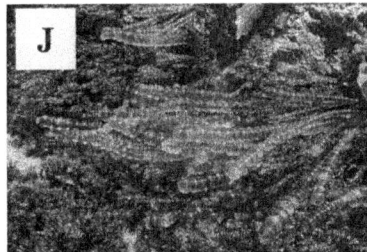

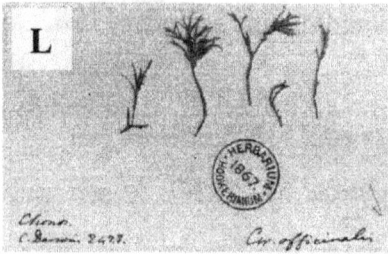

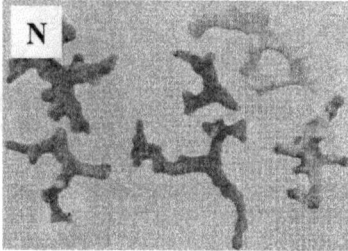

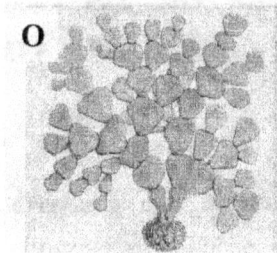

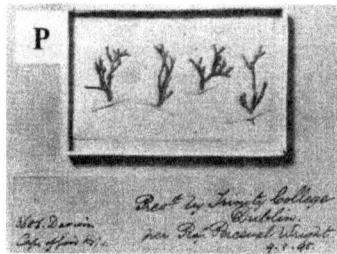

Figura 1. – A – Jania micrarthrodia; B – Amphiroa beauvoisii; C – Caulerpa webbiana; D – Melobesia mamillaris; E – Halimeda opuntia; F – Corallina officinalis (collected in the Falkland Islands); G – Fucus giganteus (Macrocystis pyrifera); H – Amphiroa orbigniana; I – Corallina officinalis var. chilensis; J – Chaetomorpha coliformis; L – Corallina officinalis (collected in the Chonos Archipelago, Chile); M – Jania rosea; N – Phymatolithon calcareum; O – Halimeda macroloba; P – Amphiroa exilis var. crassiuscula

Santa Cruz, Argentina

Here, there were probably specimens of the type of *Fucus* (Fucales, Phaeophyceae) collected during the second week of May, when the *Beagle* was sailing between Santa Cruz and the Tierra del Fuego (Porter, 1987).

Valparaiso and Port Famine, Tierra del Fuego, Chile

The *Beagle* navigated this area during the months of August and September 1834, having Darwin collected specimens of *Corallina chilensis* Decaisne, synonymous (basionym) of *Corallina officinalis* var. *chilensis* (Decaisne) Kützing (Corallinales, Rhodophyta) (Figure 1I), whose lectotype location is Valparaiso, Chile (Silva, Basson & Moe, 1996).

Cabo Tres Montes, Chile

In this location, on December 31st 1834, they collected specimens of *Conferva clavata* var. *darwinii* J.D. Hooker & Harvey, synonymous of *Chaetomorpha coliformis* (Montagne) Kützing (Figure 1J) (Cladophorales, Chlorophyta) (Kützing, 1849; Porter, 1987) and of *Sphacelaria funicularis* Montagne, synonymous (basionym) of *Stypocaulon funiculare* (Montagne) Kützing and whose type location is Falkland (Sphacelariales, Phaeophyceae) (Silva, Basson & Moe, 1996).

Chonos Archipelago, Chile

The *Beagle* navigated through the Chonos Archipelago, in the south of Chile, between December 1834 and January 1835. In this archipelago they collected specimens of: *Corallina officinalis* L. (Figure 1L); *Bossea orbigniana* (Decaisne) Manza, synonymous of *Bossiella orbigniana* (Decaisne) P.C. Silva; *Amphiroa orbigniana* Decaisne (Figure 1H), synonymous (basionym) of *Bossiella orbigniana* (Decaisne) P.C. Silva; *Amphiroa darwinii* Harvey, synonymous of *Bossiella chiloensis* (Decaisne) H.W. Johansen; *Melobesia polymorpha* Harvey, synonymous of *Lithophyllum incrustans* Philippi (Corallinales, Rhodophyta) (Porter, 1987; Guiry & Guiry, 2009).

Galapagos Islands

Darwin was at the Galapagos Islands from September 15th until October 19th 1835 and, during that period, observed and collected various algae of the following species: *Melobesia calcarea* (Pallas) Harvey and *Lithothamnion calcareum* (Pallas) J.E. Areschoug, both synonymous names of *Phymatolithon calcareum* (Pallas) W.H. Adey & D.L. McKibbin (Figure 1N) (Corallinales, Rhodophyta) (Porter, 1987; Guiry & Guiry, 2009).

King George Sound, Australia

The *Beagle* docked at King George's Sound from March 6th until 14th 1836. Regarding this location, Darwin wrote in his Journal: "We have been here for eight days and I do not remember, since we left England, having spent such a boring and uninteresting period" (Barlow, 1933). In the rocky intertidal he collected samples of: *Amphiroa stelligera* Decaisne, synonymous of *Metagoniolithon stelliferum* (Lamarck) Ducker; *Jania rosea* (Lamarck) Decaisne (Figure 1M); *Corallina chilensis* Decaisne, synonymous (basionym) of *Corallina officinalis* var. *chilensis* (Decaisne) Kützing; *Jania tenuissima* Sonder, synonymous of *Jania micrarthrodia* J.V. Lamouroux (Figure 1A); *Lithophyllum darwinii* (Harvey) Foslie, synonymous (basionym) of *Melobesia darwinii* Harvey (Corallinales, Rhodophyta) (Guiry & Guiry, 2009).

Cocos-Keeling Islands, Indic Ocean

Situated in the Indian Ocean, northeast of Australia, these islands are approximately 580 miles southeast of Java and form two coral atolls densely covered by coconut trees. The *Beagle* docked at the Cocos-Keeling Islands from April 1st to 12th 1836 and during this period, Darwin collected specimens of *Halimeda macroloba* Decaisne (Figure 10) that, contrary to what Darwin supposed, were not coralline algae but members of the Halimedaceae class (Chlorophyta) (Porter, 1987; Guiry & Guiry, 2009).

Cape of Good Hope, Simon's bay, South Africa

The *Beagle* was anchored at Simon's bay from May 31st to June 18th and Darwin must have collected at that location various specimens of *Amphiroa exilis* var. *crassiuscula* Harvey (Figure 1P), whose name is synonymous to *Amphiroa beauvoisii* var. *crassiuscula* (Harvey) Yendo (Corallinales, Rhodophyta) (Guiry & Guiry, 2009).

Bibliographical References

BARLOW, N. (Ed.). (1933). *Charles Darwin's Diary of the Voyage of H.M.S. Beagle*. Cambridge: Cambridge University Press.

BARLOW, N. (Ed.) (1958). *The Autobiography of Charles Darwin 1809–1882*. London: Collins.

CLERCK, O., Bolton, J.J., Anderson, R.J. & Coppejans, E. (2005). *Guide to the seaweeds of KwaZulu- -Natal. Scripta Botanica Belgica* 33: 1-294.

DARWIN, C. (Ed.) (1838–1843). *The zoology of the voyage of H.M.S. Beagle, under the command of Captain FitzRoy, during the years 1832 to 1836*. 5 pts. London: Smith Elder.

DARWIN, C. (1839). *Narrative of the surveying voyages of His Majesty's Ships Adventure and Beagle, between the years 1826 and 1836, describing their examination of the southern shores of South America, and the Beagle's circumnavigation of the globe*. Volume 3. *Journal and remarks, 1832–1836*. London: Henry Colburn.

DAWSON, E.Y. (1953). Marine red algae of Pacific Mexico. Part 1. Bangiales to Corallinaceae subf. Corallinoidae. *Allan Hancock Pacific Expeditions* 17: 1-239, Plates 1-33.

GUIRY, M.D. & Guiry, G.M. (2009). *AlgaeBase*. World-wide electronic publication, National University of Ireland, Galway. http://www.algaebase.org/

HARVEY, W.H. (1847). *Nereis australis,* or algae of the southern ocean: being figures and descriptions of marine plants, collected on the shores of the Cape of Good Hope, the extra-tropical Australian colonies, Tasmania, New Zealand, and the Antarctic regions; deposited in the Herbarium of the Dublin University. Part 1. pp. i-viii + 64, Plates I-XXV. London: Reeve Brothers.

HARVEY, W.H. (1858-1863). *Phycologia australica*. Vols 1-5. Plates I-CCC.

HUISMAN, J.M. (2000). *Marine Plants of Australia*. University of Western Australia Press, Nedlands, Western Australia.

KEYNES, R. (2000). *Charles Darwin's zoology notes & specimen lists from H.M.S.* Beagle. Cambridge: Cambridge University Press.

KÜTZING, F.T. (1849). *Species algarum*. pp. [i]-vi, [1]-922.

MONTAGNE, C. (1842). *Prodromus generum specierumque phycearum novarum*, in itinere ad polum antarcticum...ab illustri Dumont d'Urville peracto collectarum, notis diagnosticis tantum huc evulgatarum, descriptionibus verò fusioribus nec no iconibus analyticis jam jamque illustrandarum. pp. [1-]16. Parisiis [Paris]: apud Gide, editorem.

OLIVEIRA, E., Österlund, K. & Mtolera, M.S.P. (2005). *Marine Plants of Tanzania. A field guide to the seaweeds and seagrasses*. pp. 267.

PORTER, D. M. (1985). The *Beagle* collector and his collections. In Kohn, D. (Ed.) *The Darwinian Heritage*. Princeton: Princeton University Press: 973–1019.

PORTER, D. M. (1987). Darwin's notes on *Beagle* plants. *Bulletin of the British Museum (Natural History) Historical Series* 14, No. 2: 145-233.

SILVA, P.C., Basson, P.W. & Moe, R.L. (1996). Catalogue of the benthic marine algae of the Indian Ocean. *University of California Publications in Botany* 79: 1-1259.

SLOAN, P. R. (1985). Darwin's invertebrate program, 1826–36: Preconditions for transformation. In Kohn, D. (Ed.) *The Darwinian Heritage*. Princeton: Princeton Univ. Press; 71–120.

WEBER-VAN BOSSE, A. (1904). Corallinaea verae of the Malay Archipelago. *Siboga-Expeditie Monographie* 61: 78-110.

WOMERSLEY, H.B.S. & Johansen, H.W. (1996). Subfamily Corallinoidea (Areschoug) Foslie 1908: 19. In: *The marine benthic flora of southern Australia – Part IIIB – Gracilariales, Rhodymeniales, Corallinales and Bonnemaisoniales*. (Womersley, H.B.S. Eds), pp. 288-317. Adelaide & Canberra: Australian Biological Resources Study & the State Herbarium of South Australia.

Figure Credits

Figure 1: A – Huisman, J.M. (2000); B – F. Leliaert in Clerck, O., Bolton, J.J., Anderson, R.J. & Coppejans, E. (2005); C – Huisman, J.M. (2000); D – Jan Christian Sørlie (Forskning.no); E – Oliveira, E., Österlund, K. & Mtolera, M.S.P. (2005); F – Porter, D.M. (1987); G – Harvey, W.H. (1858-1863); H – Porter, D.M. (1987); I – Colin Bates (Algaebase.org); J – Nuytsia@Tas (Flickr.com); L – Porter, D.M. (1987); M – Huisman, J.M. (2000); N – Guiry, M.D. (Algaebase.org); O – Harvey, W.H. (1858-1863); P – Porter, D.M. (1987).

Anna Carolina K. P. Regner
Universidade do Vale do Rio dos Sinos, Brasil

THE "INTERPLAY OF THE ACTUAL AND THE POSSIBLE" IN THE *ORIGIN OF SPECIES*

What is original in Darwin's explanation lies in his effort to answer the crucial question he poses in *The Origin of Species*, that of how new species are produced in Nature. His work is also original in terms of the argumentative strategies employed. These strategies are related to the principles of the general structure of his argument, as demonstrated in his *particular whole-part movement* (the way in which he refers backwards and forwards to specific arguments in the development of each chapter), in his *comparison of points of view* (where he affirms the superior explanatory power of his theory over that of "creationism"), in the *treatment of difficulties, objections and exceptions* (the way in which his theory is able to account for even those cases which are apparently more unfavourable to it), in his fair evaluation of the *weight of reasons* (the interrelationship of the facts and reasons referred to within the context of his explanation), in his *appeal to the explanatory power of his "one long argument" as a whole* (the phrase he uses to refer to his treatise), and in the *interplay of the actual and the possible* (which is one of Darwin's most innovative strategies, and the subject of this analysis[1]).

The strategy adopted by Darwin for the *interplay of the actual and the possible* consists of three parts overall. The first of these clarifies the concept of *possibility*, particularly of how the principle in question can be viewed in terms of the theory by establishing what the reader should **not** expect from it (i.e. *what is not possible*), or by exploring the *absence of logical impossibility* or the *presence of factual possibility*. In the second part (in the light of what is possible in principle and what is really possible), Darwin establishes *what is possible in certain particular situations*. In the third part, he determines *what is actually given in terms of what can really be given*. He uses a variety of mechanisms in the *Origin* to reinforce specific *possibilities*, and does not always do this by means of a generalisation or something which leads to a generalisation. An occurrence may be "highly probable" *if it can be clearly conceived* by specifying examples through careful weighing of the evidence, or by the fact that it cannot be doubted. In the *Origin*, "probability" includes both *possibility* (the conceptual and/or factual possibility of an occurrence or of a determined explanatory

---

[1] Other strategies used by Darwin include the *appeal to ignorance*, to the *advance of research*, to the *psychological, sociological and ideological conditions and values of investigation and of the scientific community*, to the *authority of well-known scientists*, to the *familiarity* of the evidence, to the *progressive character* of the minds of those who Darwin expects to support his theory, and to the *cognitively revolutionary* nature of his theory.

hypothesis) and *proof*, which indicates a particular degree of expectation in relation to each prediction or retrodiction. Darwin often begins an argument by establishing what is "conceivable", and concludes by saying "it is, therefore, highly probable...", as he does when referring to studies analogous to his carried out by Landois:

> "But *it is conceivable* that the now utterly lost branchiœ have been gradually worked in by natural selection for another purpose: for instance, Landois has shown that the wings of insects are developed from the tracheœ; *it is therefore highly probable* that in this great class the organs which once served for respiration have been actually converted into organs for flight." (Darwin, 1872, p.148) – *our italics*.

Since it places the real in the sphere of the possible, and is more than a merely heuristic resource, Darwin's strategy "reinforces" our knowledge of Nature as a system within which "probablilities" and "tendencies" express the effective way of being of Nature itself. The ontological premise of a uniformity in the process of Nature as a complex system, and the epistemological allow imagining *possible* occurrences and establishing *possible* explanatory frameworks. The joint examination of the range of logical-conceptual and factual *possibilities*, from what is *actually* given and what is *ignored*, transforms *possibility* into a legitimate explanatory condition. In the absence of any evidence to the contrary, the inference of *possible* past conditions for the determination of actual occurrences is a satisfactory explanation, as is the inference of *possible* conditions to explain the absence of a determined occurrence. "Probable" is not the same as "doubtful", but rather encompasses the exploration of objectively *possible* alternatives. Thus, according to Darwin, we must conclude from the fact that various domestic species are completely fertile amongst themselves (even though they may descend from two or more wild species) that either the parent species initially produced hybrids which were completely fertile, or that the hybrids which were subsequently created then became fertile. The latter alternative, originally proposed by Pallas, seemed to Darwin to be by far the most probable and the most difficult to doubt, and his selection of this alternative was preceded by a detailed discussion (Darwin, 1872, p.240-241). Within the sphere of the exploration of possibilities, probability may also reflect the impossibility of excluding other possibilities, as is the case when we admit that "it is probable" that strictly contemporaneous forms have been accumulated over large areas of the same parts of the world, but "we are far from having any right to conclude that this has invariably been the case and that large areas have invariably been affected by the same movements" (Darwin, 1872, p.300).

It is true that Darwin also admits that a given occurrence can also be considered "not probable" *vis-à-vis* the evidence we have at our disposal. For example, given what we know about the great geological changes which occurred in other parts of America during the Ice Age, it is not probable that sediment was deposited during this period near the estuary of the Mississippi to a depth at which marine animals can best flourish (Darwin, 1872, p.276). Known facts can exclude the probability of other occurrences, especially in the case of hypotheses which can in some way conflict with Darwinian theory. In terms of support for this theory, the focus is on "what is not impossible". For example, "there is nothing improbable" in the case of a given insect which has varied and rudely resembled the features of its exterior, to become more or less green, if its exterior so becomes, leading to protective mimicry and natural selection by preserving those modifications which are useful (Darwin, 1872, p.182). In the artful game of possibilities and impossibilities, probabilities and improbabilities, the argumentation in favour of Darwin's theory emerges victorious by means of the *refutation of objections* which are made against it (Darwin, 1872, p.299-300).

The absence of "logical impossibility" can be considered as a "reason" for the acceptance of a determined explanatory hypothesis. The theory therefore benefits from the discussion of *what may or may not be probable* in the process of the action of natural selection (for example, in delicate subjects such as sterility between species). This clarifies its scope and thereby makes possible new advances in intelligibility. In such situations we can see that *the interplay of the actual and the possible* is not a trivial one, but is rather an instrument which allows Darwin to delve into, with the greatest possible conceptual rigour, questions which cannot be answered immediately, and establish the explanatory power of his theory. In the final analysis, the range of *possibilities*, supported by what is *actually* given, and with the *impossibilities* removed, reinforces the theory through which and by which the gates are opened to what is *real*.

By means of the interplay between the real and what is not given, what is ignored and why, and what is possible, *difficulties* are explained, or rather clarified, restructured, dissolved (seen as "apparent" or "misplaced") or responded to (i.e. considered to have some "real" basis which needs to be dealt with). The starting point for this process is always to try and *understand the difficulty*, and to clarify its substance. The explanatory task may end there and then, having demonstrated that *there is no difficulty* to be discussed, nor any objection to be responded to. Alternatively, understanding the difficulty can make room for a *discussion* of the largest number of relevant factors possible, which can then lead to arguments which are sometimes long and complex, and which comprise a range of different elements, e.g. facts, plausible premises, comparison with the explanatory power of alternative views, considerations relating to the cognitive faculties, and successive reassessments of the evidence available. The ultimate aim of dealing with objections is, in a certain sense, to render them "apparent". If they have a "real" basis, this is not only related to Darwinian theory, but is due to *difficulties* in terms of our current cognitive and investigative resources, or to *difficulties* which are intrinsic to any theory in the determination of such a complex object.

Difficulties become apparent through the clarification which Darwin's theory provides, or through analysing the basis of the difficulty concerned. This is what happens in the case of the most serious objection levelled against the theory, that of the absence of numerous transitional forms (Darwin, 1872, p.265). This absence is explained by the obvious incompleteness of the geological records available at that time. In the light of explanations provided for the movements in the surface of the earth, of considerations relating to conditions of fossilization, and of the conditions which Darwin's theory states as being propitious to the appearance of new forms, this lack of evidence was only to be expected (Darwin, 1872, p.275 and p.288-289), as was the *impossibility* of completely reconstituting the fossil chain, without which the transitional forms could not be conclusively classified (Darwin, 1872, p.134-135, p.189, p.264, p.255-277, p.278, p.279-280, p.289, p.313 p.408). When it is *possible* to find evidence favourable to Darwin's theory, paleontology provides it (Darwin, 1872, p.282, p.284, p.287).

The conjunction of factors which, according to Darwin's theory, interfere in the possibility and characterisation of the evidence do not only explain the absence of the latter but also the presence of "apparent" *counter-examples*, which can be given in the form of exceptions to the rules which are clearly determined by the theory. These exceptions can be dealt with as they are allegedly few in number and, once the circumstances have been clarified in order to demonstrate that there has been interference of other factors without affecting the validity of the rule, the anomaly subsequently disappears. This is the case with the apparent exception to the rule of similarity of the endemic productions of islands and the nearby continent (Darwin, 1872, p.354-355). Some exceptions may appear to be directed at the core of the theory, e.g. certain facts of geographical distribution of species produced in comparatively recent times (Darwin, 1872, p.320-322). Even in these cases, however, clarification of the facts involved cause the anomaly to disappear. There then comes into play, in addition to the resources provided by the "new" geology (which is integrated with the view of the theory of natural selection), conjecture related to means of migration, which is explored at the level of *factual possibilities* (Darwin, 1872, p.343-344 and p.352-353). The explanation of the facts of geographical distribution is a good example of the role of conjectures, i.e. "adequate" assumptions for the elimination of *difficulties*, which have originated, in their turn, from unsound suppositions (Darwin, 1872, p.30, p.320-330 and p.303-306).

The strengthening of the explanatory possibilities of the theory (in *favourable situations* and in Darwin's adroitness at dealing with the objections raised) allows Darwin to reassess the available evidence and place it within the framework of the positive argumentation of his theory, or redirect its target. His strategy of initially weakening the objection raised is part of a discussion which begins by relativising the weight of the said objection and its initial impact. Another part of his strategy is to recognise the seriousness of the objection, which helps to increase the *possibility in principle* that the theory will be able to deal with these *difficulties* (Darwin, 1872, p.206). If it can be shown that the theory can account for even the most intricate cases – such as that of the sterile ants (Darwin, 1872, p.229-232) – the superiority of Darwin's theory will have been established once and for all, Questions which are central to the theory of natural selection are necessarily outside the scope of *actual* evidence, and thus lend decisive importance to the *interplay of the actual and the possible*, as in the case of two serious difficulties: the formation of a complex organ such as the human eye, and the acquisition of complex instincts by natural selection.

In the case of the formation of the human eye by natural selection, the appeal to the *explanatory power of the theory as a whole guarantees, in principle, the possibility* of its production by natural selection (Darwin, 1872, p.156). The objections raised are explained as "equivocal" (Darwin, 1872, p.151-152). Darwin affirms that it is necessary to use faculties such as reason and imagination, indeed *reason should overcome imagination* (Darwin, 1872, p.143-144, p. 145, p.146 and p.404), analysing every aspect of the difficulty in minute detail, and searching for favourable evidence in analogous situations (Darwin, 1872, p.147). We should discard what is not relevant to the issue in question, such as the demand for simultaneousness of the different useful variations (Darwin, 1872. p. 170), filling in the gaps so that we can rationally take account of the different aspects involved in the premises which impinge on the theory. At the core of the objection is another question which will also be raised about the development of other organs and structures: how, in the initial stages, without the obvious utility of the developed form, can minute variations be useful? Would they not simply be lost among all the others? Darwin's strongest argument in answer to these questions is the *possibility in principle* of these occurrences and of the action of natural selection (Darwin, 1872, p.183-185), which explains very successfully a large number of facts, as well as *the inexistence of conclusive evidence to the contrary:*

> "Although the belief that an organ so perfect as the eye could be formed by natural selection, is enough to stagger any one; yet in the case of any organ , if we know of a long series of gradations in complexity, each good for its possessor, then, under changing conditions of life, there is no logical impossibility in the acquirement of any conceivable degree of perfection through natural selection. In the cases in which we know of no intermediate or transitional states, we should be extremely cautious in concluding that none can have existed, for the metamorphoses of many organs show what wonderful changes in function are at least possible" (Darwin, 1872, p.165).

The difficulty in the case of the explanation of the acquisition of complex instincts (which correlate to other significant structural and physiological modifications) can be measured by its application to what may be the most difficult case of all, that of the sterile ants. By means of this case, Darwin intends to *"prove" the validity* of his principal claim, that of the general power of natural selection (Darwin, 1872, p.233). This *discussion* begins, as in the case of the formation of the human eye, by weakening the objection via reference to the *factually encountered possibility* that insects can become sterile (which is therefore not impossible in principle). The objection is weakened even further in the case of social insects, since natural selection will act in accordance with what is good for the community. Darwin restates the difficulty in order to continue discussing it: the sterile ants display considerable differences to the males and females of the ant colony. By putting it in this way, he treats the *difficulty* by focussing on *possible factors of interference.* It is important to remember that changes may be produced not only by the direct action of natural selection, but as the effect of laws of correlation, that natural selection can apply to the family, and that analogous situations related to plants can be examined. The climax of the difficulty is thus concentrated on the occurrence of castes of sterile ants, which is then removed by reference to *occasional empirical findings* by *different authorities* of gradations and differentiations between sterile ants belonging to the same niche, and by the always strong *appeal to the power of the theory which, in principle, can be attributed to natural selection* in order to explain the preservation and accumulation of useful variations (Darwin, 1872, p.229-232). Both in factual and theoretical terms this is not impossible but, on the contrary, there is *an (increasingly) strong possibility* for this explanation.

The *possibility in principle* of accounting for objections and the *impossibility of proof to the contrary* reinforce the legitimacy of the explanatory premises within the realm of the *possible* by responding to the difficulties raised and constructing explanatory pillars for facts where Darwin's theory is clearly superior (Darwin, 1872, p. 301, p.341, p.343-344, p.352-353, p..360, p.365, p.375, p.410), thereby enhancing the credibility and viability of the theory of natural selection. Darwin's explanatory effort exploits the realm of the *actual* to the maximum, and extends the frontiers of the *possible* to their outer limits.

Bibliography

DARWIN, C. (1987). *Charles Darwin's Notebooks, 1836-1844.* Ed. Paul H. Barret et al. Ithaca: Cornell University Press.

DARWIN, C. (1872). *The Origin of Species by Means of Natural Selection or the Preservation of Favored Races in the Struggle for Life* .6th Edition). London: John Murray.

Jacinta Maria Matos
Faculdade de Letras, Universidade de Coimbra, Portugal

DARWIN'S *VOYAGE OF THE BEAGLE* AS SCIENTIFIC TRAVEL WRITING: THE ORIGINS AND EVOLUTION OF A GENRE

In a recent review in the *Times Literary Supplement*, Richard Lewontin lamented that the vast majority of books on Darwin which have been published as part of the on-going celebrations still follow, with few exceptions, the Suetonian ideal of history--as-biography. He bemoans the failure to privilege a wider contextual approach and to engage with "the history of evolutionary thought before Darwin" and/or with "the socioeconomic milieu" in which he and his contemporaries worked (Lewontin, 2009: 19).

Far be it from me, an amateur in the field of evolutionary theory, coming as I do from literary and cultural studies, to attempt to redress that balance. My more modest intention in this paper is simply to read Darwin's *Voyage of the Beagle* in the wider context of English travel writing, and to place the author in an evolutionary line stretching from the Renaissance to the present day in terms of one of travel writing's more distinguished and influential subgenres: the scientific travel book.

The story will have to be told briefly and succinctly, leaving aside the many ramifications and subspecies, mutations and adaptations to changing external conditions. Some links will have to be completely missed, but the telling will, I hope, provide a 'view from elsewhere' in a gathering predominantly made up of historians and social scientists.

The origins of scientific travel writing can be traced back to the Discoveries and to the new epistemologies required by the opening up of a whole new world to European scrutiny and appropriation. The written accounts of explorers, buccaneers and adventurers took the shape of travel narratives where the marvellous and the factual vied with each other for supremacy and the fantastic and the outlandish happily coexisted with the most detailed and thorough descriptions of the material reality of these new lands. This (to us) odd mixture both defines the early form of the genre and provides the impetus for its evolution. The outcome of the struggle was entirely predictable: the need to validate the strange tales of amazons and men with no heads placed individual experience and observation at the centre of knowledge and redefined truth as an empirical process legitimized by sensory perception.

In this sense, questions about the rhetorical construction and presentation of texts became fundamental and a new discourse based on the eye-witness account and on a systematic recording of external detail changed the make-up of the travel tale forever. Diaries and journals provided the immediacy and authenticity the form required. Literary devices such as voice and point of view, as well as narrative strategies like plot structure and temporal organization had to be developed to substantiate the incredible, and to make it believable to a European audience. In the absence of other material evidence or as a complement to it, the authority of the written account came to be of paramount importance as a guarantor of the truth of the tale. Ultimately, the marvellous and the monstrous had to go, displaced by the necessity of mapping a true geography, because only the real can be subdued, conquered and colonized.

This new episteme (centred on curiosity, observation and empirical proof) opened up the possibility for the creation of modern observational science, and travel writing both benefited from and contributed to a new cultural environment which strongly relied on the invention of a language to describe the visible. In the next few centuries, travel books would be instrumental in the creation of an inventory of the world and in the development of what Mary Louise Pratt has called the Enlightenment's "planetary consciousness" (Pratt, 1992: 5), which underlies the imperial project. As Europeans first charted the outline of continents and then penetrated their interior, the discourse of travel helped in the necessary mediation between Europe and its Others; that process of translating the foreign into the familiar and of transforming the amorphous, unruly and chaotic into something intelligible and meaningful by means of the structuring power of discourse.

By the time Darwin set sail on the *Beagle,* he had a long line of ancestors behind him, from Hakluyt and Dampier to Humboldt, Cook and Mungo Park, some of whom he explicitly acknowledges in his text. He also benefited from the expansionist drive of English imperial power and the increased sophistication of its methods and practices. In the words of Eric J. Leed, "old forms of travel were redesigned [...] as scientific expeditions, mobile structures of intellectual labor designed for the accumulation of information" (Leed, 1991: 178). Or, if you prefer Stephen Greenblatt's formulation, Europeans possessed a "mobile technology of power" (Greenblatt, 1991: 9) comprising war ships, navigational instruments, attack dogs, lethal weapons and (let us not forget) writing – the means to preserve and reproduce whatever knowledge was being systematically and deliberately compiled. A network of diplomatic, business or personal connections also provided the English traveller with effective logistic support, which literally spanned the five continents dominated by an Empire where the sun never set. Travel had become a highly specialized professional activity, clearly geared towards the formation of the imperial archive and the creation of a global, comprehensive and unified system of knowledge.

By this time, the conventions of scientific travel writing were well established: a first-person narrative of a journey, undertaken with the purpose of gathering knowledge about the natural world (as part of a scientific expedition or as a lone adventure), alternating between the personal account of the protagonist's progression through foreign lands and the description of landscapes, people, plants and animals he/she encounters in his/her travels. Darwin also inherited a wide reading public composed not only of fellow scientists but also and predominantly of curious amateur naturalists, enthusiastic armchair travellers and avid readers of adventure stories – in short, the traditional audience of the travel book. In an age when science still shared a common language with the arts and the humanities, scientific travel writing was more than a mere sub-product of the discourse of science; rather, it was part and parcel of the process of production and dissemination of knowledge in the metropolitan centre. To this large educated audience, an audience equally interested in both the personal adventure and the intellectual debate, the idea that travel and knowledge are inextricably linked was nothing new. For centuries English culture had been revering heroic venturers who travelled in great danger and discomfort to far away lands just to bring back news of a different world.

The *Voyage of the Beagle* stands squarely in this English tradition, and Darwin's text undoubtedly evolved from it. But at the same time, it also includes elements from adjacent forms of travel writing and related types of traveller. The family resemblances are there, with the philosophical traveller in his search for the origins of civilization and civility; with the pilgrim seeking the sacred place, now located in the secular realm of the natural world; with the young upper-class gentleman going on his Grand Tour to polish his education by means of a *peregrinatio academica* through the recognized centres where learning was available to the inquiring mind; with the Romantic picturesque traveller, designing new ways of looking at scenery and fashioning a vocabulary to read all the elements that compose a landscape. Darwin's text can even claim a family connection with the famous (or should we say, infamous) stereotype of the 'Englishman abroad' – that arrogant, self-serving figure, as impervious to the sensibilities of the native cultures around him as he is to the weather.

And from scientific travel writing itself, Darwin inherited the structural contradictions and paradoxes of a hybrid genre, poised between the subjective and the objective; between narration and description; between the recognition of difference and the need to familiarize and domesticate; between an essential condition of mobility and flux, and the stasis and fixity required by a normalizing conceptual framework. Among all the other subspecies of an essentially mongrel genre, scientific travel writing is perhaps the one which is fraught with the deepest contradictions. To say that 'scientific travel writing' is, by its very nature, an oxymoron, may not be too much of an exaggeration. The balance it aims for is at best precarious, trying to reach an equilibrium between the centrality of the 'I' whose personal fortunes and misfortunes are the focus of the traveller's tale, and the effacement demanded by an epistemology which posits a radical disjunction between subject and object, privileging the materiality of the latter over the immaterial and elusive character of the former.

The *Voyage of the Beagle* is infused with these contrary impulses which pull the text in two directions at once. As one would expect, the contradictions battle it out (for the most part) in the character of the narrator, who inevitably holds centre stage in the genre of the travel narrative. He is, we feel, a shy, inexperienced, self-effacing figure, often out of his depth in the company of *gauchos* or the landed proprietors of *estancias*, almost apologetic for bringing in the personal and subjective as if they were unwelcome distractions from the more serious purpose of the enterprise. He only comes into his own, self-confident *persona* when observing the behaviour of the octopus or the changing habitat of the agouti or the difference in size of finches' beaks. He is, in fact, rehearsing the well-known trope of the anti-hero engaged in an 'anti-conquest', "[c]laiming no [...] imperial articulations of conquest" (Pratt, 1992: 38-39), merely observing, changing nothing – an innocent, disengaged traveller passing through the world and respectfully treating it as an autonomous, independent object.

When the traveller leaves, the world will carry on being what it is – or, perhaps more accurately, the world will continue to be engaged in a *process of becoming*. Change, and the mechanisms of change, is what this is all about, after all. Darwin's contribution inserted a temporal dimension in a previously static view of Nature. The paradigm was shifting from the rigidity of taxonomies and classificatory systems to more fluid preoccupations with temporal and historical change. It is tempting to say that the journey on the Beagle helped Darwin to make the imaginative leap towards evolutionary theory, not only in terms of the scientific data he gathered on the trip, but because the essential nature of 'the journey' (mobility through space and progression through time) provided him with the conceptual model he needed to think through the dynamic links between discrete, separate elements and to envisage a universe where everything is perpetually in motion. After all, as Ashton Nichols reminds us, "All scientific thinking relies on metaphors, analogies and other forms of figurative comparison" (Ashton, 2004: 19), and the metaphor of the journey is certainly one of the most permanent, pervasive and universal ways in which we give meaning to our earthly existence and shape to our passage through the world.

Darwin's journey might be said to reproduce, in fact, the archetypal journey from innocence to experience both in personal and professional terms. Travel, he claims, will build the character of the traveller and "teach him good-humoured patience, freedom from selfishness, the habit of acting for himself" (Darwin, 1989: 377) just as much – we can now say, with the benefit of hindsight – as it will turn him from an amateur naturalist into a professional scientist. Like the traveller (and the travel writer), the naturalist is a subject moving through the materiality of an objective reality: both are equally engaged in a process of inscription and appropriation; both have to deal with the strains of turning difference into familiarity, and with the difficulties involved in the assimilation of alterity and otherness; both need to devise a vocabulary and a language to make the meaningless speak in a recognizable voice; both will bring back evidence in the form of trophies or souvenirs to substantiate their tale; both want to be welcomed as heroes after having successfully been tested to their physical, psychological and mental limits. Some would say – quite correctly – that both are also complicit in a rhetoric of acquisition, the desire to possess, if not literally at least symbolically, the world around them. But both know that the world will always resist total appropriation and will continue to lend itself to further journeys of discovery.

I see the *Voyage of the Beagle* as one among many travel books, an exemplary text of a particular moment in the history of the genre, when 19th century self-confidence mapped new spaces of knowledge and power, and the British imperial gaze roamed the earth looking for origins and explanations or beginnings and conclusions that would legitimize the civilization they had created. But this, of course, is only part of the story.

And clearly the Victorian age did not mark the final evolutionary stage of scientific travel writing – it has not become extinct. It has managed to survive in the very adverse external conditions of a postmodern world of mass tourism and mass information, a world which has been systematically and thoroughly studied, labelled, catalogued, photographed, documented and filmed. How can scientific travel writers like John Hatt, Benedict Arnold or Redmond O'Hanlon compete with the visual exuberance of a David Attenborough? They do, and quite successfully, judging by the record sales of their books and the high reputation they enjoy. The new generation of writers can no longer experience the same wonder and excitement of discovery, nor are they engaged in the quest for a Grand Narrative which will bring all the unruly diversity of Nature into one single, unified plot line. In their journeys, they travel through the pages of Humboldt, Wallace or Darwin as much as through the jungles of Borneo or the tropical forests of the Amazon. Reality is no longer unmediated, a blank slate on which you can imprint your vision. A layered writing, a palimpsest of meanings is all that they can claim to offer. But they are happy to keep alive and augment the legacy, and for them Darwin will always be a distinguished ancestor, albeit of a different species.

Bibliography

DARWIN, Charles (1989), *Voyage of the Beagle*. Harmondsworth: Penguin Books. [1839]

GREENBLATT, Stephen (1991), *Marvellous Possessions. The Wonder of the New World*. Oxford: Clarendon Press.

LEED, Eric. J. (1992), *The Mind of the Traveler. From Gilgamesh to Global Tourism*. New York: Basic Books.

LEWONTIN, Richard (2009), "Why Darwin?" in *Times Literary Supplement*, 28 March: 19-22.

NICHOLS, Ashton, ed. (2004), *William Wordsworth, Charles Darwin, and Others. Romantic Natural Histories*. Boston and New York: Houghton Mifflin Company.

PRATT, Mary Louise (1992), *Imperial Eyes. Travel Writing and Transculturation*. London: Routledge.

Palmira Fontes da Costa

Faculdade de Ciências e Tecnologia, Universidade Nova de Lisboa, Centro Interuniversitário de História das Ciências e da Tecnologia

THE MEANING OF MONSTROSITIES IN CHARLES DARWIN'S UNDERSTANDING OF THE ORIGIN OF SPECIES

Beings who clearly deviated from their species in one or more traits have been a subject of great interest and debate by physicians and natural philosophers since at least the 16th century.[1] Yet, by the early 19th century, the mechanism of their origin and their meaning for the understanding of the natural world was still controversial. Nevertheless, monsters obviously showed that new traits could appear among members of a species and sometimes in a very extreme manner. Moreover, although the majority of monstrous animals died at an early age and some had problems in terms of reproduction, various works had also shown the inheritance through various generations of some forms of monstrosity. Their appearance was therefore relevant for understanding variability in the natural world.

In his seminal work, *On the Origin of Species by Means of Natural Selection* (1859) Charles Darwin (1809-1882) introduced the theory that populations evolve over the course of generations through a process of natural selection, and presented a body of evidence showing that the diversity of life arose through a branching pattern of evolution and common descent. His theory required the ubiquity of change in nature and the centrality of variation among individuals of the same species throughout the history of the natural world. What kind of role, if any, did Darwin attribute to the appearance of monstrosities in explaining the variation of nature and ultimately the origin of new species?

During Darwin's life the understanding of animal and vegetable monstrosities underwent profound changes and teratology emerged as a new branch of scientific knowledge. What was the impact of these new studies on Darwin's thought? This paper addresses this question by focusing not only on some of Darwin's works but also on his notebooks on the transmutation of species and personal correspondence. I will argue that Darwin's frequent references to this topic in his personal notebooks and letters should not be neglected and is useful for a better understanding of the development of his ideas on the problem of the origin of new species.

---

[1] See Daston, L. and Park, K. *Wonders and the Order of Nature, 1150-1750*. New York: Zone Books, 1998; Fontes da Costa, P. *The Singular and the Making of Knowledge at the Royal Society of London in the Eighteenth Century*. Newcastle: Cambridge Scholars Publishing, 2009

Monstrosities and the laws of variation

It seems to have been John Henslow (1796-1861) who first alerted Darwin to the importance of monstrosities. In a letter to his great mentor and former teacher of Botany at the University of Cambridge, dated 3rd July 1840, Darwin remembered how Henslow's lectures had called his attention to the fact that "monsters were sometimes curious".[2] Together with the letter, he sent Henslow an orange with the shape of cow horns from the family orchard at Down House.

Various scholars have pointed out that Henslow was fundamental in Darwin's scientific education and career. He not only provided Darwin with the best education in natural history of the period and with the opportunity to travel on the *Beagle*, but he also called his attention to a new subject: the centrality of intra-species variation in the understanding of the natural world, a problem that later became fundamental to Darwin's programme of research and ultimately to the publication of his work *The Origin of Species* (1859) as well as to other related books that he published afterwards.[3]

In his studies of intra-species comparisons, Henslow often attached two or more pressed plants of the same species to a single sheet of paper, clearly showing any differences between the individuals. Many of his specimens now held at the Botanical Garden of the University of Cambridge, which he directed for several years, also show "monstrosities", that is, unusually shaped specimens where some feature or features deviated from the typical form. It is very likely that Darwin saw some of these specimens.

Darwin included only a few references to monstrosities in *The Origin of Species*.[4] He defines monstrosities as a "considerable deviation of structure in one part, either injurious to or not useful to the species, and not generally propagated".[5] This definition is significant since, by stressing the general non-inheritance of monstrosities, it rules out their importance in the process of transformation of species. Darwin also remarks on "the reappearance of minute dangling horns in hornless breeds of cattle, more especially, according to Youatt, in young animals, – and the state of the whole flower in the cauliflower" and notes that "we often see rudiments of various parts in monsters". However, he doubts "whether any of these cases throw light on the origin of rudimentary organs in a state of nature".[6]

A different picture emerges if we look at Darwin's notebooks on the transmutation of species and his personal letters. During the voyage of the *Beagle* Darwin recorded his observations in a series of field notebooks. After returning to England, he also began to use them to record theoretical speculations. Darwin's notebooks on the transmutation of species reveal in detail his research and gradual illumination of the species question. Interestingly, they have several references to monstrosities. Some of them are just notes on news of monstrous births in various parts of the world that

---

[2] Darwin Correspondence Project, Letter 573 — Darwin, C. R. to Henslow, J. S., 3 July [1840].

[3] David Kohn, Gina Murrell, John Parker, Mark Whitehorn, "What Henslow taught Darwin", *Nature* 436 (2005) 643-645.

[4] Darwin, *On the Origin of Species*, 1859, pp. 8, 11, 14, 131, 155, 443.

[5] *Ibid.*, p. 44.

[6] *Ibid.*, .p. 45

he had noticed in the published literature of the period. Such is the case of a "Female pig apt to produce monsters in the Isle of France" or a "Madagascar oxen with an hump", both from *The Edinburgh Journal of Natural History*.[7] Also from another journal, *L'institut* (1838, p.414), Darwin records that the author, Mr. Guyon, points out the existence of more monstrosities in Africa than in Europe.[8]

Darwin's notebooks show also that he was especially interested in the possible relevance of monstrosities for the appearance of variety in nature. He knew from various authors that, just like mules, "dreadful monsters [are] abortive".[9] However, he also notes in one of his notebooks, how some monstrous traits such as those that appear in six-fingered people are hereditary.[10]

One of the first English authors who had dealt with the problem of the origin of monsters and proposed an hereditary principle for at least some kinds of monstrosities was John Hunter (1728-1793). In his essay "On Monsters", Hunter recognized that there must be a principle of monstrosity and whether it "be coeval with the first arrangement, or arise in the progress of expansion, is not easily determined in many [instances of monstrosity]; but it is certainly not the case in all; for many take place at a late period, and would seem to be owing to accident, or to some immediate impression; but still there must be a susceptibility for such, which susceptibility must be original".[11] Moreover, Hunter acknowledged that some monsters had an 'hereditary principle' and that, once formed, they had the 'principle of propagating their monstrosity.'[12] He also discussed whether particular species were subject to peculiar monstrosities.[13] Hunter's essay was only published posthumously in 1861, but Darwin's notebooks on the transmutation of species show that he knew the work through Richard Owen (1804-1892).[14]

The notebooks reveal also that Darwin had read the most recent works on teratology. He describes Etienne Geoffroy Saint-Hilaire's *Philosophie Anatomique*, dealing more specifically with monsters, as "worth reading" and, in a letter to Hooker, refers to the fact that he has "just finished three huge volumes by Isidore St Hilaire on animal monsters, and a nasty curious subject it is".[15] The work of these authors become

---

[7] Notebook B: [Transmutation of species], CUL — DAR 121, page sequence 192.

[8] Notebook D: [Transmutation of species], CUL — DAR 124, page sequence 74.

[9] Notebook D: [Transmutation of species], CUL — DAR123, page sequence 192.

[10] *Ibid.*

[11] John Hunter, "On Monsters", *Essays and Observations on Natural History, Anatomy, Physiology, and Geology*, ed. By R. Owen, Vol. 1, 239-251, London: John Van Voorst, Paternoster 1861, p. 240.

[12] *Ibid.*, p. 246. John Hunter supported this view with the fact that he had seen three *spinae bifidae* in the children of one family, two hare-lips in the children of the same parents, as well as other cases.

[13] *Ibid.*, p. 248.

[14] In one of his notebooks on the transmutation of species, Darwin particularly stressed Hunter's remark that monsters are formed at an early stage, that is "at the very first formation, for this reason, that all supernumerary parts are joined by their similar parts, viz. a head to a head", Notebook D: [Transmutation of species], CUL-DAR123, page sequence 55.

[15] Notebook B: [Transmutation of species], CUL-DAR121, page sequence 116; Letter 847 — Darwin, C. R. to Hooker, J. D., 31 Mar [1845]. Darwin is referring to Isidore Geoffroy Saint-Hilaire's *Anomalies de l'organisation chez l'homme et les animaux au traité de teratólogie* (1832-7).

especially valuable in Darwin's elaboration of *The variation of animals and plants under domestication* (1868), a book that attempted to explain the mechanisms of variation and inheritance. Indeed, of all works published in Darwin's lifetime, this is the one where it is possible to find the greatest number of references to monstrosities.[16] Darwin emphasizes the importance of Isidore Geoffroy Saint-Hilaire's law on the affinity of homologous parts and its relevance in explaining the origin of double monsters: "this is perhaps best seen in monsters with two heads, which are united".[17] However, he also notes that lately it has been admitted that:

> the production of double monsters is explained in a different way and as being due to the spontaneous divarication of the embryonic mass into two halves. This, however, is effected by different methods. But the belief that double monsters originate from the division of one germ, does not necessarily affect the question of subsequent fusion, or render less true the law of the affinity of homologous parts.[18]

Darwin points also to the usefulness of the law of mutual affinity in explaining other cases of monstrosities:

> Isidore Geoffroy gives a number of instances of two or more digits, of two whole legs, of two kidneys, and of several teeth becoming symmetrically fused together in a more or less perfect manner. Even the two eyes have been known to unite into a single eye, forming a cyclopean monster, as have the two ears, though naturally standing so far apart. As Geoffroy remarks, these facts illustrate in an admirable manner the normal fusion of various organs which during an early embryonic period are double, but which afterwards always unite into a single median organ. Organs of this nature are generally found in a permanently double condition in other members of the same class. These cases of normal fusion appear to me to afford the strongest support in favour of the present law. [19]

He remarks, however, that "Adjoining parts which are not homologous sometimes cohere; but this cohesion appears to result from mere juxtaposition, and not from mutual affinity".[20]

Darwin also refers to the French naturalist Alfred Moquin-Tandon (1804-1863) who had studied monstrous plants and argued for the tendency in homologous parts to unite during their early development as one of the most striking laws governing the production of monsters. He further emphasises that the law throws clear light not only on the production of monsters but also of many normal structures which have evidently been formed by the union of originally distinct parts.[21]

---

[16] There are 10 references to monstrosities in volume 1 and 46 references in volume 2.

[17] Darwin, *The variation of animals and plants under domestication*, 2nd volume, p. 352.

[18] *Ibid*, p. 353.

[19] *Ibid.*, p. 341. Isidore Geoffroy Saint-Hillaire presented his ideas in *Histoire génerele et particulière des anomalies de l'organization chez les animaux ou Traité de teratology*, Paris, 1832-1836.

[20] Charles Darwin, *The variation of animals and plants under domestication*, 2nd volume, 1868, p. 341.

[21] *Ibid.*, p. 342.

Therefore, in *The variation of animals and plants under domestication*, Darwin considers monsters as one extreme case of variation in nature and he refers particularly to Etienne Geoffroy Saint-Hillaire's law of mutual affinity to explain their occurrence. According to this explanatory framework, most monstrosities would be due to problems occurring during the early development of the organism, namely to arrested development.[22] Darwin is also aware that "many congenital monstrosities are inherited" and that "other malformations are rarely or never inherited".[23] He specifically observes that monstrosities can be a cause of sterility since "great deviations of structure, even when the reproductive organs themselves are not seriously affected, sometimes cause plants to become sterile".[24] In addition, he remarks that close interbreeding could lead to monstrosities and that domesticated organisms are much more liable to produce them.[25]

Despite the various references to monstrosities in *The variation of animals and plants under domestication*, Darwin does not discuss any possible relationship between their appearance in nature and his transformist ideas on the origin of species. What possible reasons were there for his silence on this matter?

Monstrosities and the transformation of species

The notebooks on the transmutation of species reveal that Richard Owen suggested to Darwin that "the production of monsters, which follow certain laws according to species, present an analogy to the production of species".[26] Hence, much before writing the *Origin of Species*, Darwin was alerted to the fact that monsters might be a useful model for understanding the appearance of novelty and ultimately of new species in nature.

In the concluding chapter of *The Origin of Species*, Darwin asserts his conviction on gradualism by invoking the old Leibnitizian and Linnean aphorism, *natura non facit saltum* (nature does not proceed by leaps):

> As natural selection acts solely by accumulating slight, successive, favorable variations, it can produce no great or sudden modifications; it can act only by short and slow steps. Hence, the canon of *Natura non facit saltum* which every fresh addition to our knowledge tends to confirm, is on this theory intelligible.[27]

Darwin's emphasis on gradualism explains, at least in part, why the possible relationship between the appearance of monstrosities and the transformation of species might have seemed problematic to him. Monstrosities represented the possibility of the existence of extreme changes in nature and, therefore, were not compatible with his

---

[22] Darwin, *Variation of animals under domestication*, p. 57.

[23] *Ibid.*, p. 24.

[24] *Ibid.*, p. 166.

[25] *Ibid.*, pp. 263; 417-418.

[26] Notebook B: [Transmutation of species], CUL — DAR 121, page sequence 163.

[27] Darwin, *On the Origin of Species*, p. 471.

gradualist views. This is probably one of the reasons why Darwin only occasionally mentions monstrosities in *The Origin of Species*. However, shortly after the publication of the work, in one of his letters to Charles Lyell, dated February 18th 1860, Darwin frankly admits that he "had been too cautious in not admitting great and sudden variations" in his book.[28] This remark was motivated by a recent attack on his work by the botanist William Henry Harvey. On the basis of the study of the plant *Begonia frigida*, Harvey had argued that in some cases new species could have originated through the abnormal development of the existing form.[29] In the letter to Lyell, Darwin admits that one of the problems of having had to present his theory in a shorter version than he originally intended, was the absence of relevant matters.[30]

Indeed, in the fuller manuscript written between 1856 and 1858, usually referred to as the "big species book", Darwin had included a section on monstrosities.[31] In this section, he discusses the work of the main contemporary authors on the subject, Étienne Geoffroy Saint-Hilaire and his son Isidore on animal monstrosities and Moquin Tandon on vegetable monstrosities. Darwin remarks that all of these authors have insisted "on the law that monstrosities in one animal resemble normal structures in another".[32] He doubts, however, that "in a state of nature new species arise from changes of structure in old species so great & sudden as to deserve to be called monstrosities". He notes that, if it "had this been so, we should have had monstrosities closely resembling other species of the same genus or family; as it is comparisons are instituted with distant members of the same great order or even class, appearing as if picked out almost by chance". In fact, all the cases of monstrosities which resemble normal structures which he could find were not in allied groups. Furthermore, Darwin does not believe, "that structures could arise from any sudden and great change of structure so beautifully adapted as we know them to be, to the extraordinarily complex conditions of existence against which every species has to struggle".[33] Yet, he admits that possibility in the rarest instances.

The problem of the possible existence of sudden variations in nature is again addressed by Darwin in a letter to his close friend, the botanist Joseph Hooker (1817-1911):

> As the "Origin" now stands Harvey's is a good hit against my talking so much of insensibly fine gradations; & certainly it has astonished me that I sh^d be pelted with the fact that I had not allowed abrupt & great enough variations under nature. It would take a good deal more evidence to make me admit that forms have often changed by *saltum*.[34]

---

[28] Letter from William Henry Harvey, professor of Botany at Trinity College, Dublin, *Gardeners' Chronicle and Agricultural Gazette*, 18 February 1860, pp. 145-6.

[29] *Ibid.*

[30] Darwin referred always to his book *On the Origin of Species* as his "abstract".

[31] Charles Darwin's Natural Selection Being the Second Part of his Big Species Book Written from 1856 to 1858, edited from manuscript by R. C. Stauffer, University of Wisconsin, Madison, 1999.

[32] Ibid., p. 319.

[33] *Ibid.*, p. 319.

[34] Darwin Correspondence Project, Letter 2705 — Darwin, C. R. to Hooker, J. D., [20 Feb 1860].

In another letter to Charles Lyell, Darwin mentions the case of a monstrous Gold-fish with analogous fish in state of nature and the case of monstrous eels examined by Louis Agassiz (1807-1873) but he reaffirms that he still feels "excessively doubtful whether such abrupt changes have more than very rarely taken place – changed by *saltum*".[35]

The aforementioned letters to Lyell and Hooker are revealing since they present a less categorical view on gradualism than that Darwin had argued for in *The Origin of Species*. In the letters, Darwin does not completely refute the existence of abrupt changes in the history of life. Instead, he admits the possibility that, although very rarely, they might have taken place. It is significant, but not surprising, that Darwin was only open to confessing a breach of uncertainty on his gradual view of the transformation of species in private letters and to two of his closest friends.

The view that sudden, inexplicable change and the production of monstrosities were casual factors in the production of new species had been argued by the Swiss palaeobotanist Oswald Heer (1809-1883). Darwin was aware of Heer's views and wrote a letter to Asa Grey (1810-1888) in search of reassurance that Heer's supposition was wrong: "Do you not consider such cases as all the Orchids next thing to a demonstration against Heer's view of species arising suddenly by monstrosities: it is impossible to imagine so many coadaptations being formed all by a chance blow.[36]

It was Camile Dareste (1822-1899) who fully addressed the implications of monsters for transformism. He considered that several races and species had a teratological origin since several anomalies were compatible with life. Dareste worked on the artificial production of monsters. He corresponded with Darwin who praised him for his efforts in understanding the origin of monstrosities:

> I thank you for your very kind letter, & for the present of your pamphlet. Whether or not many persons in France are at present interested in your subject of Teratology I feel thoroughly convinced that the time will come when your labour & that of all the few others who have worked on this subject will be highly valued. Therefore I am glad to hear that you intend to publish a book on this subject.[37]

Later, in his *Descent of Man* (1871), Darwin refers to Dareste's work on monstrosities as "full of promises for the future".[38]

Dareste's main work, *Recherches sur la production artificielle des monstruositées, ou Essai de tératogénie experimentale* (1891), was only published after Darwin's death. It included a tribute to Darwin and the promise that his programme of research on monsters would finally solve the mysteries behind the origin of species:

---

[35] Darwin Correspondence Project, Letter 2707 – Darwin, C. R. to Lyell, Charles, 23 Feb [1860].

[36] Darwin Correspondence Project, Letter 4196 – Darwin, C. R. to Gray, Asa, 31 May [1863].

[37] Darwin Correspondence Project, Letter 5547 – Darwin, C. R. to Dareste, G. M. C., 23 May 1867. The pamphlet was Dareste, Camille. 1862. Mémoire sur la production artificielle des monstruosités. *Annales des Sciences Naturelles* (Zoologie) 4th ser. 18: 243-76.

[38] Darwin, *The Descent of Man*, p. 388. Darwin refers also to Dareste in *The variation of animals and plants under domestication*, Vol. 2, pp. 289, 331, 340

Je serais heureux si les considerations que je viens de developer pouvaient engager les jeunes savants qui debutant dans l' etude de la zoologie a me suivre dans une voi qui, j' en serait certain, les conduira à d' importantes découvertes (...) Un des maitres les plus illustres de la science actuelle a dit dans un de ces derniers ouvrages que mes experiences son plaines de promeces pour l' avenir (Darwin, De la descendence de l' homme, p. 388). Ces paroles de M. Darwin m' encourajent a continuer les etudes auxquelles j' ai voué ma vie, etudes qui me ont déjà permis de etablir les lois de la formation des monsters, et qui me permettront, je l' espere, de reunir quelques donnes pour la solution de un des plus grans problems que puisse proposer notre intelligence, celui de l' origine des espéces.[39]

Concluding Remarks

It is in Darwin's work *The variation of animals and plants under domestication* that we can find more references to monstrosities as an extreme case of variability in nature. This work reveals that he knew of the recent findings in teratology. Nevertheless, in his published works, the English naturalist does not make any direct reference to the possible relation between the appearance of monstrosities and the origin of new species. Yet, a different picture emerges if we consider Darwin's notebooks on the transmutation of species and his personal correspondence. These documents show that Darwin was conscious of this possible relationship. One of the possible reasons for avoiding the issue in his published works, as I have pointed out, might have been the challenge that it posed to his gradualist view of change. In addition, throughout his life Darwin was very cautious about theoretical speculations. He probably thought that he needed much more evidence to be convinced of the possible relationship between monstrosities and the appearance of new species. Nevertheless, we have also seen that in his encouragement of Dareste's work, Darwin was open to new paths in the understanding of the natural world even if they might contradict some of his treasured suppositions.

Bibliography

Manuscripts at Cambridge University Library (http://darwin-online.org.uk)

Darwin Correspondence Project:

Letter 573 — Darwin, C. R. to Henslow, J. S., 3 July [1840].
Letter 2705 — Darwin, C. R. to Hooker, J. D., [20 Feb 1860].
Letter 2707 — Darwin, C. R. to Lyell, Charles, 23 Feb [1860].

---

[39] Camille Dareste, *Recherches sur la production artificielle des monstruositées, ou Essai de tératogénie experimentale*, 1891, p. 41.

Letter 4196 — Darwin, C. R. to Gray, Asa, 31 May [1863].

Letter 5547 — Darwin, C. R. to Dareste, G. M. C., 23 May 1867

Notebook B: [Transmutation of species], CUL — DAR 121.

Notebook D: [Transmutation of species], CUL — DAR 123 and CUL-DAR124.

Published works

DARESTE, Camille, *Recherches sur la production artificielle des monstruositées, ou Essai de tératogénie experimentale.* Paris: C. Reinwald et C^{c}Éditeurs, 1891.

DARWIN, Charles, *Natural Selection Being the Second Part of his Big Species Book Written from 1856 to 1858*, edited from manuscript by R. C. Stauffer, University of Wisconsin, Madison, 1999.

DARWIN, Charles, *The variation of animals and plants under domestication*, 2nd volume, London: John Murray, 1868.

DARWIN, Charles, *On the origin of species by means of natural selection, or the preservation of favoured races in the struggle for life.* London: John Murray, 1859.

DARWIN, Francis (ed). *The life and letters of Charles Darwin, including an autobiographical chapter.* vol. 2. London: John Murray, 1887.

FONTES DA COSTA, P. *The Singular and the Making of Knowledge at the Royal Society of London in the Eighteenth Century.* Newcastle: Cambridge Scholars Publishing, 2009

HUNTER, John, "On Monsters", *Essays and Observations on Natural History, Anatomy, Physiology, and Geology*, ed. By R. Owen, Vol. 1, 239-251, London: John Van Voorst, Paternoster, 1861.

KOHN, David, Gina Murrell, John Parker, Mark Whitehorn, "What Henslow taught Darwin", *Nature* **436** (2005) 643-645.

MOQUIN-TANDON, Alfred. *Éléments de Teratologie Végétal.*, P.-J. Loss, Libraire-Éditeur: Paris, 1841.

SAINT-HILLAIRE, Etienne Geoffroy, *Philosophie anatomique, des monstruosités humaines*, Paris,1822.

SAINT-HILLAIRE, Isidore Geoffroy, *Histoire génerele et particulière des anomalies de l'organization chez les animaux ou Traité de teratologie,* Paris, 3 vols., 1832-1836.

Maria Manuela Alvarez

Departamento de Ciências da Vida, Faculdade de Ciência e Tecnologia, CIAS, Universidade de Coimbra, Portugal

THE CONTRIBUTION OF GENETICS TO THE EVOLUTION OF EVOLUTION

Introduction

Some 150 years ago, in 1859, Darwin explained why the changes operated in organisms are transmitted from generation to generation, disappearing or becoming more common, depending on their contribution to survival. Later on, between 1936 and 1947, this idea was combined with others, which preceeded from genetics, which was still to be discovered in Darwin's time, and from several others disciplines of Biology. From this combination a new evolutionary paradigm emerged, the Modern Synthesis or the Synthetic Theory of Evolution, which connected inherited genetics and natural selection. According to this conceptual framework the changes operated in organisms are produced by genetic mutations: i) if they contribute to improve organism's fitness they become more common in the population gene pool, and eventually, became part of the species heritage; ii) after gradual accumulation, over successive generations, genetic mutations will originate new species. The Synthetic Theory of Evolution was, and still is, accepted by most biologists and can be considered as a natural update of Darwin's theory as a consequence of subsequent scientific advances i.e. as an evolution of Evolution

The general acceptance of the Modern Synthesis did not prevent the questioning of some of its assumptions. One of them regards the evolution of species over geological time. The evolutionary change by accumulation of genetic mutations proceeds in two levels: within a single species, that contributes to population differentiation over a time scale of generations; and between species, responsible for the onset of new species and other taxonomic groups over geological time. These two scales of evolutionary change are often referred to as microevolution and macroevolution, respectively. While it is often assumed that macroevolution is just an extrapolation of microevolution, the discovery of new phenomena that are not easily explainable within the current paradigm hampers the reconciliation of these two fundamental evolutionary levels.

In the turn of the 20th century, new scientific and technological developments gave a new vision of life, far more complex than that which served as the basis for the Synthetic Theory. In the mid 60s and late 90s genetics experienced two major technological and conceptual revolutions: the molecular revolution, and the "omics" revolution. Both provided new information on organism's variation, and new insights on the forces responsible for their origins. The purpose of this article is to provide a brief recapitulation of genetics' conceptual advances during the 20th century, and the discipline's impact on the history of evolutionary theory.

"The Eclipse of Darwinism" and the consolidation of the principle of natural selection

In Darwin's time, the concept of heredity was dominated by two powerful myths. One of them assumed that parental acquired characteristics should be transmitted to the future generations. The other claimed that offspring characteristics were of some intermediate value between those of its two parents, as a result of the mixture of both their blood during the conception – blending inheritance.

In his book entitled *The Variation of Animal and Plants under Domestication*, published in 1868, Darwin developed a theory of inheritance in which small particles, called "gemmules", were assumed to be shed by the organs of the body and carried in the bloodstream to the reproductive organs where they accumulated in the germ cells. After the union of the two gametes, the gemmules were combined in the zygote so that the offspring would be an analog constructed about the mean of the parental values. This concept of heredity was not compatible with that of natural selection since any advantageous change produced in a singular organism would be diluted in the next generation. "This effect is very similar to that which is obtained when a drop of paint is added to a litre of water: no matter how useful the paint may be in the future, there is no way of recovering the drop" (Dennet, 1995).

At the time Mendel had already demonstrated that the hereditary factors transmitted by both parents to the progeny do not combine, but were passed intact as discrete units. Mendel also proposed rules for the transmission of the hereditary factors, which could be easily observed in the lab through selective cross-breading of chosen lineages. Mendel's experiments were published in 1866 but were largely ignored until 1900, many years after his death.

Mendel's inheritance theory was presented in Great Britain by William Bateson, at a meeting of the Royal Horticultural Society in May of 1900. Classical Darwinists, also known as biometricians, considered Mendel's heredity incompatible with natural selection. They reasoned that if hereditary units passed intact throughout generations as Mendel suggested, they couldn't accumulate changes susceptible to natural selection's scrutiny. Moreover, Mendel's traits were considered largely trivial and non-adaptive. These statements opened a debate between biometricians and Mendelians, originally focused on the clarification of the basis of inheritance. Mendelians were partisans of both models of evolution by natural selection and Mendelian inheritance, however, some of them saw in large effect mutations an opening for the possibility of saltation, the opposite idea of gradual evolution. Darwin was profoundly inspired by the concept of gradualism, and it became the foundation of his theory of evolution. This concept postulated that all geological and evolutionary changes were slow, gradual, and quantitative.

Mendel's work became the foundation of a new discipline in biology, genetics, and its "hereditary factors" were later termed the genes. As it gained recognition and importance in the scientific community, in the 20 years that follow the re-discovery of Mendel genetics, Charles Darwin's conception of evolution by natural selection was considered a theory with a major flaw. He could offer no plausible mechanism to explain the mode of inheritance. During this period, the scientific challenges to Darwinism led many to abandon the theory. Morphologists remained faithful to a morphological ideal, paleontologists tended to be Lamarkists; and all of them agreed that evolution progressed in abrupt steps, it was not gradual. Julian Huxley (1942) used the phrase "The Eclipse of Darwinism" to describe this state of affairs.

In 1918 the statistician Ronald Fisher compared the inheritance of traits measurable by real values, with Mendel predictions. He reached a value of significance of 0.99997, which means that in 100 000 simulations only 3 did not fit on Medelian predictions, from which he concluded that the discontinuous nature of Mendelian inheritance was compatible with continuous variation and gradual evolution. Through this statistical demonstration, Fisher reconciled biometricians and Mendelians. However, the experimental proof that Mendelian genes could be mutated was known only in 1927, with the first artificial mutation induction performed by Joseph Muller. By bombing male fruit flies with X-rays, Muller caused the mutation of their genes and noted that the offspring featured new malformations. The idea that the genes were singular molecular entities that could be changed over time provided the experimental support that the theory of natural selection needed to be accepted by the scientific community. Mutation was described as the mechanism responsible for the production of variant forms of a gene, called alleles. This discovery became the foundation of modern genetics.

The birth of Population Genetics and the discovery of a new mechanism of evolution: the random genetic drift

Through the study of the transmission of heritable traits, the causes of their stability and change, genetics appeared, in the beginning of the 20th Century, as the science that would provide the complete understanding of the evolutionary process. Mendelian genetics originally focused on organism's heredity under controlled experimental conditions, using selected organisms and traits. However, to understand biological evolution, it would be necessary to study the heredity of organisms in the natural environment, where they reproduce randomly within populations. To accomplish this goal Ronald Fisher, Sewall Wright and John Haldane redefined the concept of evolution as the variation of allele frequencies over successive generations. The concept of population was also redefined as a group of interbreeding organisms. Population's properties, such as population subdivision and structure, and effective population size, were tested to estimate their influence on gene frequencies variation, besides natural selection.

Population thinking provided a new scenario for cross-breeding and inheritance. Within populations of limited size parents will produce millions of sperm cells and thousands of eggs cells. From these numerous gametes produced in each generation only a small fraction will be united to form a zygote. The stochastic nature of the gametes sampling process could be responsible for allele's frequency variation. Sewall Wright (1929, 1955) demonstrated that if this effect accumulates for several generations, it may cause the fixation or elimination of genetic variant forms, and thus, generate microevolution. The variation of genetic diversity due to stochastic processes became known as "random genetic drift". Its contribution to the origin of species was intensively debated. At the core of the debate was the assumption that natural selection could be excluded from the process.

Fisher, Wright and Haldane succeed in merging both Darwinian natural selection and Mendelian inheritance theories. The concept of population was central to their approach which became known as "population genetics".

The birth of the Modern Synthesis

The Theory of Population Genetics was based on sophisticated mathematical models that approximate reality. In this context, "population" was an idealized group of organisms, assumed to be adhering to the assumptions of a theoretical model (e. g. random mating). Those mathematical formulations have kept field naturalists apart from this new approach. Until a second triumvirate, composed by Theodosius Dobzhansky, Gaylord Simpson and Ernst Mayr translated the theory of population genetics into empirical practice. One major achievement of this work was the demonstration that populations had far more genetic variability than the early population geneticists had assumed in their models, and that genetically distinct sub-populations were important reservoirs of variability, which is pivotal to the evolutionary change through time and space.

The conceptual tools supplied by the synthesis between Darwinism and Mendelism proved to be effective in the interpretation of evolutionary change within natural populations. But were they capable of explaining macroevolution? At the time, the criteria to include a singular organism in a particular species was its similarity to a standard form, which was defined by a set of morphological features. Based on this assumption, speciation was described as a process that involved the production of systematic mutations that reorganized the genome, originating singular organisms which deviated, significantly, from the standard form. These organisms, which Goldschmidt (1940) called "hopeful monsters" were the true founders of a new species. The differences between species produced by this mechanism were not of an adaptive nature, and thus, there was no place for natural selection in the speciation process.

Dobzhansky and Huxley suggested that the change in allelic frequencies could lead to the formation of new species if it occurred in isolated populations. This hypothesis was later analysed by Ernst Mayr (1942) leading to a new concept of species, the biological concept as opposed to the typological concept based on morphology. Its main idea was that species are separated from each other by reproductive barriers, which prevent gene flow among their members. In isolated populations the gradual accumulation of genetic variants with slight effect on individual phenotypes, continued for sufficiently long, give rise to reproductive barriers, and thus, to new species or higher taxonomic levels such as genera and families.

During the first part of this century several branches of Biology, such as systematics, morphology, botany, and ecology, incorporated population genetics into evolutionary thinking. From this unanimity a consensus was born about the way how evolution proceeds which was, basically, a Neo-Darwinian theory that recognized the importance of mutation and variation within populations. This synthesis became known as the Synthetic Theory of Evolution or the Modern Synthesis. At its core were three important assumptions. The first assumed that evolution is a process which develops in two phases, in the first, mutations are produced at random; in the second phase, natural selection acts on those mutations as a driving force of evolutionary change (in this process the contribution of genetic drift is not significant). The second assumption postulates that evolution is slow and gradual. The third assumed that macroevolution is an extension of microevolution; e. g. the gradual accumulation of genetic variants with slight effect, continued for sufficiently long, gives rise to new species.

For some evolutionists the Modern Synthesis was a major paradigm shift. Karl Popper claimed that the Modern Synthesis is a theory about how evolution works at the level of genes whereas Darwinism was focused mainly on the evolution of form of the organisms and species (Platnick and Rosen, 1987). It is a common thought that developmental biology is missing from the theory of evolution even after the onset of the evolution of development (evo-devo) research program in 2003 (Pigliucci, 2007).

The challenges of molecular evolution

In 1952 the complete sequence of the protein insulin became known. By the mid--50's, a considerable amount of data regarding other proteins was available allowing its comparison between species. The amino acid sequences were aligned providing a new scenario of variation between species. Surprisingly, changes did not happen randomly but in particular regions of the molecule – amino acid substitutions in insulin from cows, sheep, pigs, horses and whales, for example, were restricted to positions 8 to 10 of the sequence. Most of these changes did not affect its functional role; and the mutation rate was similar in different species. Based on these data Zuckerland and Pauling (1965) suggested a molecular clock for evolution at the molecular level. This hypothesis was the opposite of erratic tempo of evolution that was assumed at the morphological level. Later on, the molecular clock was used by Sarich and Wilson (1967) to measure the divergence time between humans and chimpanzees in 5 million years. This value was much lower than the 25 millions considered previously.

In 1969, Kimura suggested that a constant rate of evolution most likely was not driven by natural selection. Alternatively he hypothesized that most molecular changes were caused by random drift of neutral or nearly neutral mutations. This same hypothesis was suggested, independently, by King and Juckes (1969) and became known as the Neutral Theory of Molecular Evolution. The term "neutral" used in this context means that the future of different variants of a gene is determined, mainly, by genetic drift. In other words, Kimura's theory suggests that most genetic diversity exists because it does not affect an organism's survival, and not because it was chosen by natural selection.

The neutral evolution model became the foundation of several mathematical models designed to predate divergence times between orthologous amino acid sequences.

The advent of several DNA techniques such as polymerase chain reaction, and direct sequencing analysis has brought a better understanding of gene structure and function. In the late 90's the development of new algorithms for genome analysis, high speed-computers and bioinformatics have enabled fast and reliable predictions regarding evolution, physiology and fitness of the sequenced organisms. Genomic data revealed that genes evolve by duplication and that those which encode proteins are frequently conserved by tens and hundreds of millions of years, exceeding the duration of many species. Genes are now considered as an independent level of evolution, with a deep history, often different from that of the species to which they belong.

Previously, genes were considered adaptive characteristics of species, not a level of evolution. Furthermore, genomes are no longer described as well-organized libraries of genes, but complex units of information that change rapidly over time due to selection mechanisms operating at multiple levels simultaneously, as well as genetic processes of duplication, transposition, mutation, and recombination.

The new information provided by the molecular and genome studies will force biologists to connect evolutionary and molecular biology. For some of them claimed that the Modern Synthesis needs to incorporate this recent knowledge in a new expanded post-modern synthesis. However, some of its historical defenders argue that the new concepts and empirical findings of the last 20 years are implicit in the theory and, thus, any expansion of its conceptual foundations or grafting of new ideas is dispensable.

Bibliography

CAVALLI-SFORZA LL, BODMER WF 1999. The Genetics of Human Populations. Dover Publications, Inc. New York.

DENNET DC 1995. Darwin's Dangerous Idea. Touchstone. New York.

GOULD SJ 2000. O Polegar do Panda. Gradiva. Lisbon.

GOULD SJ 2002. Macroevolution. In Encyclopedia of Evolution. Ed.

HARTL D, CLARK A. 1997. Principals of Population Genetics. Sinauer Associates. Sunderland (MA).

HULL DL 2002. History of Evolutionary Thought. In Encyclopedia of Evolution. Ed. Mark Pagel. Oxford University Press, Inc. New York.

HUXLEY J 1942. Evolution: the modern synthesis. Allen and Unwin, London.

JOBLING MA, HURLES ME, TYLER-SMITH C 2004. Human Evolutionary Genetics, Origins, Peoples & Disease. Garland Science, New Deli.

MAYR E 2001. What Evolution Is. Basic Books, New York.

PAGE RDM, HOLMES EC. 1998. Molecular Evolution: a phylogenetic approach. Blackwell Science, Ltd. London.

PIGLIUCCI M 2004. Do we need an extended evolutionary synthesis? Evolution 61-12: 2743-2749.

PLATNICK NI, ROSEN DE 1987. Popper and evolutionary novelties. History Philos Life Sciences 9: 5-16.

RIDLEY M 2004. Evolution. Blackwell Science, Ltd. London.

ROSE MR, OAKLEY TH 2007. The new biology: beyond the Modern Synthesis. Biology Direct 2: 30 doi: 10.1186/1745-6150-2-30.

WRIGHT S 1955. Classification of the factors of evolution. Cold Spring Harb Symp Quant Biol 20: 16–24. doi:10.1101/SQB.1955.020.01.004

Pedro Ricardo Fonseca

FCT; Faculdade de Letras, CEIS20-Grupo de História e Sociologia da Ciência,Universidade de Coimbra, Portugal

A DISCIPLE OF RONALD AYLMER FISHER IN PORTUGAL: WILFRED LESLIE STEVENS IN THE ANTHROPOLOGICAL SCHOOL OF COIMBRA DURING THE EARLY 1940'S.

The present work studies Wilfred Leslie Stevens' (1911-1958) presence at the Anthropological Institute of the University of Coimbra during the early 1940's. Who was Wilfred Leslie Stevens? Why was he assigned? What analysis can be made of his passage through Coimbra? It was around these three questions that we elaborated our work, in an effort to locate and structure information which, on the one hand, would allow us to obtain partial and temporary answers, and, on the other hand, would favour the emergence of new topics of interest and new questions.

Who was Wilfred Leslie Stevens? Despite having carried out an extensive bibliographical research, we were unable to locate a biography or biographical summary on W. L. Stevens. The following information is, thus, the result of the conjugation of elements collected from diverse sources, including data provided by people that work at institutions to which Stevens was connected to during his lifetime.[1] Wilfred Leslie Stevens was born on the 25th of June 1911. He studied at the University of Reading and at the University of Cambridge,[2] where he obtained his bachelor's degree in Mathematics.[3] In June 1935, he initiated his PhD in eugenics at University College London (UCL), where he was assistant professor in the department of eugenics from October 1934 until June 1937, and professor from 1937.[4] It was at the Galton Laboratory of UCL that Stevens worked under the guidance of Ronald Aylmer Fisher (1890-1962) between 1935 and 1941. In 1941, due to urgent works of war, Stevens joined the department of statistics of the experimental station of Rothamsted for a few months, before moving to Portugal.[5]

---

[1] We wish to express our profound gratitude to Dayaram Nakrani and Wendy Butler of University College London (UCL), Hans Lucas and G. J. Stemerdink of the International Statistical Institute (ISI), Suzanne of the International Biometric Society (IBO), Peter Bloor from the British Council, and Professor Décio Barbin, for their valuable help.

[2] Information generously provided by Wendy Butler of the Senior Records Office of University College London (UCL), (28/05/2009).

[3] See: *Boletim da Associação Brasileira de Estatística*, Ano XVIII, Nº 52, 2º Quadrimestre de 2002, p. 43. Available at: http://redeabe.org.br/Boletins/Boletim_52.pdf (24/05/2009).

[4] Information generously provided by Wendy Butler of the Senior Records Office of University College London (UCL), (28/05/2009).

[5] See: "Mathematical Statistics at the University of Sao Paulo: Mr. W. L. Stevens", In: *Nature* 162, 56-56 (10th July 1948). Available at: http://www.nature.com/nature/journal/v162/n4106/abs/162056c0.html (28/05/2009)

His passage through Portugal is the main object of study of the present work and will be, thus, the object of a more detailed analysis. In 1947, Stevens was hired to ensure the leadership of the discipline "Mathematical Statistics and Demographical Statistics" of the Faculty of Economy and Administration of the University of São Paulo (Brazil), where he was a professor between 1948 and 1958. The elaboration of the statistical tables of R. A. Fisher and Frank Yates (1902-1994), published in 1938, benefited from the assistance of Stevens,[6] which, besides that, published dozens of articles in specialized magazines of statistics, eugenics and biometrics, as, for example: *Annals of Eugenics, Journal of Genetics, Journal of the Royal Statistical Society B* and *Biometrika*.[7] Elected member of the International Statistical Institute (ISI) in 1952,[8] Wilfred Leslie Stevens passed away in 1958.

Why was W. L. Stevens hired? The hiring of the British statistician was part of the path which one of Portugal's leading anthropologists, Eusébio Tamagnini (1880-1972)[9] had outlined for Anthropology in Portugal and, in particular, for the Anthropological School of Coimbra, during the early 1940's, i.e. only a couple of years before W. L. Stevens was hired. In 1940, Eusébio Tamagnini, along with José Antunes Serra (1914-1990) mentioned the approach of physical anthropology (the anthropological branch then predominant, as opposed to cultural or ethnological anthropology)[10] to biology, and, in particular, to genetics. This approximation, illustrated by the progressive amount of the number of biologists dedicating themselves to physical anthropology (contradicting the traditional predominance of physicians), is connected to methodological issues, with research works demanding the use of "rigorous statistical methods in judging the data and in the comparison of the various populations, along with the results of the studies on the heredity of human features".[11] E. Tamagnini and J. A. Serra defined the development of these studies as "one of the current purposes of the Institute of Anthropology",[12] to which they assigned, in line with the eugenic thought dominant

[6] See: José Maria Pompeu Memória, *Breve História da Estatística*, Brasília, Df, Embrapa Informação Tecnológica, 2004, p. 52. Available at: http://www.im.ufrj.br/~lpbraga/prob1/historia_estatistica.pdf (24/05/2009).

[7] Until 1947, the year he was hired by the University of São Paulo, Stevens had published more than twenty articles in the magazines already mentioned. Cf. *Boletim da Associação Brasileira de Estatística*, Ano XVIII, Nº 52, 2º Quadrimestre de 2002, p. 43. Available at: http://redeabe.org.br/Boletins/Boletim_52.pdf (24/05/2009)

[8] Information generously provided by Hans Lucas of the International Statistical Institute (ISI), (26/05/2009).

[9] On the history of the anthropological school of Coimbra, under the leadership of Eusébio Tamagnini, see, for example: Gonçalo Duro dos Santos, *A Escola de Antropologia de Coimbra 1885-1950: o que significa seguir uma regra científica?*, Lisboa, Imprensa de Ciências Sociais, 2005, especially pp. 122-174. (the work includes a biography, pp. 206-209., and a complete bibliographical list, pp. 226-232., of Eusébio Tamagnini); and *Cem anos de antropologia em Coimbra 1885-1985*, Coimbra, Museu e Laboratório Antropológico, 1985, especially pp. 18-22. (the book contains a detailed chronology on the anthropology at the University of Coimbra, pp. 227-233)

[10] See: E. Tamagnini and J. A. Serra, *Subsídios para a história da antropologia portuguesa* (Memória apresentada ao Congresso da Actividade Científica Portuguesa, Coimbra, 1940), Coimbra, 1942, p. 7.

[11] Idem, *ibidem*, p. 12. – our translation from the Portuguese text.

[12] Idem, *ibidem*, p. 13. – our translation from the Portuguese text.

at the time, a valuable practical application: "the eugenic and population studies constitute the basis of the indispensable social reforms for the enhanced future life of humanity".[13] It is in this context of the necessity to improve the statistical treatment of anthropometric, physiological and demographic data, that one understands the arrival of W. L. Stevens, assigned "as a statistician, to guide the application work of modern statistical methods to Biological Sciences and organize initiation courses for professors and students of the same methods".[14] The «Elementary Course of Modern Statistical Methods applicable to Scientific Investigation», headed by professor W. L. Stevens, functioned between 1942 and 1944, and is linked to a set of published studies in the series "Questões de Método".[15] It is importance to add that in hiring a "distinct student of Professor R.A. Fischer",[16] E. Tamagnini could count with the intervention of the British Council and the "Instituto para a Alta Cultura".[17] This last institution provided a subsidy of 16 000 escudos (Portuguese currency at the time) for the functioning of the course headed by W. L. Stevens.[18]

What analysis can be made of W. L. Stevens' passage through Coimbra? First, it is important to highlight that the Anthropological School of Coimbra could benefit, even if only for a limited period of time, from the services of a disciple of Ronald Aylmer Fisher – a celebrated scientist with important contributions to mathematics, statistics, biometrics and evolutionary biology (with a decisive role in the progressive conciliation between Mendelism and Darwinism, R. A. Fisher is one of the founders of population genetics and one of the main contributors to the Modern Synthesis).[19] As for the years W. L. Stevens spent in Coimbra, the data which allows us to inquire about his teaching activity is frankly scarce. We know that the course he led functioned between 1942 and 1944, but the apparent absence of Stevens' *curriculum vitae* in the archives of the University of Coimbra, and, mainly, the inexistence of annuals of the same institution for the period between 1943 and 1947 (encompassing, thus, the years during which the course led by W. L. Stevens was lectured), conditioned

---

[13] Idem, *ibidem*, pp. 13-14. – our translation from the Portuguese text.

[14] *Diário do Governo*, 11th December 1942. Quoted by: *Cem anos de antropologia em Coimbra 1885-1995*, Coimbra, Museu e Laboratório Antropológico, 1985, p. 21. – our translation from the Portuguese text. The course's subject areas were mathematics, biology, medicine, psychology, genetics, physics, chemistry and agriculture. Cf. *Revista da Faculdade de Ciências da Universidade de Coimbra*, Coimbra, Tipografia da Atlântida, vol. X, n°2, 1942, p. 308.

[15] See: *Cem anos de antropologia em Coimbra 1885-1995*, Coimbra, Museu e Laboratório Antropológico, 1985, p. 21.

[16] Eusébio Tamagnini. Quoted by: Gonçalo Duros dos Santos, 2005, p. 211.

[17] See: Gonçalo Duro dos Santos, 2005, p. 211; *Revista da Faculdade de Ciências da Universidade de Coimbra*, Coimbra, Tipografia da Atlântida, vol. X, N°2, 1942, pp.293-294. British official sources confirm the intervention of the two identities in the process. Cf. *The British Council Annual report for 1941-42* – information generously provided by Peter Bloor, Records Management Officer, The British Council, (1/6/2009).

[18] See: *Revista da Faculdade de Ciências da Universidade de Coimbra*, Coimbra, Tipografia da Atlântida, vol. X, n°2, 1942, p. 302.

[19] The evolutionary biologist and popular science writer Richard Dawkins ranks R. A. Fisher as Darwin's great 20th century successor. Cf. R. Dawkins (ed.), *The Oxford Book of Modern Science Writing*, Oxford, New York, Oxford University Press, 2008, pp. 18-19.

our investigation. What was the programme of the course? Who attended it? What bibliography was recommended? Why was it extinct after only two years? These are just some of the questions that (at least) for now, will remain without an answer. As for W. L. Stevens' scientific activity, the English statistician published many articles during his short stay in Portugal – due to the limited length of the present text, these works will not be mentioned here. It is also important to highlight that, although in Portugal, W. L. Stevens' master, R. A. Fisher, did not forget him, revealing himself informed about some important progresses made by contemporary Portuguese naturalists. On the 29th July 1944, R. A. Fisher wrote to W. L. Stevens requesting the latter to send him examples of the three species of tristyly plants which had been identified by the Portuguese botanist Abílio Fernandes (1906-1994).[20]

---

[20] See: http://digital.library.adelaide.edu.au/coll/special//fisher/corres/stevenswl/StevensWL440729a. html (28/05/2009).

Ricardo S. Reis dos Santos
Centro de Filosofia das Ciências, Faculdade de Ciências, Universidade de Lisboa, Portugal
Francisco Carrapiço
Faculdade de Ciências, Departamento de Biologia Vegetal, Centro de Biologia Ambiental, Centro de
Filosofia das Ciências, Universidade de Lisboa, Portugal

DARWIN AND MERESCHKOWSKY:
TWO IMAGES, TWO EVOLUTIONARY CONCEPTS

Introduction

With the publication of *The Origin of Species,* in 1859, the English naturalist Charles Darwin (1809-1882) revolutionized all Western thought. Regarding science, natural selection positioned itself as a paradigmatic mechanism for explaining biological evolution, and which, over time, was incorporated into new epistemological conceptions (e.g. Darwinism, neo-Darwinism, social Darwinism). In 1909, only fifty years after the publication of Darwin's important work, the Russian biologist Constantin Mereschkowsky (1855-1921) introduced the concept of symbiogenesis as an alternative explanatory mechanism for the evolution of life. In both cases, Darwin and Mereschkowsky illustrate their concepts through images. In this work we will focus on Darwin's and Mereschkowsky's epistemological experiences in the conceptual explanations of the evolution of life. We will also pay special attention to the epistemological value of image as proximity operator in the representation of concepts.

The tree and the evolutionary concept of Darwin

With the publication of *On the Origin of Species,* Darwin had in mind two distinct objectives: «first, to show that species were created separately, and secondly, to show that natural selection was the main agent of change (...) » (Darwin, quoted in Gould, 1989). The verb «to show» does not appear here by accident. In fact, it underlines Darwin's intentions of exposing, showing, making visible, evident, what he considered being the «mystery of mysteries»: the origin and evolution of species. Darwin considered his work «a long argument» which had as a guideline precisely those two above-mentioned objectives. Thus, his intention was «to show» that species were created separately, and «to show» that natural selection was the main agent of change. In this sense, Darwin was accurate in the way he «showed» those two objectives. In its hundreds of pages, *The Origin of Species* includes only a small illustration – a treelike diagram – although Darwin considered the publication of this diagram «indispensable» (Darwin, quoted in Smith, 2006). Actually, this image represents, in a summarised manner, not only the so-called textual «long argument», which serves as a contextualizing element, but also and mainly «to show» the effects of natural selection on the descendants of a common ancestor, and in particular «to show» the principle of divergence.

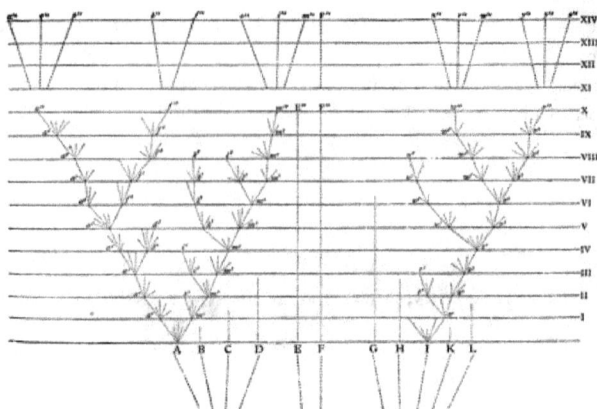

Figure 2. Charles Darwin's Diagram, On the Origin of Species (London: Murray, 1859), between pages 116 and 117
© Wellcome Library, London

Darwin's diagram (fig. 1) appears here as an interesting thought-experiment. The letters A and L represent the species of a vast gender that inhabits a particular geographical region. Each horizontal line represents a thousand, or more, generations, allowing for a vertical reading in relation to time. The punctuated lines go from A to I and are gradually ramified, representing different variations, which appear in the descendents. When one of these lines crosses the horizontal line, a small letter with a number above the line of the text indicates that sufficient variations occurred to form a distinct variety. This process continues by the horizontal line X, from which Darwin presents a condensed and simplified version of the same process. Here, we can observe that, at the end of ten thousand generations, the species A evolved into three distinct species (a10, f10, m10). After fourteen generations, it originated eight species (from a14 to m14). However, the original species A, as well as all the species and intermediate varieties, were extinct. The species B, C and D survived at least during a certain time. Just one species, F, survived during fourteen thousand generations. Of the eleven initial species presented (A to L), fifteen species emerged, very different and more distinct than the previous ones. In fact, so distinct, according to Darwin, that we can imagine the last descendants from A to I as two separate genders or at least sub-genders (Smith, 2006).

The diagram does not represent all of the evolution theory by natural selection, but ends up «showing» in a very objective manner, along with the due contextualization, Darwin's evolutionary concept. In summary, a concept characterised by a mechanism which acts passively and which is exterior to the individual. In fact, a mechanism which considers that the organisms are in constant competition due to the scarceness of resources, organisms which, due to their intra and inter-specific variations present a differential adaptation, that is, natural selection ends up preserving the better adapted organisms to a certain environment. In this sense, the species, as an individual, appear here as a selection unit and evolution occurs vertically.

The tree and the evolutionary concept of Mereschkowsky

In 1909, fifty years after the publication of *On the Origin of Species,* Mereschkowsky published in the *Proceedings Studies of the Imperial Kazan University* a paper titled *The Theory of Two Plasms as Foundation of Symbiogenesis. A New Doctrine on the Origins of Organisms*[1], where he introduces for the first time the concept of symbiogenesis: «the origin of organisms by the combination or the association of two or more beings which enter in symbiosis» (Mereschkowsky, 1909, quoted in Carrapiço & Rita, 2009). Symbiosis, according to the definition introduced in 1879 by Anton De Bary (1831-1888), means «the joint life of different organisms» (De Bary, 1879, quoted in Carrapiço & Rita, 2009). In Mereschkowsky's paper, similarly to Darwin's important work, is presented a diagram with the shape of a tree with the intention of «showing» the concept of symbiogenesis (fig. 2).

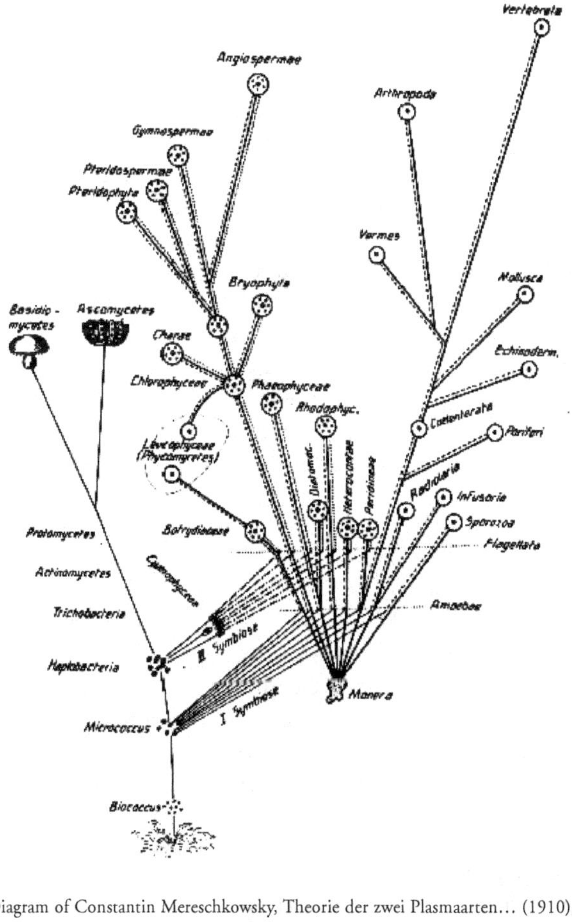

Figure 3. Diagram of Constantin Mereschkowsky, Theorie der zwei Plasmaarten... (1910), page 366

---

[1] The original article was written in Russian. One year later, Mereschkowsky published the same article in German.

This diagram, similar to Darwin's one, also reveals an experience of thought. If we compare it to the one published in *The Origin of Species,* we see two substantial differences: first, there are two evident starting points which lead to two distinct evolutionary lines of organisms equally distinct; second, there is a horizontal connection between these two evolutionary lines. These two innovations highlight a theory which Mereschkowsky had already developed in 1905 in an article entitled *Uber Natur und Ursprung der Chromatophoren im Pflanzenreich* [on the nature and origin of chromatophores (plastids) in the plant kingdom] , where he defends for the first time that chloroplasts had originated from free-living cyanobacteria; in fact, a theory which Mereschkowsky will dedicate most of his lifetime, despite opposition of all the currents of that time (Carrapiço & Rita, 2009).

The concept of symbiogenesis proposed by Mereschkowsky remained submerged until the middle of the 1960's, when Lynn Margulis (1938-2011), after several attempts, publishes an article entitled *On the Origin of Mitosing Cells* (Sagan, 1967) in which she develops the *Serial Endosymbiosis Theory,* bringing to scientific debate symbiogenic ideas. The theory developed by Margulis establishes a discontinuity among prokaryotic and eukaryotic cells, and essentially considers that mitochondria, basal bodies, flagella and chloroplasts derived from free-living prokaryotic cells, leading eukaryotic cells to be seen as the result of the evolution of primitive symbiosis (Carrapiço & Rita, 2009). In fact, the sequential endosymbiosis theory by Margulis is no more than a sort of "modern synthesis" of Mereschkowsky's symbiogenesis theory.

The epistemological implications of this concept are very interesting since symbiogenesis created new units of selection – symbiomes[2] – which appear through the integration of various parts, followed by the progressive differentiation of the whole, conferring, thus, a competitive advantage which goes beyond the traditional neo-Darwinism selection (Carrapiço, 2009). On the other hand, symbiogenesis presents not only an evolutionary mechanism in which symbiosis occurs as a vehicle of that organism, but presents itself also as a decisive operator in the production of innovative metabolic and anatomic variation on which the own natural selection can act later on.

Conclusion

The corollary of the natural selection mechanism is based on the principle that evolution occurs by a competitive process in which only the better adapted organisms are preserved. In this sense, natural selection occurs in the interface between the organism (and all its heredity charge) and the environment in which it is inserted. As a result, natural selection acts on the phenotype of the individual and has no intervention in the machine that produces variation, being limited to its preservation

---

[2] The introduction of symbiomes in scientific terminology was a conceptual change in the traditional view which has been transmitted on the structure and function of organisms, with profound consequences in biological, medical and social domains. In this perspective, each plant and each animal have to be considered as a "superorganism" – symbiome – which includes its own genes existing in chromosomes, the genes of cellular organelles (mitochondria and/or chloroplasts), as well as the genetic information of symbiont bacteria and the virus which lives in the organism. Concept introduced by Jan Sapp in 2003 (Carrapiço, 2003).

or elimination. In other words, the variation is a fact for which, according to Buffon, «there is no other solution than of the fact itself» (Jacob, 1981). However, according to this mechanism, evolution occurs in a gradual and unidirectional manner along a vertical line with origin in one point. On the other hand, the symbiogenic concept, introduced by Mereschkowsky, came to show that natural selection is not the only explanatory mechanism of biological evolution. In fact, there is more and more evidence of the multiple origins of life and horizontal gene transfer between different phylogenetic branches. Symbiogenesis positions itself as an evolutionary mechanism that does not exclude natural selection but has cooperation at its basis. In this sense, symbiogenesis can be hereby understood as a mechanism of producing difference. This differentiation results from the horizontal fusion of two or more distinct entities, which present different capabilities from their individual components, forming the so-called symbiome (Carrapiço & Rita, 2009). As a result, and without despising the excellence of Darwin's and Mereschkowsky's absolutely notorious contributions, we consider it is important to refer that the two evolutionary concepts here presented probably constitute restricted aspects of a universal law. And for that reason, we should argue that no system will explain life in all its aspects and all its details.

	Natural Selection	Symbiogenesis
Selection unit	Individual	Symbiome
Variation	Acts on variation	Produces variation
Sense of evolution	Vertical	Vertical and horizontal
Form of evolution	(Darwin, 1859) Ramified tree	(Doolittle, 2000) Reticulated tree
Evolutionary gradualism	Always	Not always

Table 1. Comparison between Natural Selection and the Symbiogenesis in its main aspects.

In a recent article, entitled *An extended evolutionary synthesis*, Pigliucci & Levy (2009) declare that «since Modern Synthesis, little has been advanced theoretically that is, Modern Synthesis constitutes a base-structure of current and future evolutionary biology, without there being a great need to revisit its fundaments» Such claim argues, thus, for an expansion of that synthesis without altering the paradigm. The same authors claim that the Modern Synthesis (the theoretical restructuration of original

Darwinism as a new discipline of Mendelian genetics and statistics) carried out in the 1930's and 1940's, did not correspond, as defended by Mayr, to a shift of paradigm in the Kuhnian sense of the word, but instead to a true synthesis of areas that, at that time, were in opposite sides (Pigliucci & Levy, 2009). This theoretical advancement, as we have seen, occurred fifty years after the publication of *The Origin of Species*. This theoretical advancement implied, or should have implied, or will imply, a paradigm shift. Curiously, this shift can be represented by two images – Darwin's and Mereschkowsky's treelike diagrams – as representative marks of two distinct but not exclusive evolutionary concepts. In this sense, both Darwin and Mereschkowsky realized the importance of image in its ability to visualize the unseen, that is, the outcome of a process (evolution) that cannot for whatever reason be performed in the laboratory.

Bibliography

CARRAPIÇO, F. – Introdução a alguns conceitos. Available at http://azolla.fc.ul.pt, 2003 (access on 1st of May 2009)

CARRAPIÇO, F. – *The Symbiotic Phenomenom in the Evolutive Context*. In Pombo, Rahman, Torres & Simon (eds) Unity of Science: Essays in Honour of Otto Neurath. Springer, 2011

CARRAPIÇO, F. & RITA, O. – Simbiogénese e evolução. In Levy, Carrapiço, Abreu e Pina (eds). *Evolução. Conceitos e Debates*, Lisbon: Esfera do Caos, 2009, 175-198

DARWIN, C. – *On the Origin of Species by Means of Natural Selection*. 1st Edition. London: John Murray, 1859 (disponível em http://darwin-online.org.uk)

GOULD, S. J. – *Quando as galinhas tiverem dentes*. Lisbon: Gradiva, 1989

JACOB, F. – *O Jogo dos Possíveis. Ensaio sobre a Diversidade do Mundo*. Lisbon: Publicações Gradiva, 1981

PIGLIUCCI, M. & LEVY, A. – Uma síntese evolutiva expandida. In Levy, Carrapiço, Abreu e Pina (eds). *Evolução. Conceitos e Debates*, Lisbon: Esfera do Caos, 2009, 199-219

SAGAN, L. – On the Origin of Mitosing Cells, *Theoret. Biol.* (1967) 14, 225-274

SAPP, J., CARRAPIÇO, F. & ZOLOTONOSOV, M. – Symbiogenesis: The Hidden Face of Constantin Merezhkowsky. *Hist. Phil. Life Sci*, 24 (2002), 413-440

SMITH, J. – *Charles Darwin and Victorian Visual Culture*. Cambridge: Cambridge University Press, 2006

Gökhan Akbay

Department of Philosophy; Middle East Technical University, Ankara, Turkey

FUNCTION, NATURAL SELECTION AND INFORMATION

Functions debate was at first a debate about teleology. The question was whether biological entities were designed by an omnipotent God or the outcomes of a natural process. Now, an omnipotent God has lost its significance as an alternative to naturalistic theories of evolution. However, the apparent harmony and complexity of the biological world still charms many scientists, including arch-evolutionists like Richard Dawkins.[1] Functions debate turned out to be a debate internal to naturalism.

The vital question in functions debate, namely the substantive question, involves the nature of functional entities. I will primarily be concerned with this question which is about the nature of functional entities. They include natural entities like enzymes, organs, systems, etc. They also include artifacts that humans produce and use. The question is whether we can find an *interesting* property that is common to all and will unite them except nonfunctional entities.

What do we mean when we say that the function of mirrors is to reflect light? And what does a biologist mean when he says "the function of hemoglobin is to carry oxygen to tissues"? For mirrors we can say they are very good at reflecting light and we use them to reflect light. We can also appeal to the design intentions of mirror producers. In the second case, we can neither find designers nor users of hemoglobin molecules. Natural functions pose more serious problems than conscious functions. In order to justify our usage of the word 'function' we should find a covering definition for both types (conscious and natural).

The most important distinction for Wright is between function and accident.[2] If we turn back to the hemoglobin example, it is a matter of fact that hemoglobin can also bind to CO (carbon monoxide), which is a lethal toxin but is not the function of hemoglobin it is rather an accidental side-effect of hemoglobin's structure. The same can be said for artifacts. The computer has many functions but I would think twice before saying "the function of computers is to make noise". This distinction is the central theme of Wright's article.

After a lengthy discussion of previous analyses of function statements, Wright proposes his own solution to the problem. For Wright, the most critical point of

---

[1] Dawkins,R., "Universal Darwinism", in Hull, D. and Ruse, M. (eds.), *The Philosophy of Biology* (Oxford: Oxford University Press, 1998)

[2] *Ibid.*

function ascriptions is to explain the reasons for the presence of functional entities[3]. For example, when we claim that the function of knives is to cut, we mean that knives are present because they cut. In the case of artifacts, the point is usually clear. An artifact may have many effects, but one effect can explain why it is there. We can use CDs for ornamenting our cars but they are produced for storing information. Wright asserts that the same point applies to biological functions as well. Hemoglobin is present because it carries oxygen. It may have other effects such as binding to CO, but natural selection has maintained and spread hemoglobin for its oxygen binding capacity.

The second substantial contribution to functions debate comes from Robert Cummins' 1975 article. The article was an attempt to explicate the real aim of functional explanations in science. According to Cummins, functional explanations have nothing to do with the presence of some entity. In contrast, functional explanations seek to explain what contribution an entity or a process makes to the capacities of a containing system. Function attributions thus explain how a containing system produces complex outcomes by means of simple processes and entities.

Cummins claims that the apparent scientific plausibility of selected-effects approaches originates from a misunderstanding of evolutionary theory. According to Cummins, selected-effects approaches falsely consider natural selection as an explanation of the presence of functional traits of organisms. For Cummins, natural selection does not determine which traits an individual has. It is determined by the genetic plan. Natural selection just explains why some traits are more frequent than others by referring to their adaptive advantages. In his own words "natural selection cannot alter a plan, but it can trim the set."[4]

Flowchart diagrams, abstract descriptions of electronic circuits or assembly lines are best examples of Cummins' approach. Consider the computer fan example I mentioned before. The function of the fan is to cool the processor. Cooling the processor is a capacity of the computer which is achieved by the inner workings of the fan. The fan can be decomposed into its simpler parts. These simpler parts contribute to the cooling capacity of the fan, hence, one can explain how the cooling capacity of the computer is realized by means of analyzing relevant parts into simpler and simpler capacities they have.

Wright's line of inquiry was elaborated by Ruth Millikan in her theory of "proper functions".[5] She constructed a theoretical definition that would unite purposeful phenomena under one definition.

Millikan adds a further constraint on functional entities: reproduction. By reproduction she means something like copying. Copying occurs when some properties of an original entity determine the properties of its descendants in a regular way. For instance, the copying machine maps the written marks of the original paper onto another sheet of paper and produces a similar paper. In copying, descendants systematically co-vary with the original entity (the ancestor or the model).

---

[3] *Ibid.* p.154

[4] *Ibid.* p.751

[5] Millikan, R. Excerpt from *Language, Thought and Other Biological Categories* in David Buller (Ed.), *Function, selection, and design*, Albany, N.Y. : State University of New York Press, 1999.

Another constraint Millikan adds is selection. For Millikan, we cannot determine the function of a trait just by looking at its present benefits. The point is that we cannot distinguish fortuitous benefit from genuine function by just looking at its present performance. How beneficial should a trait be in order to be functional? Millikan identifies two extremes regarding biological cases[6]. The first extreme is the view that the trait in question should be a necessary component of the living system. Homeostatic functions (i.e. thermoregulation in haemothermal animals and such necessary dispositions of an organism) may be a candidate for this extreme view. However, even homeostatic functions were not present in some ancestors of today's organisms. So they cannot be "necessary" in the strict sense. There are also some functions of traits that are not performed in the lifetime of an individual. Mating displays of a lonely budgie would not occur unless a friend from opposite sex is placed into his cage.

Another extreme is the view that a past token might have a function just because it has benefited only once in the reproduction of the trait. As Millikan states it, it is natural selection that draws the line between these two extremes. Hence, selection is a necessary part of proper function definitions. In her own words: "Whether something has a function is not a matter of how often it has accidentally helped out in the movement from generation to generation. Anything whatever might occasionally have done that. It is a matter of whether it was selected to help out in this way."[7]

A crucial point of Millikan's account is the reference to historical conditions. As we observed before, it is the complexity of the system and relevant simplicity of dispositions that make a causal role analysis of functions plausible. It is the explanatory aims of the researchers that determine which capacities would deserve analysis. This may be true for machines in general. They are specified by certain rules of performance. There are rules that specify the proper input, internal states and expected output. This is why abstract characterizations like flowchart diagrams are well suited to describing machines.

The central problem with Cummins' account is that it cannot capture the normative aspect of function ascriptions[8]. For Millikan, since Cummins does not ascribe functions to parts that do not actually contribute to a systemic capacity, his analysis cannot account for malfunctions. According to Millikan, an entity has a proper function not because of its contemporary dispositions. Having a function depends on history. The historical link between normativity and function is provided by natural selection.

Reference to natural selection has been seriously criticized by many philosophers. Counter examples include swampman[9] (a molecule to molecule duplicate of a person who randomly and immediately appears), screws that accidentally fall into a machine and make a functional connection[10], brand-new antibiotic resistance genes that enter

[6] *Ibid.* p.35

[7] *Ibid.* p. 38

[8] Millikan, R. (1989) "In Defense of Proper Functions". *Philosophy of Science* 56: pp. 294-295

[9] Sterelny, K. and Griffiths, P. *Sex and Death: An Introduction to Philosophy of Biology* (Chicago: University of Chicago Press, 1999), p.222

[10] Kitcher, P. "Function and Design," in Hull, D. and Ruse, M. (eds.), *The Philosophy of Biology* (Oxford: Oxford University Press, 1998)

a bacterium[11], etc. All of these attempts aim to show one thing: history is not *essential* to function ascriptions. These counterexamples seem to miss the point in a crucial respect. If Millikan were doing conceptual analysis, in other words if she were trying to determine the criterion for true usages of the term function these examples would show that including selection and even reproduction in the definition of function would lead to constant failures. However, Millikan explicitly states that she is not in search for a clarification of the older versions of function concept[12]. Rather, she was trying to find a theoretical definition of purposeful phenomena. Although she does not explicitly tell what the difference will be, I can cite one property of theoretical definitions: they may conflict with your intuitions. Consider "burning". A theoretical definition of burning would cite chemical reactions which involve oxidation. Thus, corrosion would be burning according to the theoretical definition. However, someone who lacks that theoretical knowledge would find this characterization counterintuitive. It is not a conceptual necessity that functional things have a selection history. It is how things work on our planet.

Discussions in functions debate looks very much like the intentionality debate. Just consider how many themes coincide in two fields: malfunction-misrepresentation, normativity of proper functions-normativity of content, algorithmicity of natural selection-algorithmicity of thought, etc. the list can be extended. Is the use of such similar concepts just a matter of chance or are there real similarities between two fields? In my opinion similarity is real and it is because of the semantic aspects of these two fields. By semanticity I do not mean lingual meaning. What I mean is a systematic covariance with some aspects of environment that could count as a normative relation.

The greatest problem for both of these fields is to naturalize normativity (or eliminate it). Since there is such an overlap between these fields, I think we can borrow some concepts from one and apply them to the other. I would like to borrow the concept of information from intentionality debate and investigate whether it can give us the unifying definition we want. I have two aims in this part of my essay. The first one is to explain the intuitions that led me to carry out this project. The second is to begin my investigation by finding out what kind of an information concept can give us the unity we want: unity of artifactual and biological domains, unity of proper functions and causal role functions.

I am impressed by the idea that functional structures carry information about their environment[13]. Function is, in a sense, information about the past environments where organisms evolved. All functions are selective. Their domains are specific. For instance, a bird's wings are adapted to fly only in a fluid which has a viscosity similar to the Earth's air. All of the enzymes are highly specific to their substrates. Eyes have a specific range of wavelengths for sight. It seems as if natural selection coded relevant information into our genes. The case is also relevant to artifacts. Artifacts

[11] Sterelny, K. and Griffiths, P. (1999) p.222

[12] Millikan, R. (1989a) p.293

[13] Dennett, D. C., *Darwin's Dangerous Idea: evolution and the meanings of life.* New York : Simon & Schuster, 1996. p.198

are also domain specific. Their specificity depends on the things on which they are used. For example a pen is specific to some kinds of surfaces, you cannot write on anything. In a sense, a pen includes information about its substrate. This is the first intuition that affects me.

The second intuition comes from biological practice. The use of information concepts in biology, especially in genetics is very common. In my opinion, this is no arbitrary choice. Informational concepts fit this area well. It is apparent from the successes of this approach. Geneticists usually talk about coding, instructions and other such concepts. As I mentioned before, the use of flowchart diagrams in molecular biology also supports such an intuition. Flowchart diagrams or more detailed algorithms tell us how under specified conditions a program will respond. If these fit so well in molecular biology, can we conclude that there really is information about those conditions coded into the organisms themselves? Let me clarify this point. In biochemical pathways molecules are depicted as activating or inhibiting each other. For instance we can describe a pathway like this: if there is this much bicoid proteins nearby, activate such and such genes and begin segmentation, else do nothing.

These are just intuitions and need clarification. The first point of clarification regards the concept of information. What kind of an information concept should we have in order to account for these facts? There are two types of information concepts in use. One was first discovered by Claud Shannon. Shannon's information concept measures the nonaccidental correlation between variables.[14] For instance, smoke gives information about the presence of fire because they show a correlation. Another example may be the bell's ringing. This sense of information is only inferential.[15] To account for functions, we should find another concept of information. We need it in order to capture normative aspects of functions.

The second type of information is called "semantic information". As Dretske describes it, semantic information depends on nomic regularities between the source and the signal[16]. Semanticity is not identical to meaningfulness. According to Dretske, the difference between information and meaning is that having the information that P automatically guarantees having any other nomically or analytically nested information. Analytical nesting is logical implication. Nomical nesting is making some state of affairs necessary by means of a law of nature. For example "this ball is red" carries the information that "this ball is not blue" because it implies that logically but it does not mean that.

I claim that this semantic concept of information can give the unified notion of function. First of all, it is normative but it also accords with a synchronic analysis. Secondly, whatever the physical details of coding information are, both design processes and natural selection can code relevant environmental information into artifacts and organisms.

[14] Godfrey-Smith, P. "Information in Biology" in Hull, D. and Ruse, M. (Eds.), *The Cambridge Companion to Philosophy of Biology*, (Newyork: Cambridge University Press, 2007), p.106

[15] *Ibid.* p.107

[16] Dretske, F. *Knowledge and the flow information,* (Cambridge, Mass. : MIT Press, 1981), p.72

Rita Serra

CES-Centro de Estudos Sociais, Faculdade de Economia, Universidade de Coimbra, Portugal

DARWIN, EVOLUTION AND PROGRESS

Since the publication of *The Origin of Species*, 150 years ago, and the popularization of Darwinism, a lot has been said about Darwin's ideas and their implications in various sciences. One of the most revolutionary aspects of Darwin's concept of Evolution is that the adaption of species to local contexts occurs based on an evolutionary process without direction or intent. However, Darwin's Evolution is a metaphor frequently used to support Western society's belief in Progress as a process of intentional development towards a better world (Gould, 1988). In the text I aim to reflect on Darwin's legacy regarding these two forms of understanding the world – Evolution versus Progress – which are often rivals and lay the base of diverging proposals for the intervention in natural and social systems. I will start by briefly indicating how the concept of Darwin's Evolution is used to explain the emergence of complex systems so that further on I can compare it to the modern paradigm of development based on determinist systems.

The concept of Darwin's Evolution gave us a world without a creator or engineer. The changes which happen to species are not the result of a plan or intention, they are not more capable *a priori*, and are not moving towards a perfect world. On the other hand, the appropriation of Darwin's concept as Progress leads us to believe that evolution advances gradually in the direction of greater perfection. In the vision of Progress, the engineer is replaced by evolution's own mechanism. The world we live in is seen as the best of possible worlds, in which other worlds were eliminated by the "executioner" of natural selection (Gould, 1988). This world obeys the laws of nature and believes that there are answers with greater success than others *a priori* in order for us to adapt to an environment that is insensitive to our will.

François Jacob (1989), in his book *The Possible and the Actual*, uses a curious metaphor for biological evolution without an engineer: it would be great if we did photosynthesis, that way we would not need to work to obtain energy, we would just have to stay in the sun. Why don't we? Because somewhere on the path to evolution, this solution stopped being possible. If we have to imagine a Creator, the most appropriate metaphor for evolution is not one of an engineer, but of a gadgeteer who improvises with what he has at hand as one does bricolage, transforming arms into wings, legs into fins, using the materials available for new uses. The success of a gadgeteer is in always having materials available to reuse, in the proverbial sense of "he who saves what has no worth will always have what he needs". But there is still another important consequence in replacing the engineer for a gadgeteer: the second does not have a plan, he improvises, and therefore, the world which he produces is not the best of possible worlds. It is simply a world that functions (or goes on functioning) in the most varied contexts. The diversity of contexts selects a diversity of possible responses in which various solutions can coexist. In this sense, a certain ecological niche can be occupied by various species with different life strategies, from parasitism to free living, from rapid growth to slow, from mass reproduction to unique descendants, from specialists to generalists. The "game rules" which determine what is possible are not the universal "laws of nature", but contextual. For example, some species of fungus invest in sexual reproduction in situations of food scarceness and in nutritionally rich environments they just grow. The driving force of evolution depends as much on the existence of diversity of solutions to deal with environmental challenges as well as on the existence of barriers (geographical, temporal, seasonal, ethological or others) that limit the contexts to which the species adapt. The process of the creation of species – speciation – is a reflex of this creating force of diversity and barriers. Where a species begins and ends is a constant debate subject in the scientific world, but it is unanimous that species exist as groups of delimited organisms by some sort of criteria[1]. According to the evolutionary concept of species, these are defined as groups of organisms isolated genetically from others that just exchange genetic information amongst themselves.

The barriers lead to the existence of species with colective identities, but the coexistence of these identities forces them to relate. Again, there are diverse forms of possible interaction, from competition to altruism, that are not always determined just by the species but also by the context. For example, certain funguses can behave as symbionts or tree parasites, according to the health state of the plant. The interaction among species also conditions the evolutionary path of each species, a process which is called co-evolution. This concept was highly popularized in the evolutionary study of predators and prey, but can be stretched to the abiotic environment, since the modifications of living beings are capable of modifying the environment itself and affect the entire ecosystem (as plants notoriously did with the production of oxygen). Due to environmental changes the adaptation of species never results in a perfect world, because the species live in environments of constant change. Change rhythms are not constant and periods of certain stability can be interrupted by catastrophic events (Gould, 1988). For all that has been said, Darwin's evolution without a path of various groups of individuals in delimited contexts and with various possibilities of interaction in a world in constant change results in a complex system. Consequently, the paradigms of Evolution based on Darwin's idea are not deterministic, but enriched of explanatory power regarding complex systems: we can explain the evolutionary path of a species, but we cannot predict what will happen in the future. The connecting link of evolution is its history and game rules that limit the universe of possible

---

[1] Species are not "natural" groups. The concept of species is a human construction and various notions exist according to schools of classification and operative criteria (Serra, 2005). The biological concept of species defines it as groups of individuals that reproduce amongst themselves and originate fertile descendants. However, this criteria cannot be operated on living beings that reproduce asexually or parasexually (ex.: fungus, bacteria...), or possess cultural and physical barriers that led them to reproduce in controlled environments (ex: dog and wolf, a male Saint Bernard and a female Chihuahua, among others). The evolutionary concept of species is one of the "common denominators" used by the scientific community.

solutions, but the final result of evolution is unpredictable, because it does not depend on progressive adaptation of the species to the environment but on the co-evolution of species with the environment.

In "Development Betrayed", Richard Norgaard (1995) compared the concept of co-
-evolution to the concept of Progress which is at the base of development standards promoted by Western societies. The concept of progress has its roots in deterministic sciences that consider the world static and determine mechanic models capable of prediction when the "laws" that govern systems are decoded. The myth that we can progress towards a determined path, for example, sustainable development, is based on the assumption that we can control nature through science and get effective governance models based on rational social organization. According to Norgaard, the premises to development deem it to failure, for not recognizing that reality results from the co-evolution of ecological and cultural systems, which are complex and non deterministic. If we want to have new ways of thinking about the future, we have to look at the world with the eyes of complex sciences. To further explain this point of view, one of the examples presented by Norgaard is the co-evolution of plagues, pesticides, institutions and policies of the United States. Before World War II there were only inorganic pesticides (ex: sulfur) and some of the products in the market were not efficient. The regulation emerged as a way to protect farmers from false publicity and the consumers from dangerous contaminants in the food, while easing the development of new chemicals on behalf of the industry. In the 1940's a new type of pesticides was discovered: organic (ex: DDT), which initially were very effective and so widely used as opposed to the inorganics. But these new chemicals created resistance in insect populations in a few years, and the problems started. The reemergence of plagues occurred when the application of chemicals stopped and other plagues emerged to occupy agroecological niches unoccupied by the initial species. The response of the agroengineers and the chemical industry to these problems was to recommend more applications of pesticides. Despite entailing more economic costs, this recommendation made sense to the eyes of individual farmers that saw no other choice, but, collectively, caused more problems to resistance. Some researchers presented proposals of integrated protection programs based on ecosystemic approaches that included crop rotation, biological control and other measures applied in a coordinated manner; but these programs were only adopted by a minority of farmers. At the time when scientific information of the dangerous effects of organic pesticides on the environment was getting bigger, scientists and activists stimulated the environmental conscious which led to a new regulation to protect the environment and the health of rural communities. These more demanding regulatory requisites slowed the response of the chemical industry to produce new and more effective compounds due to administrative procedures imposed by environmental institutions. These delays in the development of new products led to an increase in their cost. Few companies managed to support the research costs and operate under imposed norms, which led to the restructuring of the industrial fabric in few companies of bigger dimensions. The new pesticides produced were less toxic to people, but more expensive and demanded more care and knowledge to apply them. The farmers managed to buy these products when the price of agricultural goods was high, in the beginning of the 1980's they were desperate when there was a break in prices. It was during this

time that the Department of Agriculture supported the implementation of integrated protection programs, but the adherence to these programs is still limited and the agroecosystems were so modified that they cannot simply stop using pesticides entirely. It is evident that at the beginning of pesticide application, nobody could predict these environmental, social and economic problems. But in this case it is also evident that the responses of the institutions did not occur in a direct way to the problem, but according to political interests of those affected by the problem, from the industry to the environmentalists, which according to "the game of the possible» culminated in an indirect response which influenced the evolution of plagues and pesticides.

The difference between the aspirations of modern development and its achievements can be explained through the co-evolutionary paradigm, where the degradation and scarceness of natural resources, the scientific inability to give answers, the public sectors' inability to deal with bureaucratic obstacles derived from competing political interests and with ethic, cultural and religious diversity, reflect that the application of deterministic approaches to complex systems are condemned to failure. The crisis of modernity can be interpreted as symptoms of inadaptation to ecological and cultural systems, since the environmental crisis are, in a final analysis, crisis of social organization and cultural character.

The deterministic approaches are established on the assumption that there are universal ways of solving problems through science which are independent from contexts, and therefore legitimize centralised answers based on expert knowledge scientifically recognised which led to the homogenization of local contexts by imposition, sometimes by force, of valid answers *a priori*. The barriers that support the diversity are seen as obstacles to this hegemonic universalisation towards an ideal of unique progress. On the contrary, the co-evolutionary alternative legitimises plural approaches, decentralized and more contextualised. Instead of selecting *a priori* better solutions, the co-evolutionary paradigm opens political spaces to the participation of forms of scientific and traditional knowledge towards decision making. The co--evolutionary paradigm of Richard Norgaard is in its essence, emancipatory, because instead of substituting a legitimate form of knowledge by another without altering the hierarchy of powers, it favours the distribution of power. This conceptual evolution does not imply the destruction of deterministic approaches to contexts where they are well adapted as certain areas of chemical engineering, physics, biology and economy, among others. It simply defends that they cannot apply deterministic approaches to complex systems and hope for success.

The co-evolutionary paradigm as a model of development raises a series of questions. Which are the criteria to decide and intervene in complex systems when we know that the result of our actions is unpredictable? How do we create a space for dialogue and understanding among forms of distinct knowledge and uneven powers? The benefit of co-evolution as an alternative paradigm is not the best way to answer these questions, but it is a starting point, the destitution of our cosmic arrogance (Gould, 1988), the unique solutions, the legitimisation for a participative management of resources, the application of alternative pedagogies, like feminists, for the redistribution of power (Buchy, 2004). If there are no correct ways to understand the world, the best is to constantly submit science to the scrutiny of skeptic inquiry and maintain an open mind to evolve in our ideas. This is the most important legacy Darwin could have left us.

Bibliography

BUCHY, Marlene. 2004. The Challenges of 'Teaching By Being': The Case of Participatory Resource Management. Journal of Geography in Higher Education, 28, 35-47p.

GOULD, Stephen Jay. 1988. O mundo depois de Darwin. Editorial Presença, Lisboa, 244p.

JACOB, François. 1989. O Jogo dos Possíveis. Gradiva, Lisboa, 141p.

NORGAARD, Richard. 1995. Development Betrayed: the end of progress and a coevolutionary revising of the future. Routledge, London e New York, 280 p.

SERRA, Rita. 2005. Micoflora das uvas portuguesas e seu potencial para a contaminação das uvas com micotoxinas, com destaque para a ocratoxina A. Centro de Engenharia Biológica da Escola de Engenharia da Universidade do Minho

Ricardo S. Reis dos Santos

Centro de Filosofia das Ciências, Faculdade de Ciências, Universidade de Lisboa, Portugal

EVOLUTION, PROGRESS AND THE CONFUSION OF THINGS

Introduction

In the preface of his book titled *Darwin's Dangerous Idea*, the North-American philosopher, Daniel C. Dennett writes: «Darwin's evolution theory by means of natural selection always fascinated me but, during the years, I met a surprising variety of thinkers that cannot hide their discomfort towards this great idea and that manifest it with an attitude that goes from persistent skepticism to declared hostility. I found not only laymen and religious men but also secular philosophers, psychologists, physicists and even biologists that would prefer that Darwin was wrong» (Dennett, 1995). This means that evolution is, from its beginning, affected by a certain short-sightedness in relation to its principles and mainly regarding its implications.

Actually, Darwin's ideas challenged, not only all conceptions about the origin of animals and plants, but also about the actual regularity of the world, and mainly the purpose of human life. Victorian society experienced moments of great convulsion. There was a popular conviction that Darwin had murdered the idea of God and that one day, jokingly, had entitled himself the «Devil's chaplain» (Browne, 2006). Thomas Henry Huxley, a close friend of Darwin, gave us a good snapshot of those moments writing in the *Westminster Review*: «Everyone read the book of Mr. Darwin, or, at least, gave an opinion on his merits or demerits; pietists, whether laymen or ecclesiastic, discredited it…; fanatical devotes denounced it with ignorant censorship; elders, of both genders, considered it a dangerous book, and even wise men… cited antiquated authors to demonstrate that the author is no better than an anthropoid (…)» (Huxley, quoted in Avelar *et al.*, 2004). Rapidly, pamphlets started circulating in the streets ridiculing Darwin, in the cafes lords gathered to give their opinion on the horrendous idea that we all descend from a monkey, in the newspaper cartoons caricatured the origin of the species.

With the publication of *The descent of man and selection in relation to sex*, in 1871, the criticism intensified. It was not just the fact that Darwin proposed that living beings should not be considered creations of a divinity, but mainly the fact that this theory took Man off the pedestal of moral superiority. As Browne (2006) noted, «Biblical fundamentalism is mainly a modern concept, and not Victorian. That which Darwinism challenged in the Victorian period was the transformation of life in an amoral chaos, without any sign of divine authority or sense of design or purpose». The implications of Darwin's ideas were, in all domains, too profound and affected the fabric of our more fundamental beliefs. The jesuist priest Adam Sedgwick, who had been Darwin's professor when he studied theology at Cambridge, wrote harsh words opposing this theory: «(...) I cannot conclude without expressing my profound rancor for the theory, for its materialism full of determination...; for its total disregard for final causes, indicating an understanding without morality on behalf of its proposers» (Sedwick, 1860, quoted in Avelar *et al.*, 2004). In 1882, an engraving was published in *Punch's Almanack* illustrating man's evolution, with the inscription that «Man is but a worm». This scenario of a possible origin from a worm insinuated by this almanac with the purpose of causing controversy is a serious thing. Already in the 18th century, when it was suggested that spermatozoids were worms, the Catalan professor Monravá, who taught in the Faculty of Medicine at Campo Santana, used to say to his students: «Sons of worms? This to me is worse than being sons of a bitch!» (Monravá, quoted in Pinto-Correia, 1999).

As François Jacob (1981) said, «the Darwinian conception has, thus, a fatal consequence: the current living world, as we perceive it around us, is just one of many possible. (...) It could just as well be different. It could even not exist.». It is precisely this contingency, this chance, and this vulgarization of the human species that will be controversial. So this is the reason why resistance persisted in time and was mainly assumed as an aspect of absolute truth. Hegel wrote somewhere that humanity will only be satisfied when it lives in a world created by itself. Human solipsism is the most evident face of this resistance.

The march of progress: iconographical overview

The Swiss naturalist Charles Bonnet (1720-1793) was probably the major enthusiast of Preformation, a theory of reproduction that emerged in the second half of the 17th century and which caused feverous debates among the most brilliant minds of the period. Bonnet dedicated himself to the study of insects and developed, along with René Antoine de Réaumur (1683-1757), an interesting work on parthenogenesis, and ended up by definitively demonstrating that water fleas had «virgin births». With only 25 years of age, Bonnet published a treatise on insectology where he presented the idea of a scale of natural beings. It is curious to note that we can assume this scale as a modified version of Aristotles's *scala naturae* which is, in the end, a scheme of classification by divisions (*diaireses*) corresponding to «natural beings». The sequence of these divisions is based on the logic of progression which goes from the simple to the complex, ending with man.

Figure 4. Scale of natural beings, according to Charles Bonnet (1745)

Charles White (1728-1813), a distinguished British doctor, published in 1799 his *Regular Gradation in Man*, where he presented the diversity of vertebrates in a linear gradation that goes from birds to crocodiles and dogs, passing through monkeys and ends in the human groups with the Caucasian model on the top. These are his words: «In who, but the European, could we find the arched noble head containing a similar quantity of brain (…)? And the perpidencular face, prominent nose, rounded chin? The variety of features and perfection of expressions (…) the rosy face and coralinian lip?» (White, 1799).

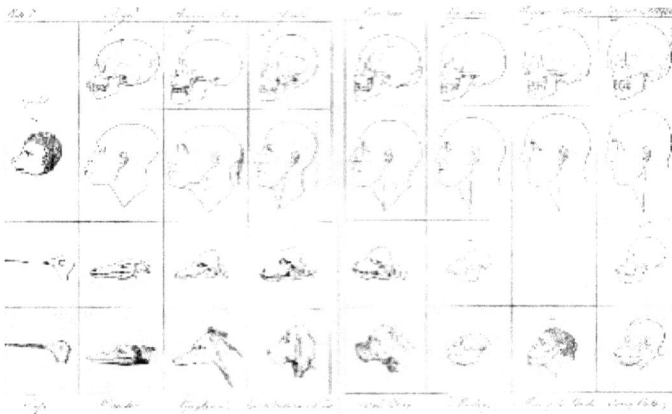

Figure 5. Linear gradation of vertebrate, according to Charles White (1799)

This tradition of placing man at the top, in a clear vision of the world based on the mental scheme of «us and the others», has never disappeared. Even with Darwin, and especially after Darwin, this human inevitability and superiority ends up being a part of the structuring of Western thought. A canonical representation of evolution based on the principle that life starts with the simple and restrict and progresses always vertically to more and better was then produced and popularized. In this sense, evolution becomes synonym of progression. We find in Henry Fairfield Osborn (1857-1935), a North-American geologist, a good example of this type of representation. In the progressive evolution of the human brain, Osborn represents the brain of a chimpanzee as the least evolved, followed by *Pitechanthropus*, *Piltdown*, *Neanderthal*, and finally *Homo sapiens*, as the most evolved. The progression is revealed in terms of the volume of cerebral mass, this means, it starts with the smallest and most simple and progresses into more and more complex, and thus, better.

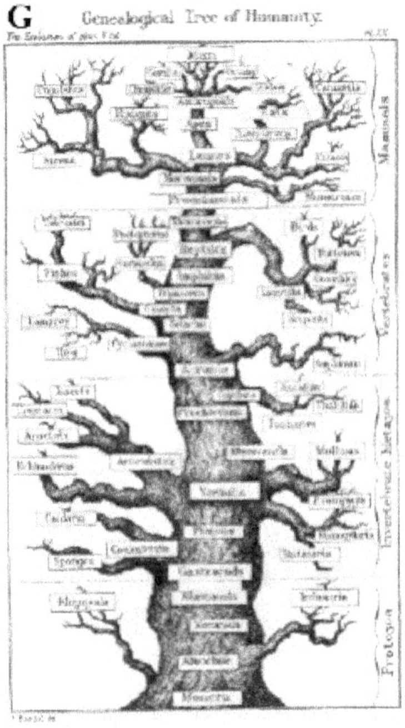

Figure 6. Genealogical tree of humanity, by Ernst Haeckel (1874)

Ernst Haeckel (1834-1919), brilliant promoter of Darwin's theory and his correspondent, in his work *Anthropogenie* (1874) included a genealogical tree of humanity. In this tree we find once more the canonical representation of evolution, this means, at the base of the tree the most simple beings and at the top the most complex. Furthermore, he hierarchies groups – protozoa, invertebrate metazoans, vertebrate, mammals – creating an order that gives a certain idea of ascendant movement, a progression that has the end at the top.

Figure 7. Set of illustrations representing the march of progress[1]

But even now we keep using this kind of iconography. The march of progress turned itself into a marketing concept. Evolution is progress and therefore the march is the trail that evolution has to walk towards a state of near perfection. This means that man is in the frontline of the evolution process. Behind him are all the others and, in front of him, nothing. These common iconographies of evolution are taken so serious that they end up being used in daily folklore, with immediate effects on the apprehension of the concept by the public. And they are even used in the representation of prejudices, stereotypes, and sexist jokes (fig. 4).

Álvaro Cunhal: notes on Darwin's work

Álvaro Cunhal (1913-2005), a distinguished Portuguese politician of the 20th century developed a careful critical analysis of Darwin's main ideas. In a letter dated October 6th 1951, censured by the country's dictatorial regime of the time, Cunhal complains about «the true campaign of silence on Darwin's work» that was established in Portugal and advances with an explanation for such situation: «Such campaign of silence can be understood. Evolutionism in biological sciences (as well as in geology), without taking into consideration all it affirms and implicates about the origin of man and the world, brings (however with Darwin's intention) the particularly undesirable idea that human societies also evolve; also in human societies nothing is permanent and eternal» (Cunhal, 2007). Furthermore, Cunhal criticises the limitations of Darwin in analyzing man's social life and intellectual activity: «Responding to an author who had offered him a fundamental work on political economy, Darwin

---

[1] Despite all efforts, it was not possible to identify the source of these images. But because of its importance we decided to include them here. To the author(s) we express our sincere apologies.

wrote that he was only a naturalist and nothing understood of those issues... The answer was not sincere, because Darwin had drank from Malthus his *Struggle for life* and his "natural selection". However, that response explains his impossibility to see beyond the closed horizon of his extract. (...) Thus, his inability to understand that quantitative transformations alter into qualitative, and the consequential evolution in abrupt leaps, in the biological, as well as social field. From here we can appreciate his despise for "savages", his racism, his antifeminism, his marked British and *whig* spirit. Only ideologists of a new and ascending extract could, and did, break these limitations, overcome these difficulties and solve the problem of the evolution of man as a distinct evolution (from the moment he created and used work instruments) from the evolution of other living species. Darwin could not achieve that: from that moment, man, with a conscious purpose, started to act on nature and transform it» (Cunhal, 2007). Karl Marx (1818-1883), in a letter sent to the German philosopher Friedrich Engels (1820-1895) dated June 18th 1862, wrote «(...) Darwin reconnaît chez les animaux et les plantes sa propre société anglaise, avec sa division du travail, sa concurrence, ses ouvertures de nouveaux marchés, ses 'inventions' et sa malthusienne 'lutte pour la vie'. C'est le *bellum omnium contra omnes* de Hobbes (...)» (Marx, 1862, quoted in Pereira, 2003), that is, for Marx, Darwin's work was no more than a mirror of the economic and social logic of Victorian England.

Cunhal and Marx demand a certain social perspective from Darwin that would somehow correspond to a certain way of viewing the world. The connection of Darwin's ideas with the ideologies of Malthus is, for that reason, the identification of evolution with certain social issues, mainly the most polemical, which introduces a certain confusion of things, a confusion which ends up influencing the discursive folklore of our days. And so, the accusations, the prejudice and the fixations appear. Darwin is considered racist, antifeminist and the British people are considered to have an evil spirit.

Conclusion

John Gray, a charismatic British thinker, published in 2002 a brilliant book, entitled *Straw Dogs. Thoughts on Humans and Other Animals*. In the preface of the soft cover edition, Gray wrote the following: «Darwin's theory would not light up such a scandal if it had been formulated in a Hindu India, Taoist China or Animist Africa. In the same manner, it is only in the post Christian cultures that philosophers dedicate themselves so devotedly to the reconciliation of scientific determination with the belief in the exclusive ability of human beings to chose their way of living. The irony of the Evangelic Darwinism is that it uses science to corroborate a vision of humanity which comes from religion» (Gray, 2002). This same thinker makes a strong criticism to humanism in this book, considering it only a metamorphosis of Christian doctrine. In this sense, Gray considers humanism not a science, but a religion, this means, a belief that humans can make a world better than the one they have lived in until now. It is precisely due to this utopia that humanists seek Darwin to fundament their faith in progress, forgetting that the idea of progress is a secular belief of the Christian belief in Providence, and that, paraphrasing Karl Kraus, is condemned from the beginning to «celebrate Pyrrhic victories over nature».

Darwin showed us a world where there is no progress. To insist on a connection between science and progress is to use abusively science for dangerous social means, not only because man will never live in a world created by himself, but because it erodes the foundation of scientific knowledge. This corrosion leaves science susceptible to a hostile environment leading to the appearance of anti-scientific movements which proliferate in later sections with very specific missions.

The reason why people are against evolution is not because of science. The reason why people are against evolution or resist to its arguments, is because they think evolution, as it was taught to them, represents a way of life constitutionalised in a certain political, social and economical system. That was exactly what happened with Cunhal, Marx, Engels, among others. On the one hand, they saluted the possibility of change, but on the other criticized what it was, in the end, an interpretation of themselves, of something that was intrinsically sterile in terms of ideology. In this sense, what is in debate is not evolution as a scientific fact, but a certain social perspective, a certain vision on the way we live in our daily life. The confusion of things remains in the fact that evolution is not perceived as a science, but as a representation of a certain way of life that we can after consider good or bad, this is, that can then be submitted to moral judgement. It is precisely for this reason that debating with creationists, for example, is completely useless, because it is a debate which will not make any difference to evolution: only arbitrary points of view are discussed on a certain way of life of human beings and, as Jacob (1981) well noted, «nothing is so dangerous as the certainty of being right».

Bibliography

AVELAR, Teresa; MATOS; Margarida & REGO, Carla. *Quem Tem Medo de Charles Darwin? O Problema da Selecção Natural.* Lisboa: Relógio d'Água Editores, 2004

BONNET, Charles. *Traité d'Insectologie, premier parte.* Paris: Durand, 1745

BROWNE, Janet. *Darwin's Origin of Species – A Biography.* 2006 (Portuguese Translation by Ana Falcão Bastos and Cláudia Brito. Lisboa: Gradiva, 2008)

CUNHAL, Álvaro. *Obras Escolhidas de Álvaro Cunhal. 1935-1947.* Tomo I. Lisboa: Edições Avante, 2007

DENNETT, Daniel. *Darwin's Dangerous Idea.* 1995 (Portuguese Translation by Álvaro Augusto Fernandes. Lisboa. Temas e Debates, 2001)

GRAY, John. *Straw Dogs. Thoughts on Humans and Other Animals.* Granta Publications, 2002. (Portuguese Translation by Miguel Serras Pereira, Lisboa: Lua de Papel, 2007)

HAECKEL, Ernst. *Antropogenie: Keimes-und Stammes Geschichte des Menschen.* Leipzig: Engelmann, 1874

JACOB, François. *The Possible and the Actual.* Pantheon Books, 1981 (Portuguese Translation by Luis J. Archer. Lisboa: Gradiva, 1981)

PEREIRA, Ana Leonor. *Darwin em Portugal [1865-1914]. Filosofia. História. Engenharia Social.* Coimbra: Livraria Almedina, 2001

PINTO-CORREIA, Clara. *O Mistério dos Mistérios. Uma História breve das teorias de reprodução animal.* Lisboa: Relógio d'Água Editores, 1999

WHITE, Charles. *An account of the Regular Gradation in Man, and in Different Animals and Vegetables; and from the Former to the Latter.* London, 1799

Susana A. M. Varela
Faculdade de Ciências, Departamento de Biologia Vegetal, Centro de Biologia Ambiental, Universidade
de Lisboa, Portugal

SEXUAL SELECTION AND THE CULTURAL INHERITANCE OF
FEMALE MATING PREFERENCES

Since Darwin (1879) hypothesized that female mating decisions may drive sexual selection, that questions like how females gain information about potential mates, and what benefits they receive from choosing particular males as mates, remain key issues in behavioural ecology, and still generate large debate (see reviews in Barnard 2004 and Andersson & Simmons 2006). Because female preferences for males with particular traits can cause important skews on male reproductive success (Wade & Pruett-Jones 1990), studying the ecological forces that may affect preference is critical for understanding the diversity of male secondary sexual traits, the differences between the sexes in mating outcomes, the trade-off between multiple matings and survival, the role of sexual conflict in limiting female decisions, and ultimately the evolutionary processes of sexual selection (Barnard 2004).

Independent mate-choice

Female mating preferences can be variable between and within populations, and explanations for this variation usually assume that preferences remain fixed throughout the lifetime of the organism and result from strong genetic influences (e.g. Kirkpatrick & Ryan 1991; Barnard 2004; Andersson & Simmons 2006). Fisher (1930) was the first to formalize such a genetically based hypothesis by means of a theoretical model, in which he assumes that females find the phenotypic characteristics of certain males attractive, and that both male characteristics and female preferences are genetically heritable. Due to skewed reproductive success towards the most attractive males, both attractive traits and the preference for them spread through the population, leading to the evolution of traits more and more exaggerated over generations. Ultimately, however, this runaway process will be stopped by natural selection, as trait size reached the point where its reproductive advantage is outweighed by its survival (Barnard 2004).

Several experimental studies were able to provide evidence for the covariance between male traits and female preferences, as predicted by Fisher's runaway model (reviewed in Barnard 2004). However, the debate still persists on the kind of underlying mechanism that may be at the origin of such a co-evolutionary response. (1) According to Fisher (1930), females prefer males with certain phenotypic traits due to a genetic predisposition in preference that is acquired by chance. Alternative hypotheses, however, suggest that (2) female genetic preferences are not arbitrarily acquired, but that they are an evolutionary response to genetic indicator cues on the utilitarian benefits (good genes) that a male can provide to the female as a mate (Barnard 2004; Andersson & Simmons 2006). Genetic indicators of quality are based on correlations between a sexually selected trait and the phenotypic condition of its possessor. Since those traits are costly to the males, only robust individuals in good condition can afford to develop them (the *handicap principle*, Zahavi & Zahavi 1997). (3) Female preferences may also involve phenotypic traits that reflect the ability of the male to provide non-genetic advantages that would increase the survivorship and reproductive potential of his offspring, such as a high-quality territory, increased fecundity from nuptial food gifts, protection and parental care (Barnard 2004). Finally, (4) the preference of females for a particular male ornament can simply result from a female sensory bias if that kind of preference had initially been selected for other reasons, but that do not confer at present any reproductive advantage (Barnard 2004). There is considerable empirical support for all these mechanisms, and since they are not mutually exclusive and most probably co-occur, the challenge is to learn how to distinguish between them and to estimate their relative importance for the evolution of female mating preferences and male attractive traits (reviewed in Andersson & Simmons 2006).

Non-independent mate-choice

Another important factor that might equally affect the evolutionary dynamics of sexual selection, and that has been largely ignored until recently, is that female-mating preferences may not always be independent, and therefore not fixed. Because Darwin didn't know about the existence of genes, he described sexual selection as «the habitual or even occasional preference by the female of the more attractive males», and that such preference, although not fixed, «would almost certainly lead to their modification; and such modifications might, in the course of time, be augmented to almost any extent, compatible with the existence of the species» (Darwin 1879, cap. 14). Our present knowledge about genes and genetics has allowed us to better understand the evolutionary process in its whole. However, it is a mistake to ignore the influence of non-genetic mechanisms on sexual selection. In fact, genetically inherited information may not be enough to assess male heterogeneity in quality. As a complement to females' genetic predisposition for males with particular traits, mating decisions may be influenced by the choices of other females, that is to say, by the social information that is provided inadvertently by the mating decisions of conspecific-model females (Nordell & Valone 1998; Valone & Templeron 2002; Wagner & Danchin 2003; Danchin et al. 2004; Danchin & Wagner 2008).

The use of inadvertent social information (generally known as public information) may, indeed, be a more parsimonious and reliable approach to the mate-choice process (Danchin et al. 2004). Because it is extracted from the direct observation of the success and failure of conspecifics engaged in the efficient performance of their mating activities, it thus reflects conspecifics' genotypic dissimilarity in quality, providing reliable information on with whom to mate. It could have therefore evolved as a direct adaptation to assess more effectively the quality of potential mates. Furthermore, because it integrates, in a unique observation, the various qualities required in a mate, it reduces the time and energy invested on independent trial-error attempts (Brooks 1998; Nordell & Valone 1998; Valone & Templeton 2002; Danchin *et al.* 2004).

One consequence of using public information to decide with whom to mate is the copying of successful conspecific choices by multiple individuals attempting to benefit from the same favourable mating conditions (Wagner & Danchin 2003). Mate-choice copying occurs if the mating preference of a (observing) female for a particular (target) male increases or decreases, depending on whether that male mated previously or was avoided by other (model) females (Pruett-Jones 1992). Prospecting females should be observed copying other females only when their discriminating ability is inadequate (Nordell & Valone 1998). When this is not the case, females should rely first on their own experience to efficiently assess male quality (e.g. Gibson & Höglund 1992; Brooks 1998; Nordell & Valone 1998). When females lack the ability to discriminate between two males of different quality, observing the choices of more experienced females should allow them to mate with the best male (Nordell & Valone 1998; Wagner & Danchin 2003). Finally, observing females will choose mates entirely on the basis of true copying only if they are directly exposed to the mating interactions of model females, which is the only way of obtaining direct information about male attractiveness or quality (Danchin *et al.* 2004).

The first comprehensive series of laboratory studies about social influences on mate choice are that of Dugatkin & Godin (1992), using guppies (*Poecilia reticulata*) as subjects, and that of Galef & White (1998), using japanese quails (*Coturnix japonica*). Taken together, the results of both these studies provide strong evidence that the attractiveness of a previously non-preferred male to an observing female is markedly increased after she sees him mating. Several other empirical, theoretical and experimental studies in a variety of vertebrate groups (see reviews on Galef & White 2000, Danchin et al. 2004, and Valone & Templeton 2002), have been providing evidence that animals actually use public information to chose their mates. More recently, my co-authors and I (Mery & Varela et al. 2009) have analysed, in *Drosophila melanogaster*, if the mating preferences of an observing female for males of contrasting phenotypes (developmentally stressed *versus* unstressed) increased or decreased, depending on whether the males mated previously or were avoided by other (model) female. In the same way as with the other experiments, prospector females increased their preference for the previously non-preferred male (the stressed one), by increasing the time they spent near him. This is the first study providing evidence of mate-choice copying in an invertebrate species, suggesting that such a strategy is probably widespread in nature.

The cultural inheritance of female mating preferences

When placed on the general framework of animal communication and learning, conspecific copying may lead to the transmission of behavioural patterns among individuals in a process that may be similar to the cultural transmission of traditions in humans (Danchin *et al.* 2004; Laland & Janik 2006; Danchin & Wagner 2008). However, for copying to result in the cultural inheritance of mating preferences, individual females must not only copy the mate choice decisions of other females, but they should also tend to repeat this type of behaviour by generalizing their socially induced preference for a particular male to other males that share his distinctive characteristics (Brooks 1998). Such social generalization of female mating preferences has been described in some mammal (e.g. Whiten *et al.* 1999), bird (e.g. White and Galef 2000*b*) and fish species (e.g. Dugatkin *et al.* 2002; Godin *et al.* 2005).

For instance, White & Galef (2000*b*), in an additional set of experiments with japanese quails, allowed focal females to see an artificially coloured male (with red or blue colour patches in their chest feathers), or a pseudo-mutant male (with three albino feathers glued to its crown) either mating with a model female or standing alone. In a second step, each focal female was allowed to chose between two new males, one red and the other blue, or one a pseudo-mutant and the other a normal--looking male (with three normal feathers glued to its crown). In both experiments, the authors found that those focal females that had seen a red, blue or pseudo-mutant male mate with a model female were more likely to mate with another red, blue or pseudo-mutant male, than were those focal females that had seen an empty cage or a red, blue or pseudo-mutant male standing alone in the cage.

Dugatkin *et al.* (2002) and Godin *et al.* (2005), in their experiments with guppies, found that individual females not only copy the observed mating preferences of other females for initially non-preferred less coloured males (Dugatkin 1998), but also that (1) an initial act of mate-choice copying had affected the mating preferences of significantly more observer females, tested consecutively in a series (Dugatkin *et al.* 2002); and that after copying (2) individual female guppies were significantly more likely than expected by chance to generalize their copied preference for the same male phenotype when presented with different males one day later (Godin *et al.* 2005).

In our experiments with fruit flies (Mery & Varela *et al.* 2009), we have likewise manipulated male attractiveness by showing an observing female a sequence of males of two artificially coloured types, with one type being accepted and the other rejected for copulation. Prospector females preferably mated with the colour type of the males they had previously observed copulating over males of the rejected type, suggesting that female *Drosophila* can also generalise socially learned information.

The ability shown in vertebrates to generalise from individuals to categories indicates a sophisticated level of cognition that can expedite the transmission of female preferences to other individuals (Danchin & Wagner 2008), and therefore accelerate the spread of novel male traits through a population (White & Galef 2000*b*; Godin *et al.* 2005), even if there is no inherent genetic preference for those traits (Agrawal 2001). Evidence that mate-choice copying and social generalisation also exist in invertebrates (Mery & Varela *et al.* 2009) greatly expands the potential of these processes to affect the evolution of female mating decisions, to induce socially biased mate choice, and thus to increase the opportunity for sexual selection to occur (Wade & Pruett-Jones 1990; Pruett-Jones 1992; Galef & White 2000; Mery & Varela *et al.* 2009).

However, understanding to what extent such a cultural mechanism of mate choice (1) can consistently modify selection pressures for certain male traits, (2) induce reproductive isolation between populations with different cultural traditions, and, ultimately, (3) favour the emergence of new species, are questions that are only now being proposed, meaning that future studies on these issues should be promising.

References

AGRAWAL A.F. 2001. The evolutionary consequences of mate copying on male traits. Behavioral Ecology and Sociobiology 51: 33-40.

ANDERSSON M. & SIMMONS L.W. 2006. Sexual selection and mate choice. Trends in Ecology & Evolution 21: 296-302.

BARNARD C.J. 2004. *Animal behaviour. Mechanism, development, function and evolution.* Pearson Education Ltd, Harlow.

BROOKS R. 1998. The importance of mate copying and cultural inheritance of mating preferences. Trends in Ecology & Evolution 13: 45-46.

DANCHIN É., GIRALDEAU L.A., VALONE T.J. & WAGNER R.H. 2004. Public information: from nosy neighbors to cultural evolution. Science 305: pp. 487-491.

DANCHIN, É. & WAGNER, R. H. 2008. Cultural Evolution. In *Behavioural Ecology*, eds. Danchin, É., Giraldeau, L.-A. & Cézilly, F., pp. 693-726, Oxford University Press, Oxford.

DARWIN C.R. 1879. *The Descent of Man and Selection in Relation to Sex.* John Murray, 2nd edition. London.

DUGATKIN L.A. 1998. Genes, copying, and female mate choice: shifting thresholds. Behavioral Ecology 9: 323-327.

DUGATKIN L.A. & GODIN J.G.J. 1992. Reversal of female mate choice by copying in the guppy (*Poecilia reticulata*). Proceedings of the Royal Society of London Series B-Biological Sciences 249: 179-184.

DUGATKIN L.A., LUCAS J.S. & GODIN J.G.J. 2002. Serial effects of mate-choice copying in the guppy (*Poecilia reticulata*). Ethology Ecology & Evolution 14: 45-52.

FISHER R.A. 1930. *The genetical theory of natural selection.* Clarendon Press, Oxford.

GALEF B.G Jr. & WHITE D.J. 1998. Mate-choice copying in japanese quail, *Coturnix coturnix japonica*. Animal Behaviour 55: 545-552.

GALEF B.G Jr. & WHITE D.J. 2000. Evidence of social effects on mate choice in vertebrates. Behavioural Processes 51: 167-175.

GIBSON R.M. & HÖGLUND J. 1992. Copying and sexual selection. Trends in Ecology & Evolution 7: 229-232.

GODIN J.G.J., HERDMAN E.J.E. & DUGATKIN L.A. 2005. Social influences on female mate choice in the guppy, *Poecilia reticulata*: generalized and repeatable trait-copying behaviour. Animal Behaviour 69: 999-1005.

KIRKPATRICK M. & RYAN M.J. 1991. The evolution of mating preferences and the paradox of the lek. Nature 350: 33-38.

LALAND K.N. & JANIK V.M 2006. The animal cultures debate. Trends in Ecology & Evolution 21: 542-547.

MÉRY F.[1], VARELA S.A.M.[1], Danchin É., Blanchet S., Parejo D., Coolen I. & Wagner R.H. 2009. Public versus personal information for mate copying in an invertebrate. Current Biology 19 (9):730-4. [1]These authors contributed equally to this work.

NORDELL S.E. & VALONE T.J. 1998. Mate choice copying as public information. Ecology Letters 1: 74-76.

PRUETT-JONES S. 1992. Independent versus non-independent mate choice: do females copy each other? American Naturalist 140: 1000–1009.

VALONE T.J. & TEMPLETON J.J. 2002. Public information for the assessment of quality: a widespread social phenomenon. Philosophical Transactions of the Royal Society Series B-Biological Sciences 357: 1549-1557.

WADE M.J., PRUETT-JONES S.G., 1990. Female copying increases the variance in male mating success. Proceedings of the National Academy of Sciences of the USA 87: 5749–5753.

WAGNER R.H. & DANCHIN É. 2003. Conspecific copying: a general mechanism of social aggregation. Animal Behaviour 65: 405-408.

WHITE D.J. & GALEF B.G. 2000*b*. "Culture" in quail: social influences on mate choices of female *Coturnix japonica*. Animal Behaviour 59: 975-979.

WHITEN A. et al. 1999. Cultures in chimpanzees. Nature 399: 682–685

ZAHAVI A. & ZAHAVI A. 1997. *The Handicap Principle*. Oxford University Press, Oxford.

João Arriscado Nunes

CES-Centro de Estudos Sociais, Faculdade de Economia, Universidade de Coimbra, Portugal

THE STAKES OF DIVERSITY AND SEXUAL SELECTION: ON NORMATIVE COMMITMENTS IN EVOLUTIONARY BIOLOGY

Diversity is a key political issue in contemporary societies. It is an established biological concept as well – witness the growing importance of biodiversity as a topic in the life sciences – and a recurrent subject of debate among those claiming a Darwinian allegiance. This paper is a preliminary incursion into the way debates over diversity within evolutionary biology are being articulated as inextricably scientific and political, through a focus on a recent challenge to sexual selection theory.[1]

I

What's the real story about diversity in gender and sexuality? How much diversity exists in other vertebrate species? How does diversity evolve in the animal kingdom? And how does diversity develop as individuals grow up: what roles do genes, hormones and brain cells play? And what about diversity in other cultures and historical periods, from biblical times to our own? Even more, I wondered where we might locate diversity in gender expression and sexual orientation within the overall framework of human diversity. Are these types of diversity as innocent as differences in height, weight, body proportion, and aptitude? Or does diversity in gender expression and sexuality merit special alarm and merit special treatment? (Roughgarden, 2004: 1-2).

These are the questions Joan Roughgarden, an evolutionary biologist from Stanford University, set out to answer.[2] In her recent work, Roughgarden discusses an impressive body of literature, ranging from biology and biotechnology to the social sciences and religion. She draws on criticisms and/or different interpretations of published research and on her own first-hand research in ecology, from field observation to mathematical modelling, to propose an alternative view; and she locates the origin of her inquiry

---

[1] The discussion that follows is heavily indebted to philosophical pragmatism, and in particular to the work of John Dewey (1991), and close to those of philosophers of science and science studies scholars like Rouse (2002), Barad (2007), Longino (2002), Clough (2003) and Mol (1999). Although their positions are not coincident, they all propose some version of what I call the constitutive normativity of science, a theme central to feminist philosophy and social studies of science. For a more detailed discussion, see Nunes, 2008.

[2] See, Roughgarden, 2004; 2009; Roughgarden et al, 2006, and the discussion in Kavanagh, 2006.

in a concern with accounting for and explaining diversity in relation to sex, gender and reproduction, and the political and social implications of her views and those of her intellectual interlocutors. An appendix to one of her books (Roughgarden, 2004) presents a set of recommendations for public policy.[3]

Roughgarden's engagement with diversity is rooted in both her scientific work as an ecologist and evolutionary biologist and in her experience as an activist, transgender woman and her exposure to the variety of expressions of sexuality and gender in human society. Academia and academic disciplines do not fare well when addressing – or failing to address – these questions, as Roughgarden emphatically points out: "(...) each academic discipline has its own means of discriminating against diversity... all our academic disciplines should go back to school, take refresher courses in their own primary data, and emerge with a reformed, enlarged, and more accurate conception of diversity." (Roughgarden, 2004: 3).

How does Roughgarden articulate her engagement with sexual selection theory as both a scientific and political critique and how does she deal with lines of argument anchored in different and potentially conflicting normative commitments?

II

Darwin's *The Descent of Man, and Selection in Relation to Sex* (Darwin, 1981) addressed the momentous issue of the place of humans in evolution and also set the frame for subsequent treatments of sexual reproduction across species and for theoretical approaches to the evolutionary advantages of sexual reproduction. The second volume discusses sexual selection, the "third" mode of selection, besides natural and artificial selection (Darwin, 1996; 1875). Roughgarden's reading of *The Descent* and of its legacy in evolutionary biology takes a path which is different from previous engagements with Darwin's accounts and arguments. She actually makes a case for the need to abandon the theory of sexual selection, despite all the difficulties associated with the canonical status of Darwin and of his work, with the authority associated with the theory and with the "gravity of discrediting a discipline's master text" (164)[4]:

> (...) Darwin's theory of natural selection as the creative force molding diversity seems certain to continue as the major element of evolutionary theory, even as discussion continues about the source of variation. By contrast, the third component of Darwin's theory, sexual selection, should not, in my opinion, be resuscitated (164).

This move is justified by the difficulty of smoothing over the factual difficulties associated with the theory and the belief that the theory "has promoted social injustice and that overall we'd be better off both scientifically and ethically if we jettisoned it" (164). In a later passage, this convergence of scientifically flawed and ethically objectionable

---

[3] Responses to Roughgarden's book – and her own comments on the responses – are available at http://www.joandistrict6.com/reviews.

[4] Page numbers with no other indication refer to Roughgarden, 2004.

features is associated with the context of Victorian England and its persistence in contemporary evolutionary biology with traits of modern societies:

> Darwin conceived his theory in a society that glamorized a colonial military and assigned dutiful, sexually passive roles to proper wives. In modern times, a desire to advertise sexual prowess, justify a roving eye, and disregard the female perspective has propelled some scientists to continue championing sexual selection theory despite criticism of its accuracy (168).

Roughgarden is not alone in her criticism. She claims affiliation to a lineage of critics, explicitly quoting feminist biologists like Sarah Hrdy or Patricia Gowaty, going one step further, however, in proposing that the theory be abandoned altogether (168). But the obstacles ahead are formidable: sexual selection stands as "evolutionary biology's first universal theory of gender", resting upon Darwin's claim, "based on his empirical studies", that "males and females obey nearly universal templates", namely those of the "eager" and more passionate male and of the "coy" female. (164).

Darwin discussed the display of "showy and virile" males to be chosen by females as the explanation for the "eagerness of males and the "coyness" of females; the assumption of universal struggle among males for access to females as a universal template for social life in animal species, and the view of diversity within a species as a "hierarchy beginning with superior individuals and winding down to the 'retarded'". Darwin's theory thus postulated a "diversity-repressing and elitist" view, "stressing a weeding out of the weak and sickly and naturalizing male domination of females" (165).

These views, however, contrast with both earlier writings and some passages of his 1871 work: "In his earlier writings..., Darwin viewed diversity favorably across species within an ecological community, imagining that each species fills a special niche in nature". This contrast is related to Darwin's different assessments of diversity within and diversity between species, and this contradiction "plagues our society today, from biology and medicine to politics and law" (165). Darwin, as an "experienced naturalist", did consider what he called "exceptions" to the general pattern he described, acknowledging differences across species in the way males "acquire" females and females "choose" males or variations in the distribution of initiative and passivity between males and females, but nonetheless "privileging the narrative of the handsome warrior", with no attempt at further discussing or explaining "exceptions". (165-6).

Similar remarks are made on Darwin's failure to acknowledge that many animals "do not align with a simple sexual binary", although he was well acquainted with barnacles, which are simultaneous hermaphrodites. The same holds for sex-role reversals, which he mentioned but briefly characterized as rare, a question still lacking adequate study (166). Darwin seemed to be unaware of same sex-sexuality and "gender multiplicity in the sense of coexisting alternative reproductive and/or life history strategies within each sex", as well as of any consideration of the functions for mating other than their contribution to reproduction (166-7).

But Roughgarden also keeps a tab on Darwin's contributions which anticipated or opened up significant lines of inquiry, such as "the theory of parental investment based on the relative cost of egg and sperm"; the distinction "between traits contributing mostly to survival in the physical environment and those contributing mostly to reproduction in the social environment"; for "acknowledging many exceptions"; for anticipating many of the concepts still employed today"; and for "attributing evolutionary status to females", at a time when the notion that females were capable of choice was controversial (167).

Notwithstanding these contributions, Roughgarden's final assessment of Darwin's theory of sexual selection is that it

> comes down to whether the underlying metaphor is correct. Is selection in a social context the natural part of artificial selection for show? Does social life in animals consist of discreetly discerning damsels seeking horny, handsome, healthy warriors? Is the social dynamic between males limited to fighting over the possession of females? Does diversity within a species reflect a hierarchy of genetic quality? (167)

The assessment of contemporary versions of sexual selection theory is more severe: it makes "matters worse by adding new mistakes, morphing what Darwin actually wrote into a caricature of male hubris", the major ones being, first, the reliance on what Roughgarden calls the "expensive-egg-cheap-sperm-principle", which would explain the alleged persistence of the showy male and the coy female pattern but is based on an "accounting mistake that Darwin did not make": "Darwin referred to the total energy expended by each sex in reproductive effort over a lifetime as being equal. The second mistake is the elevation of "deceit into an evolutionary principle":

> Darwin claimed that warfare to secure control over females is the universal social dynamics among males. Therefore, cooperative relations, especially those between members of the same sex, appear to falsify the social template that Darwin claims is universal. The contemporary work-around is to postulate deceit. Today's sexual selectionists have produced a proliferation of "mimicries": sexual mimicry, female mimicry, egg mimicry, and so forth. By postulating these types of mimicry, the spirit of warfare and conflict is preserved but driven underground, turned into guerrilla combat. Yet in no case have any of the mimics been shown to be fooling any other animal, and the circumstances suggest that the animals are in fact perfectly aware of what is happening. The sexual--selectionist picture of nature is not pretty. Not correct either (168).

In other words, given the status of evolutionary theory in Western conceptions of the world, of nature and of humanity, is it possible to frame debates within the field by drawing a boundary between *matters of fact* and *matters of concern* (Latour, 2005) which reach beyond disciplinary worlds?

III

Roughgarden is not just arguing for an alternative, but equally legitimate, position within the space of evolutionary science.[5] She indicts the positions she criticizes for

---

[5] Roughgarden's alternative approach to sexual selection is what she names social selection, and is presented and discussed in detail in Roughgarden, 2009.

failing to live up to adequate standards of scientific evidence and argument, but she also attacks the failure of those positions to engage with the consequences of what they stand for scientifically for those who are affected by it – be they humans or non-human living beings.

Roughgarden's approach may be described as an instance of what John Dewey called *inquiry*, "the controlled or directed transformation of an indeterminate situation into one that is so determinate in its constituent distinctions and relations as to convert the elements of the original situation into a unified whole" (Dewey, 1991: 108). The "indeterminate situation" arises from the critical questioning, both scientific and political and moral, of sexual selection as a theory and as a normative statement on the way the world is. It opens up a space for scrutiny of the empirical and experiential record and for setting it against established theoretical and political statements. Inquiry is an active and collaborative involvement with the world, a work of discovery which redefines the status of earlier commitments or hypotheses and allows matters of concern and matters of fact to emerge as mutually defining. It allows a convergence towards a new "determinate" situation – expressed in a theoretical framework and/or a set of political recommendations – which, in turn, is open to further inquiry as new challenges arise to prevailing claims to scientific and moral truth, themselves viewed as "warranted assertibilities" (Dewey, 1991), to be put to the practical test of their effects in the world. Roughgarden's inquiry does not leave her initial questions and commitments unchanged. Engaging with the research record, with theoretical debates and with her own work as a biologist allows the triggering of questions and moral and political commitments to be extended, complemented and revised, emerging in the end as a set of renewed commitments, more robustly anchored in a personal and collective journey through diversity in nature, culture and religion, but also open to new challenges.[6]

Bibliography

BARAD, Karen, 2007, *Meeting the Universe Halfway*. Durham, North Carolina: Duke University Press.

DARWIN, Charles, 1996 [1859] *The Origin of Species*. Oxford: Oxford University Press.

DARWIN, Charles, 1981 [1871] *The Descent of Man, and Selection in Relation to Sex*. Princeton: Princeton University Press.

DARWIN, Charles, 1998 [1875], *The Variation of Animals and Plants under Domestication*. Baltimore: Johns Hopkins University Press (2 volumes).

DESMOND, Adrian, and MOORE, James, 2009, *Darwin's Sacred Cause: How a Hatred of Slavery Shaped Darwin's Views on Human Evolution*. Boston and New York: Houghton Mifflin Harcourt.

DEWEY, John, 1991 [1938], *Logic: A Theory of Inquiry*. The Later Works, Volume 12. Carbondale: Southern Illinois University Press.

KAVANAGH, Etta (ed.), 2006, "Debating Sexual Selection and Mating Strategies", *Science*, 312: 689-697.

LATOUR, Bruno, 2005, *Reassembling the Social*. Oxford: Oxford University Press.

---

[6] Desmond and Moore (2009) have brilliantly shown how the whole of Darwin's work was inextricably driven by his scientific and moral commitments, and in particular by the "sacred cause" of opposing slavery and demonstrating the common descent of all human beings.

LLOYD, Elisabeth A., 2008, *Science, Politics and Evolution*. Cambridge: Cambridge University Press.

MOL, Annemarie, 1999, "Ontological Politics: A Word and Some Questions", in John Law and John Hassard (eds.), *Actor Network Theory and After*. Oxford: Blackwell Publishers.

NUNES, João Arriscado, 2008, "O resgate da epistemologia"". *Revista Crítica de Ciências Sociais*, 80: 45-70.

ROUGHGARDEN, Joan, 2004, *Evolution's Rainbow: Diversity, Gender, and Sexuality in Nature and People*. Berkeley: University of California Press.

ROUGHGARDEN, Joan, Meeko Oishi and Erol Akçay, 2006, "Reproductive Social Behavior: Cooperative Games to Replace Sexual Selection", Science, 311: 965-969.

ROUGHGARDEN, Joan, 2009, *The Genial Gene: Deconstructing Darwinian Selfishness*. Berkeley: University of California Press.

ROUSE, Joseph, 2002, *How Scientific Practices Matter*. Chicago: University of Chicago Press.

Maria Helena Santana
Faculdade de Letras, Universidade de Coimbra, Portugal

LITERATURE AND DARWINISM:
AN INCURSION IN PORTUGUESE NOVELS FROM THE END OF THE 19TH CENTURY

It has become common to consider *The Origin of Species*, published in 1859, a scientific and cultural revolution. With this controversial work, Darwin gave Science a new paradigm, which allowed natural history to be rewritten. From the cultural point of view one sees a rupture with the romantic ideal of harmony between Man and Nature, since the principle which regulates life is no longer harmony but struggle and resistance. The anthropocentric conception of the world also suffered a correlative disturbance, especially after the publication of *The Descent of Man* in 1871. Mankind lost its central status in Nature, simply becoming an element of the zoological order, a descendent of superior mammals. At the same time, admitting the assumption that biological life did not come from nothing, complete and almost perfect as we know it, the Darwinian theory shook the foundations of the Divine Creation doctrine, which fed the Western World's vision during centuries. The idea of a programmed world for the welfare of humanity loses support when facing a Nature that acts in an autonomous manner, defining its own course aside from human design.

No sector of culture would be able to ignore such a profound provocation. Attentive and worshipping the science of its time, literature could not keep astray from this phenomenon: it contributed to popularize the theory, eventhough questioning it. I will now illustrate some aspects of the literary reception of Darwinism in the last quarter of the 19th century, summing up a previous reflexion[1].

Natural selection, sexual selection

As is generally known, the impact of the Darwinian theory outside of the academic environment was not immediate. In most European countries it was only after the 1870's that it became widespread among the general public and was discussed in the newspapers and magazines. Portugal also had keen enthusiats, as proved by the important study of Ana Leonor Pereira[2], although the first Portuguese translations

---

[1] Maria Helena SANTANA, *Ciência e Literatura na Ficção do século XIX*, Lisboa, INCM, 2007, pp. 46-54 and 237-265.

[2] Pereira, Ana Leonor – *Darwin em Portugal (1865-1914)*, Coimbra, Almedina, 2001, pp. 66-85.

appeared rather late. In the 1880's the readers were sufficiently familiarised with the principles of natural selection and the struggle for life; originally scientific concepts, they had now turned into cultural stereotypes.

The theme of the "struggle for life" was, without a doubt, the most productive within the writers of this period, which often used the expression as a metaphor for social violence. Hardly any writer frees himself/herself from who does not use this "magic formula"[3] to act out the dramatic conflicts, through characters who are described, invariably, as strong and weak, winners and losers. Teixeira de Queirós, one of the pioneers of Portuguese naturalism, defines the modern novel as a study of the "great conflict of life", this is, the human reaction to natural forces which oppress (the environment, the will, the body); and says that in this struggle, the individual, being weaker, is almost always defeated[4]. The same conception appears in some of the most influencial writers of this period. It is the case of Thomas Hardy or Zola, for example, who represent the relationships between individuals and classes under the sign of rivalry and "predation"[5].

Effectively, one of the senses emerging from Darwinian narrative is precisely a blind and voracious Nature, eliminating the less suitable in its triumphant march; and not even Darwin's awed gaze regarding fecundity and perfection conceals a natural history marked by violence. On the other hand, so-called social Darwinism came to legitimate readings in the opposite direction: if some agreed that the principle of the survival of the fittest predicted a society more free and evolved (as the positivists believed[6]), others saw the opposite, selfishness and competition aggravating social conflict. In this perspective, the "struggle for life" acts as a metaphor of the capitalist society.

In more pessimistic writers, the Darwinian world was translated effectively as predation – "the horror of a universal struggle in the midst of universal blindness", as Antero de Quental would say. Fialho de Almeida faces civilization's advance as a new form of barbarism, bringing the intrinsic bestiality of the human being to surface:

> Everywhere the aquaphobia of profit: modern life incompatible with ancient honesty: and in the hunt for gold, the strongest hunter was almost always the guiltiest. And in the complete carnage of that struggle of wild animals and beasts, which is life, João da Graça saw, crawling in the shadows, the ant colony of the sad, the helpless,

---

[3] "Comme la *synthèse des contraires,* qui a fait fureur, notamment en histoire, la *sélection du plus apte* est une de ces formules magiques qui ont le don d'obséder les esprits où elles sont entrées. (...) Les romanciers qui ont le plus à se louer de la bienveillance du public ne nous parlent que des *batailles de la vie*;": Gabriel TARDE, "Darwinisme naturel et darwinisme social", in *Revue Philosophique de la France et de l'Etranger,* vol. XVII, 1884, p. 607.

[4] Prologue to *Os Noivos (Comédia Burguesa),* Nova edição, Lisboa, Parc. A.M.Pereira, 1896. All translations mine.

[5] Cf. George LEVINE, "By Knowledge Possessed: Darwin, Nature, and Victorian Narrative", in *New Literary History,* 24, 1993, pp. 363-91. Gillian BEER, *Darwin's Plots. Evolutionary Narrative in Darwin, George Eliot and Nineteenth-Century Fiction,* London, Ark Paperbacks, 1985; Robert J. NIESS, "Zola et le capitalisme: le darwinisme social", in *Les Cahiers Naturalistes,* 54, 1980, pp. 57-67.

[6] Cf Fernando CATROGA, A Militância Laica e a Descristianização da Morte em Portugal (1865--1911), Coimbra, Univ. Coimbra, 1988, p. 262).

the beaten children with no fathers, men without work, women without the right husband, families without shelter, [...] a sort of zoological fatality, unbreakable ...[7].

This issue was also debated by two scientists in the pages of *A Caridade em Lisboa* (Charity in Lisbon), of Teixeira de Queirós. Manuel de Sá, a skeptical radical, sees in the spectacle of life in society a total absence of justice and rationality; thus developing fantasies of mass destruction, and even proposing general sterilization. Julião, a Bacteriologist, has a different perspective on this matter, coming from what he observes in test tubes:

> The inequality among living beings is a natural fact. This principle is spread all over the universe: for some to live it is necessary that others die; the weak are perpetually devoured by the strong, by those that have the impulse to attack and better defend themselves in resistance [8].

The selection of the fittest articulates along with another theme which also had great repercussion in nineteenth-century novels: sexual selection. According to Darwinian theory, the evolution of species determines the choice of sexual partner; it is so in the animal world and so should it be in the human world. In the end, as Schopenhauer taught us, love is no more than a pretext: in Nature all is summed or should be summed up in an instinctive orientation under the disguise of procreation; i.e., the perfecting of the species is the unconscious factor of social attraction. This idea is made clear in *O Crime do Padre Amaro* (The Crime of Father Amaro), of Eça de Queirós. Dr. Gouveia, a positivist, explains to the unhappy boyfriend his situation under the light of the selection of the fittest: "I see what it is. You and the priest, he says, both want the girl. As he is the smartest and most decided, he got her. It is natural law: the strongest steals, eliminates the weakest; the female and the prey belong to him"[9]. In another novel of the time, the main character invokes the same argument to justify adultery with a married woman: "Nature does not know fidelity and infidelity; beings are attracted by natural selection, there was no escape from this law"[10]. Later on, he would recognize it as a falacy and would reject the materialistic science which inspired him.

The human problem that these characters portray is the conflict (or even contradiction) between natural law and social order. Society generated its own codes and does not allow Nature to function freely. In his book *The descent of man, and selection in relation to sex*, Darwin reflects on various factors which intervene in the process of human sexual selection. On the one hand, he refers to the choice of more attractive pairs, noticing that such criteria do not always relate to higher biological success. On the other hand, he highlights that civilisation introduces perverse elements – of course, the incidence of choice, predominantly male, but also the criteria by which it

---

[7] Fialho de ALMEIDA, "Três Cadáveres", in *O País das Uvas*, Lisboa, Livr. Clássica Editora, 12th edition, 1982, p. 288.

[8] Teixeira de QUEIRÓS, *A Caridade em Lisboa*, Lisboa, Parc. A.M.Pereira, 1901, p. 160.

[9] Eça de QUEIRÓS, *O Crime do Padre Amaro*, critical edition, Lisboa, INCM, 2000, pp. 581.

[10] Jaime de Magalhães LIMA, *Transviado*, Lisboa, Empresa Editora, 1899, p. 65.

governs itself: wealth, social position and intellectual attributes ("mental charms" in women, "intellectual powers and energy" in men).

Let us return to literature. In *A paixão de Maria do Céu* (The passion of Maria do Céu), of Carlos Malheiro Dias, the theory of sexual selection embodies very curious aspects, since it is alegorised in the content of the text. It is called "Romantic Novel", due to being projected in the historical scenary of the French invasions. In summary, it is about a fatal passion of a young aristocrat girl who was seduced by an official of the Napoleonic army, ending up abandoned to a miserable existence. The main theme of the text regards the loss of national sentiment, caused by the chaos which followed the royal familiy's escape and the Portuguese befriending the invader. Thus, in the novel, a Darwinian sociological thesis is drawn: social disorder stimulates vital competition; sexual selection is done on the basis of instinct, without considering reason or virtue: "Everywhere women are selective such as animals; her apetite imperious as tirany" – adds the narrator. The decadence of the people of Lisbon is easily explained through the physical and psychological strength of the invaders:

> The woman avenged the impoverished generations, exhausted, not virile due to the Inquisition and the praying, broken into grotesque corsets, coward noblemen and fraternity brothers. The Portuguese women were delirious with the French as the Romans had been delirious with the Sabines, falling anxious and breathless in the white and strong chest of those fighting and preying adventurers, robust animals of devastation and of harassment... [11].

What is really at stake is the dissolution of traditions, the pernicious contact between two races with different "natural histories": one sentimental and devout; the other daughter of the Revolution, used to violence. In the turbulent 18th century Lisbon something similar happened to what had occurred in the Roman Empire: an "epidemic of heroism", followed by moral decadence.

Evolution / regression

At the end of the book *The Descent of Man,* Darwin stated that the human being could be proud of civilization, but could not forget his origins: "He who has seen a savage in his native land will not feel much shame, if forced to ackowledge that the blood of some more humble creature flows in his veins". The simian origin of man was, undoubtedly, the most thrilling and controversial theme of Darwinian theory. Among the most interesting literary texts are those dedicated to reconstructing the birth of human beings – the *homo sapiens*, as we would say today – which comes to substitute Adam and Eve in the Bible.

In 1880 an important book, *Elementos de Antropologia* (Elements of Anthropology), was published in Portugal. The author, Oliveira Martins, proposes to "translate the

---

[11] Carlos Malheiro DIAS, *A Paixão de Maria do Céu. Novela Romântica.* Lisboa, Livr. Editora Tavares, Cardoso e Irmão, 1902, p. 243-4.

myths in the positive language of science", this is, he offers to rewrite the Book of Genesis according to Darwinian theory. Due to the lack of documentary elements, the author uses his imagination to reconstruct the past: The story of Caliban[12], the first man, is actually more of a literary than a scientific construction. We accompany his development through a succession of episodes, scenaries and pitoresque details, as in a novel: the discovery of the body, the weapons... the discovery of speech, art, love. Evolution is complete at the moment in which Caliban reaches social consciousness ("the last of the acts of creation – humanity").

Eça de Queirós was inspired by this book to write one of his most beautiful short-stories: "Adão e Eva no Paraíso" (Adam and Eve in Paradise). This text, published in 1897 is a philosophical narrative of a humorous tone. The irony of the text results in the mixture between the biblical allegory and post-darwinian narrative of the origins: the first man is called Adam, but no longer lives in Eden: born in an imperfect Earth, populated by dangers – the terrible fauna of the Tertiary Period.

> Adam, the Father of Men, was created on the 28th of October, at two in the afternoon...[13].
> In those times, my friends, the Sun still rotated around the Earth (...). So, in a thick and dark forest, a certain being, slowly releasing its grasp from the branch of a tree where he had been perched during that centuries long morning (...) on his two feet, steadied himself with strenuous energy, stood, spread his free arms, took a vigourous step, felt the difference from his animality and conceived the fascinated thought of what he *was,* and what he truly *had been!* God, who had supported him, in that moment created him [14].

Adam's first steps, thoughts and terrors certainly come from the book of Oliveira Martins, as well as various other previous episodes, where "the abominable days of Paradise" are told. The two authors also converge in the representation of love which, according to Oliveira Martins, constitutes the beginning of man's socialisation. Eça acts out the biblical episode in the same way, interpreting it in favour of Eve: "It is Eve who cements and breaks the big angular rocks of the construction of humanity."

In the final part of the novel, Eça refuses scientific sources to build, in an entire creative freedom, the tender moments of the original family. Yet, once again, the two texts coincide with each other when the narrator questions the sense of the story (or of History). When Martins describes the orangutan ancestor, he questions the sadness in his eyes "by chance – who knows? – predicting the infinite misery reserved for his descendance..."[15]. Eça's text develops this suggestion as well. Maintaing the ironic discourse, it contrasts the happy life of the orangutan with the suffering of Mankind,

---

[12] The name comes from a character of Shakespeares, a "savage" in a remote island in the play *The Tempest.*

[13] Eça de QUEIRÓS, "Adão e Eva no Paraíso", *Contos*, Lisboa, Livros do Brasil, s.d. (In fact, there was an Anglican bishop in the 17th Century, James Usher, which fixed the date of creation of the world as the 23rd of October of the year 4004 a.C.).

[14] Eça de QUEIRÓS, *Contos*, Lisboa, Livros do Brasil, s.d., p. 122.

[15] Oliveira MARTINS, *Elementos de Antropologia*, 5ª ed., Lisboa, Guimarães Editores, 1987, p. 65.

condemned to have a soul. Unaware of the problems of conscience, the orangutan lives in the peace of God:

> He returns to his tree early and lying in the leafy net, slowly abandons himself in the pleasure of dreaming, in an awakened dream, similar to our metaphysics and our epics but [...] a dream all made of certainty. [...] This is how the orangutan spent his day, in the trees. And how did man, the cousin of the orangutan, spend his day in the cities? Suffering – for having the superior gifts that the orangutan lacks! Suffering – for dragging with himself, unrecoverably, that incurable evil which is his soul! Suffering – because our Father Adam, did not dare to declare in reverence to the Lord: "Thank you, oh sweet Creator, give the Earth governance to whom you better choose, to the elephant or the kangaroo, while I, knowing better, return to my tree!...[16].

Fialho de Almeida explores the same theme (paradise lost), in the novel "A Dor" (The Pain)[17]. The text takes the form of a dialogue between God and the first man, highlighting the consequences of the transformist theory. Questioned on the differences which separate the human being from the orangutan (his immediate ascendant), God answers with a comparative anatomy lecture: facing open skulls of the father and grandson, He explains the map of cerebral circumvolutions; locates the humps of instinct and intellect; guarantees the transmission of intelligence and of "patrimony of ideas". The moral of the fable is that God gave man reasons to feel privileged amongst the beings of Creation but also gave him the inherent suffering of his condition; the weight of having a conscience is the poisoned gift of evolution: "And since then that vain animal, judged as the most perfect and the most free of living beings, became the miserable slave who, for all eternity, screams under the wip of his tyrant – the tyrant called Thought".

I end this incursion with a brief reference to atavism – the dark side of Darwinist anthropology. The principle that evolution is processed in a gradual but not simultaneous way had awakened the interest of the anthropologists in the so-called wild or primitive communities, where it would be possible to observe the previous stages of development[18]. Certain primitive tribes seemed to demonstrate this phenomenon, maintaining themselves immobilised in ancestral forms.

Fialho de Almeida was interested in this issue. In several of his rustic tales, the characters find themselves at the limit of differentiation between man and animal; they are not "wild" in the usual sense of the term but represent forms of rudimentary existence. Domingas, a shepherdess in "Idílio Triste" (Sad Idyll), had always lived in a rustic environment, in almost complete isolation; she could hardly speak and her gestures had a marked animalistic mimetism. One day she met a man and became pregnant without knowing: obeying an unconscious impulse, the girl prepared

---

[16] ID., *Ibid.*, p. 152.

[17] Fialho de ALMEIDA, "A Dor", *Contos*, Lisboa, Livr. Clássica Editora, new edition, s.d. pp. 315-20 (1st edition 1881).

[18] Darwin, in *The Descent of Man*, refers to impressive testimonies on wild tribes, out of his own experience and the abundant bibliography in this area; a German researcher, quoted by L. Büchner, affirmed inclusively having recognized in Abyssinia a race of black people with tales!

a shelter filled with animal skins, "...as a wild rabbit, preparing the burrow for her babies"[19]. In the tale "Os Pobres" (The Poor) a similar story is told, of a wretch who society excludes, transforming him in a typical case of reversion: his body acquired the aspect of a "domesticated orangutan" due to hard work and total abandonment. One night he encounters a vagabond in his cabin; the two make love in a wild orgy, and separate, without interest or memory, like animals[20].

Literature contributed in this way to produce living documents of Paleontology. These marginalised or handicapped beings are for naturalists a sort of fossil from the ancient days of human evolution[21]. At a time in which many scientists questioned the possibility of a return or involution, the doubt was pertinent: if there were evidence of reversion in the zoological world, why shouldn't the same principle apply to humans?

The literary texts analysed so far display anxiety and nostalgia. Nostalgia of the ancient divine Nature, lost forever in the books of poetry; anxiety facing the revelation of the new narrative on the origins, where the elected species, forgotten by God, finds it difficult to recognise itself. By transforming Adam and Eve of the fable into the "furry troglodytes" of science, Darwin disillusioned the world, evicting the King of Creation from his kingdom. Apparently there was another Story of Life, a story without a moral, without predestined heroes and perhaps without a *happy ending* – a story which was starting to be written.

---

[19] Fialho de ALMEIDA, "Idílio Triste", in *O País das Uvas*, Lisboa, Clássica Editora, 12th edition, 1982, pp.183 ss.

[20] ID., *Ibid.*, pp. 67 ss. (1st edition 1893).

[21] Oliveira Martins, in the Introduction of *Elementos de Antropologia*, states categorically: "For the anthropologist they are of the same worth, this is, as documents of a remote age, the human monsters and the collective monsters – deaf-mute, the cretins, the microcefalus – and the wild societies."

Alves Jana
Faculdade de Letras, Universidade de Coimbra, Portugal

Darwinists, but not much

«Darwinism is just a scientific theory not yet proven.» This could be the beginning of an intervention at a congress on Darwin. But, undoubtedly, such a statement would not be adequate to the situation.

Actually, Darwinism is a well accepted scientific theory in the scientifically informed intellectual environment. Or better, in an intellectual environment equipped with a scientific culture and way of thinking.

However, if it is true that Darwinism is a generally accepted theory, it is not certain that it is accepted in all its consequences. In this case, we could say that we tend to be Darwinists, but not much. That is, because we accept the biological theory, but do not incorporate it, do not insert it in the way we think about things and the world beyond the specific environment of its genesis. As if we stated, in physics, that the Earth revolves around the Sun but continued to think of ourselves as the centre of the Universe.

Darwinism is a scientific theory. However, it is rooted in the general history of thought. As such, it is a scientific theory, but it is not just "one more" scientific theory. It is mainly a new paradigm, a new model of thinking about man and his place in the Universe.

Accepting Darwinism is overcoming the Platonic and Cartesian dualism. Since Plato man is thought of as a rational soul and material body. Or better, since Plato man is thought of as mainly an immaterial and rational soul. However, he is unfortunately imprisoned in a material body which is strange to him and from which he should free himself to become what he truly is, spirit. With Descartes, in the Modern Age, this paradigm of thinking about man maintained and reinforced itself with the assertion of a self transparent Cogito. Man continues to be seen as a different substance of the material world, a reality apart and of an immediate rational nature.

We know that this anthropological model was happily married to biblical tales until the 19th century. It was then that things started to go wrong and the Cartesian Cogito was publically "humiliated". The roles of Nietzsche, Marx and Freud are recognized in this humiliation. Here, in particular, Darwin's action is of interest. But it is part of a continuous line which must include other scientists like Galileo and Newton, and, later on Gödel, Heisenberg, Konrad Lorenz and even António Damásio.

In succeeding steps, we shift from a paradigm of a man separated from nature to a man as an integral part of the only nature. In the same manner, we shift from an immediately rational and sovereign Cogito to a man that is flesh of the world, but that, through an evolutionary process, becomes rational and capable of more abstract and unpredictable behaviors from the most elementary levels of the evolutionary scale.

In this new paradigm, man is not a reality apart from nature, nor does he belong to a metaphysical order. He belongs to a physical and biological world, and everything about him is the result of an evolution that produced music and religion, poetry and mathematics and even evolutionary theory itself.

Accepting Darwinism is not just accepting a scientific theory and functioning with it inside the domain of biology. It is to change the paradigm and take due anthropological consequences. It is to refuse a dualist anthropology of thousands of years of tradition and adopt a new anthropology. A new anthropology which is necessary to build from and beyond a way of thinking that is rooted in the most various domains of western thought as well as from the practices of that thought. It is important to highlight that for 2500 years we have been thinking of man and acting in the world according to a dualist matrix, which is why this way of thinking and acting has shaped Western intelligence itself and became the own nature of Western thought. Darwinism is, therefore, a challenge to rethink all that we have come to think and do for 2500 years inside the metaphysical and dualist matrix that has, in the meantime, gone through a radical crisis.

We have to think about man beyond this crisis. We have to rethink man's status towards himself and towards the History of evolution of which he is a part. We have to think about the status of Reason itself.

Let us briefly remember that even the Cartesian Cogito was geometric, aiming for clarity and distinction, in a thought process in which evidence was the rule of distinction between all and nothing. The truth, or better, the Truth was rational, clear and distinct, therefore absolute and a-historical. The rational view was panoptic and absolute in an undeniable universality. And Science (necessarily with capital letter) was an absolute knowledge and, therefore, definite in its undeniable universality. And Man, also with capital letter, was by nature Lord of the Universe and, by the power of Cogito, a creator, or even better, a pantocrator, capable of sovereignly dominating the World and putting it to his service. And, due to the absolute nature of the Cogito, this adventure could only have a happy ending, with the construction of Paradise on Earth , not on the uncertain hereafter.

However, World War I and World War II showed that this new religious faith gave us Hell more easily than the promised Paradise. And the atomic bomb showed that human intelligence is as much constructive as it is destructive. And the obvious ecological catastrophe showed that sovereign intelligence was mainly the arrogance of a-critical intelligence, incapable of knowing its limits.

The Cartesian Cogito is dead. But its lost soul still roams inside our way of thinking concretely. As if Darwin had never existed.

We continue to suppose that there is a transcendent order that guarantees that things are as "they should be" and "will be". So, we excuse ourselves from doing what needs to be done, because we believe that what happens is the result, not of what we do or of the present forces, not of our work and our organization, but of a superior order that rules what happens and from which we can, we have the right to expect, what we want to happen.

We continue to speak as if we held the entire Truth. In fact, we do not understand, in the world of knowledge and lively action, that all the affirmation is just of a superior animal on two legs, equipped with a brain, capable of rationalizing a point of view, always a point of view, always from his place in the world. That is why, we continue to speak as if we had a panoptic point of view, exterior to and above the world.

We continue to assert man as a rational being, when everything shows that he is, above all, a living being, an animal that lives and feels, and can achieve certain levels of rationality that do not revoke but might integrate his sensitivity.

We continue to insist on a clear and distinct discourse, confusing truth with the so-called rational. We forget that what is said is always a Siamese brother to what is not said. Moreover: that which is not said, therefore the unknown, is always more extensive and more decisive than what is said and known. The history of sciences itself should have taught us, over the last two hundred years, to look at the following two hundred years of science and, thus, diminish the relative importance of what we are proud to know today.

The Japanese, who did not have Plato and Descartes, did not need Darwin to figure out that what is too clear ofuscates and blinds more than it enlightens and allows to be seen. Father Arrupe, superior general of the Jesuits, said that it was frequent for a Japanese catechumen to object towards a systematic exposition: «Father, that which you are explaining is too clear to be true.»[1] That is precisely why, Easterners always mantain what is not said as an important part not to forget with what is possible to say. And Paul Ricouer, for example, said long ago that only narratives can say what Wittgenstein advised to silence.

We continue to want to know just through the discourse we make and not, never, through what the silence can reveal and the discourse can never say. Annie Lehmann says that she and her husband refused the diagnosis that nothing could be done to recover their son Jonah from profound autism and did everything they could for him to have access to what they wanted for him. They eventually had to surrender to the evidence of failure. Looking at her own story of a tireless mother, Annie reflects: «Jonah turned 25 last Fall, and when I look at him, I can't help wondering if the past years weren't some Heaven-directed scheme meant to humble us and teach us the value of acceptance.» Understanding that we couldn't change him had changed us.» Regarding Jonah, she tells us: «He remains a man of very few words. But though it took us years, we have finally learned that there was something to hear in his silence.»

We continue to think of intelligence as a metaphysical characteristic and intrinsic to the rational animal that is man and not as an ability to solve problems, phylo and ontogenetically constructed, that we can find, larger in some cases and smaller in others, in a person, organization or community. In the same way, after having evaluated for a long time the Western culture as evidently superior, we continue to evaluate that all cultures are evidently equal, as if culture was not a collective construction to solve collective problems in which value lies in and is measured by its ability to solve these problems.

We continue to think of politics as if social reality were ruled by metaphysical forces independent from the reality of facts. Much of the criticism that is done has the Platonic paradigm of the world of ideas as a basis. A criticism is always mainly

---

[1] Juan Masiá and Kotaró Suzuki, *O Dharma e o Espírito: Diálogos entre um cristão e um budista*, Coimbra, Angelus Novus, 2009, p. 94. And Juan Masiá, author of this work also says that his Japanese students objected «Your explanation is too clear to be true.» (Idem) and that a Japanese teacher of floral arrangements said to a student of hers «Your arrangement is too symmetrical to be beautiful.» (Idem). These are manifestations of a non Cartesian, non geometric way of thinking at least not in an Euclidian geometry.

the evidence of a certain criteria that underlines criticism. So, much of the criticism is still made from a Platonic paradigm of a "world of ideas" that is independent to the world of things. A paradigm that is not even Cartesian, because if it were, it would know that the facts of the world occur according to the laws of happening and not according to the abilities of reasoning.

We continue to think of education in a Cartesian format. Rational minds learn by evidence through a rational discourse of demonstration carried out by the teacher. Hence the magisterial, discursive teaching. Hence the fact that the body of the student behaves better the more absent it is. And the room is more organised if it has less action; Reasoning, which has nothing to do with the rest of the body, remains apart.

We continue to emphatically condemn religion, despite being universal in time and space, in direct proportion to its inability to show scientific evidence. Maybe Darwinism made us think of it in regard to an evolution which made man a religious being. Maybe Darwinism advised to think of religion more as a natural and cultural phenomenon as well, resulting from evolution itself. But that is unnecessary, in fact, it is forbidden, in the environment of a scientific positivism. That is also why we continue to think of spirituality as a sub product of ignorance instead of thinking of it as an area of activity which has a natural place in the process of life of a human being.

We continue to think of justice based on a Cartesian anthropology, in which principles and decisions are valued independently of a person's behaviour in a given situation. Wittgenstein had a Cartesian dream that he expressed in *Tractatus:* that it was possible to create a verbal 1 to 1 map, in which reality was represented point to point in language. Later, reality hit him and he saw that that was not possible. He even understood that there is no intrinsic rationality in the reality that can be expressed in an intrinsic rationality of language. But our justice still reads *Tractatus,* still hopes that the justice system represents the social reality point to point; and believes that the world conforms naturally and spontaneously to the supposed rationality of the way the courts function. Therefore, it is enough to judge according to the Law, for the world to remain in good order.

We mantain the secular division between science and technique on the one hand and human sciences and arts on the other. Each of the parts knows it has the Truth and thinks that the other is logically wrong from its roots. Darwinism advised to think of culture as a product of evolution, just like the sciences. But our liking for the absolute condemns us to the opposition between knowledges and powers.

We continue to think within the Cartesian Cogito model because we cannot yet get out of it. We cannot yet build an integral man, a man who, being an animal of evolution, has rational abilities to operate on and from his biological systems. In spite of António Damásio and many others having shown that the complete man cannot be thought of in terms of pure rationality.

This means we are Darwinists, but in the Cartesian sense: as if we had joined a rational discourse in a scientific context, without having incorporated it in the personal and collective system of thought and action in the world. Darwin has not happened yet.

Darwin's year is a good opportunity to reaffirm the recognition of the evolutionary theory. But, and this is what is more important now, it is an opportunity to extract from evolutionism the necessary consequences regarding what we are and how we think of ourselves and the world. And this is a work which is, in great part, yet to be done.

Daniel Rodrigues

CES-Centro de Estudos Sociais, Faculdade de Economia, Universidade de Coimbra, Portugal

EDUCATION, SCIENCE AND SOCIAL DARWINISM IN NAZI GERMANY:
FORMATION OF A SOCIETY BASED ON THE MYTH OF BLOOD AND SUPERIORITY
OF THE ARYAN RACE

Introduction

The book *On the Origin of Species by Means of Natural Selection...*, published in 1859, opposed its author, Charles Darwin, to those who opposed his ideas. By defending natural selection and evolution, the new theory shocked with the pre-existing vision according to which God was the creator of all living beings, including the human being. However, Darwin's ideas were assimilated, incorporated and even forged. The importance of Darwinism in the mentalities at the end of the 19th century is evident in their application to all areas of knowledge and in the birth of new disciplines. Such is the case of social Darwinism.

Historians saw in social Darwinism the renovation of a nationalist, racist and militarist German ideology (Weindling, 1993: 26). Ernst Heinrich Haeckel was important for the discussion between politics and Darwinism. The most important discoveries related to this issue were done in a strong patriotic environment and the belief in evolution as a natural philosophy (*Idem*: 40-41). Haeckel sought to make the connection between biology and its possible application in the organization of society. According to him, if experimental biology was capable of giving data relative to concepts such as order, hierarchy or control, it was normal to state that each citizen was a cell in the midst of social organization (*Idem*: 43). As in any political system governed by a central government, organs of the human body would be under the domain of the brain. This justified the importance of biology as a social science which, according to Haeckel, was not an autonomous science but an extension of history and archaeology (*Idem*: 42). This version was used by nationalist ideologists that saw the sustainability of their own theories in it. Being the brain the strongest and the organs the weakest, it would be necessary for one of them to subdue and dominate the other. In the words of Rudolf Hess, "... *le national-socialisme n'est rien d'autre que de la biologie appliquée.*" (*apud* Hannoun, 1997: 24). Thus, let us see how it was applied to Nazi education and science.

Race as an ideological matrix

The concept of race was never used by Darwin with the intent of classifying men, having nevertheless been attributed to him. This new concept was based on biological differences as well as psychological and/or cultural, real or imaginary differences. Physical anthropology had here an important role and, as such, the recognition on behalf of the Nazi regime, hostile to any science considered "useless". To educate ideologically became the *leitmotiv* of the Nazi educational policy. If the question of race was inscribed in the historical transformation of the West looking to dominate all the people on Earth, at a biological and anthropological level, it was necessary to apply the concept to science. However, the first Darwinist anthropologists refused to classify racial types, also condemning the racial theories of Aryan character. To insert the concept of race in scientific discourse, biology transferred ideas such as "good education" and "pure blood", originally limited to an aristocratic and moralist milieu, to anthropology. Biology and anthropology attempted to eliminate the concept of individuality, creating biological sub-species or races. Physical anthropology was taught to medicine students as a subject for the knowledge of human anatomy and the concepts of race occupied their place in the midst of medical thought.

Having the concept of race been validated scientifically, the study of its components did not take long. In his essay "*Essai sur l'inégalité des races humaines*", Joseph Arthur de Gobineau defined race as a moving force of History. However, he was merely systematizing the ideas of his time and its political elites. According to him, the "degenerate" man, also defined as man of decadence, had not preserved the same race and the same blood of his ancestors (n/d: 24), being condemned to one of two fates: to be a conqueror or to be conquered (*Idem*: 29). The vision of the world defended by Gobineau served as an answer to the imperialism and to the expansionism of European empires, among them Nazi Germany. The scientification of the concept of race opened the doors to racism as a policy of the State. Houston Stewart Chamberlain, considered one of the European fathers of racism, stated that: "Nothing transmits more conviction than the consciousness of possessing a Race [because it] elevates man above himself…" (*apud* Bruchfeld & Levine, 2000: 4), to which Adolf Hitler, leader of NSDAP, would respond in the epilogue of his *Mein Kampf* by arguing that: "A State that in a period of contamination of races protects zelously the conservation of the best elements of its own will one day become the lord of the world." (1998: 549).

More than accept the existence of human races, in which some would be pure, superior to the others and holders of the historical and political right of becoming hegemonic, it was necessary to justify such affirmation. The racist starts from biological differentiation and uses biology as a justification for his actions. The importance given by Darwinism to this science reinforced its power, moreover that its assumptions were already largely accepted. Haeckel stated in his "*Prinzipien der Generellen Morphologie der Organismen*" that "… the differences between the highest and lowest humans were greater than those between the lowest humans and the highest animals." (*apud* Weindling, 1993: 55). Despite not being a supporter of violence through expansionist militarism, his social Darwinism defended a growth of the progress through a competitive selection in culture, economy and politics, thus guaranteeing constant human progress (*Idem*: 56). If the term selection was not used by Haeckel with a racist intent, his work reflects the Nazi racial policy. If in certain cases it was about eliminating human beings of pure blood through eugenist measures; the same happened regarding the enemy. Himmler, when discussing with foreign volunteers of SS, declared that: "When we are fighting, you should all know that killing a man is no more than as killing a chicken to us." (*apud* Hassel, s/d: 215).

National socialist education and ideology

Nazi naturalism is related to the belief in the need of nature's kingdom, an idea defended by Hitler himself. E. Krieck defended that each individual had in himself his true Aryan nature, fixed in his blood (Hannoun, 1997: 18). Being innate, this nature was, however, hidden. The main objective of the educational process was the promotion of this profound nature, helping it to express itself so that each young German could become a full member of his race, with all the rights he deserves as such. The essence of each individual corresponded to his people (*Völk*) and was apprehended through the conjugation of historical, geographical and biological factors (*Idem*: 19). According to G.-S. Stent (*"Morality as a Biological Phenomenon"*), National Socialism had in social biology its orientation. This gave the party what it needed. *Völkisch* naturalism is divided in two main branches: nationalism and social biologism. If the first refers to Germanic culture, the second recovers the quetstion of blood. The theory of *Blut und Boden*, developed in the work *"Neuadel aus Blut und Boden"* by Walther Darré, Nazi minister of Agriculture and *Reichsbauernführer*, identified German blood to Nordic ground, defending that Germans were both warriors and farmers. Being a colonizing race by excellence, there would be no barrier between both social groups. According to him, the death of a German rural dweller meant the death of the German people and it was necessary to form a new nobility based on race and the colonization of new lands (to be conquered). Feelings, beliefs and actions were the result of biological and social factors, namely, blood and land (Woody: 1940: 47).

The Nazi educational system had as purpose the externalisation of the feeling of belonging to a superior race as one of its objectives. Education transformed into training (*Schulung*) and the selection became *Selektion* in the most pure Darwinist--social sense (Robinsohn, 1966: 227). Education should be linked to blood and land, being school only a part of the educational progress. Real character would be achieved by organizing the youth, their physical training and a heroic realism (Kandel: 1935: 158). This was the condition to develop the expansionist militarism at a European and world level. As a hierarchy, Nazi education was composed by the training of the body, character and intelligence, being evident some anti-intellectualism. Physical education aimed at the anatomical-physiological adaptation of the individual to his environment (Hannoun: 1997, 30) and, as a result of its role in preparing for military service, the curricular time dedicated to such training increased strongly with the Nazi education policy. On the other hand, the education of will (or character) gave them the ability to make decisions. In a letter to professor Eckhardt in 1938, Himmler stated that: "The methods of intellectual education do not interest me. Knowledge rottens youth but, if we submit it to harsh challenges, it learns to overcome fear and death." (*apud* Hassel, s/d: 175). For Hitler, the concept of physical health was connected to the racial philosophy of Nazism and contributed to the preservation of race (Lewin, 1946: 456). During education, obedience to the group was instilled in the individual. The reason was the fulfillment of a common ideal that corresponded to its culture and to the demands of his race. Quoting Heidegger, "... *l'insertion sociale* völkisch *réclame de l'individu allemand sa fusion corps et âme dans le creuset de sa race. Il n'a pas d'aspirations, pas d'attentes, de besoins, de pensées, de destins autres que ceux de son groupe (*Völk)" (*apud* Hannoun: 39). This is what was intended with the creation of the *Hitlerjugend* and the *Bund deutscher Mädel*, among others. Education transformed itself into a means used by the regime to create a people of lords, conscientious of their superiority.

Science and politics

The year of 1933 was a turning point in German science. Racial laws authorizing the expulsion of scientists of Hebraic origin and their defenders were a rude blow to German science. Doctors and biologists of the 20th century, especially in Nazi Germany, produced an ideology as a substitute of philosophy (Müller-Hill: 1989: 10). Science was allied to higher education by the role played by academics in various investigation projects. Subordinated to the State and politics, science oscillated between radical denial and secret acceptance. The Nazi program for science is clearly visible in the words of *Reichsminister* Franck, leader of German jurists, when at a conference in Tübingen, he stated that the ideas of Hitler contained "the final truths" of any scientific knowledge, having all the results to coincide with the prerequisites of Nazism. Franck went further by accepting the program of the Nazi party as the only base of scientific investigation (Olff-Nathan, 1993: 17-18).

Regarding the "science of death" (Müller-Hill, 1989), this was more than a mere solution to the Jewish issue. The application of eugenist measures on mental patients and the selection of fittest individuals are a good example of it. The adoration of blood was reflected in the promulgation of various laws, among which the "Law for the Protection of German Blood and German Honour" and the "Jewish Status". These were victories for the ideology and the policy of the State, as well as for Nazi science in general and some subjects in particular (i.e. Social Anthropology, Eugenism, Biology and Racial Hygiene…). In a speech made at the Faculty of Theology of Berlin, Professor Fisher thanked the Führer for the possibility given to scientists who studied heredity to put at the nation's service the results of their investigation as it happened with the Nurnberg Laws. In his *Erbatz*, dated from 1940, Professor Verschuer defended the necessity of distinguishing the individuals that should be eliminated from those that should be promoted through the creation of biological-hereditary files, the only way to protect the hereditary legacy and race (Müller-Hill, 1989: 25). It is still possible to see that the various sciences at the service of ideology developed uncountable projects together, as the one which gathered in 1935 the Psychology of Professor Rieffert, the Anthropology of Professor Fisher and Racial Studies of Professor Günther.

Conclusion

This article aimed to demonstrate, very briefly, implications that the radical interpretation of Darwinist assumptions had in forming a society based on the myth of pure blood and superiority of race. Nazi Germany found in racial theories and in their application to education and science their ideological base. After applying the concept of race to science, nothing else stopped a racist and racialist regime of imposing itself as a State of Law, respectful of natural law. Selection of individuals would be something natural, reflecting in human societies what already happened in nature. Darwinism found in Nazi Germany the paradigm of a State in which natural racial selection was taken to the extreme. The consequences are well known today. The distinction between *Ubermensch* and *Untermensch* and the necessity to preserve the Aryan race led to the mass extermination of members of "inferior" races. The Holocaust is, maybe, the darkest side of social Darwinism applied to a State's policy based on the myth of blood. Alfred Rosenberg, ideologist of Nazism, stated in *"Der Mythus des XX Jahrhunderts"* that, under the swastika sign, the myth of blood would give origin to a worldwide revolution. The awakening of the soul of blood would mark the end of an era of racial chaos. This position summarises in a clear way what Nazism looked for in the twelve years in which Hitler governed Germany. Education, science and also social Darwinist theories constituted only valid instruments in the eternal search of a people of lords made of racially pure men.

Bibliography

BRUCHFELD, Stéphane; Levine, Paul A. (2000) *Contai aos vossos filhos… Um livro sobre o Holocausto, na Europa, 1933-1945.* Lisbon: Gótica.

BRUNAUER, Esther Caukin (1935) "National Socialist Youth in Germany" *The English Journal.* 24(3), 196-198.

GOBINEAU, Joseph Arthur de (s/d) *Essai sur l'inégalité des races humaines.* Tome I. Paris: Librairie de Paris.

HANNOUN, Hubert (1997) *Le nazisme, fausse education, véritable dressage.* s/l: Presses Universitaires du Septentrion.

HASSEL, Sven (s/d) *Comando Reichsführer Himmler. O assalto a Varsóvia.* Mem-Martins: Publicações Europa-América.

HITLER, Adolf (1998) *A minha luta.* Lisbon: Hugin.

KANDEL, I.L. (1935) "Education in Nazi Germany" *Annals of the American Academy of Political and Social Science.* 182, 153-163.

LEWIN, Herbert (1946) "Problems of Re-Educating Fascist Youth" *Journal of Educational Sociology.* 19(7), 452-458.

MÜLLER-HILL, Benno (1989) *Science nazie, science de mort: la ségrégation des Juifs, des Tziganes et des malades mentaux de 1933 à 1945.* Paris: Ed. Odile Jacob.

OLFF-NATHAN, Josiane (dir.) (1993) *La science sous le Troisième Reich: victime ou alliée du nazisme?* Paris: Ed. du Seuil.

ROBINSOHN, Saul B. (1966) "On National-Socialist Education" *Comparative Education.* 2(3), 225-232.

WEINDLING, Paul (1993) *Health, race and German politics between national unification and Nazism: 1870-1945.* Cambridge: Cambridge University Press.

WOODY, Thomas (1940) "Principles of Totalitarian Education" *Proceedings of the American Philosophical Society.* 82(1), 39-55.

João Paulo Avelãs Nunes
Faculdade de Letras; CEIS20, Universidade de Coimbra, Portugal

NEO-DARWINISM AND POLITICO-IDEOLOGICAL CONCEPTS IN PORTUGAL DURING THE FIRST HALF OF THE 20TH CENTURY

The present paper is based on the assumption that world views that can generally be considered to be Neo-Darwinian or Socio-Darwinian play a central role in many dominant ideological trends in Western and Westernised countries, and that this was the case until at least the immediate aftermath of World War II. Except in the case of some Catholic sectors and most Socialist sub-universes, the tendency was to stratify peoples and individuals based on genetic and cultural criteria. The belief was that a countless number of behavioural attitudes and situations (both on an individual and on a collective level) resulted, directly or indirectly, from a certain set of "racial and environmental" characteristics.

The realisation of the great suffering caused by extreme cases of racism occurred just before the end of World War II and in the years immediately following the conflict. Before then, the hegemonic interpretation and assessment of "intrinsic characteristics" and the relative stratification of populations or nation states, groups of people and individuals, would have been "very radical or mildly radical" versions of Neo-Darwinian concepts. Some of the most telling examples of this outlook were the efforts made to physically eliminate European citizens of Jewish origin and other genocidal projects carried out by the National Socialist Third Reich, as well as the acts of mass violence inherent to Japanese militarist expansionism.

Thus, it could be said that social Darwinism played a core role in the transformation process of systemic ideological concepts (to a higher or lesser degree) into "truths demonstrated by science". As forms of scientism (whether they be rationalist or irrationalist), practically all the ideologies that were born in the 19th and 20th centuries strove to legitimise themselves through attributes that were supposedly scientific, according to the modern paradigm. These were: objectivity and truth, unquestionability and perennity, social prestige and the ability to intervene and transform.

In accordance with the context and with the needs of each one of the ideological trends (i.e. liberal conservative or autocratic, demoliberal, authoritarian or totalitarian), Neo-Darwinian readings took on different forms. Firstly, genetic – or racial – factors either played a crucial role or one that was only moderately relevant. On the other hand, the focus was either on the justification of profiles or individual behaviour (differentiation between "active citizens", "passive citizens" and "marginal" ones; members of the "elite", "intermediate segments" and "popular classes"), or on the explanation of the "operating mechanism" of human societies by analogy to "animal societies" (i.e. organic corporatism versus individualism and the "struggle for survival") and with the human body (i.e. intrinsic and benign values versus different, malignant or pathological sets of ideas from elsewhere).

As to the dimension of observed social phenomena, interpreted in the light of social Darwinism, the following were considered: national aspects (i.e. the relative positioning of men and women, employers or senior executives and workers, the "educated" and "uneducated", governors and the governed); colonial aspects (i.e. the guardianship of "primitive populations" by "civilized nations") and international aspects (i.e. the leadership of "superior races" and the "natural hegemony" of the more powerful states' interests). Even links "with the past" were conditioned by the wish to refer to or to highlight the founding moment of each "national race", to identify and emphasize stages of "genetic regeneration", and hide or deny moments of "contamination" by "inferior races and cultures".

Despite the apparent contradiction between theoretical concepts, the present paper aims to prove that positions that are generically defined as Neo-Darwinian were the result not only of the application of evolutionist theories, but also of creationist ones. In the former case, reasoning in which metaphors of conflict and changes in the balance between individuals, "races" or states were preferred, whereas in the latter, rhetoric of preservation or of the reconstruction of "natural hierarchies", resulting from "God's will" was dominant. Both discourses were used (either alternatively or as complements to each other) to consolidate modernist, conservative or traditionalist ideologies.

Contrary to what most authors state, one could say that Portugal also experienced many of the phenomena that took place in other countries, namely the important presence of social Darwinism in Portuguese political and socio-economic thought during the first half of the 20th century. That same influence transpired in the manner in which the historic evolution of the Portuguese elites and popular classes was viewed, as well as in the position taken as to individual features and social inequalities, and finally, in the attitude towards the characteristics and operational rules of international relations.

Amongst other factors, such as the "influence of the geographic environment", the history of Portugal was explained by successive degradation and regeneration processes of the elites' "genetic heritage", associated with a royal family of "superior race" (originating from the South Atlantic region in France). It was described as a succession of positive circumstances, which were glorified, and negative ones, which were forgotten about or hidden. Examples of negative stages included the presence of Jews (and later of "Conversos" or "Marranos"), Muslims, Black slaves and "malignant sets of ideas" because they were "foreign", "contrary to tradition" and/or "contrary to scientific evidence".

In the past as in the future, social inequalities were considered part of the core, unchangeable matrix of "national reality", resulting from the different genetic heritage of every individual (disciplined or undisciplined, honest or dishonest, intellectually able or less able), or of the organic structure of human communities, whose balance and harmony depended on the presence of differing socio-economic functions, as well as a clear and stable hierarchy. These differences were considered to be the result of "God's will" or to be "naturally unavoidable". This trend can clearly be illustrated by the efforts made in terms of the observation and recording of "anthropomorphic indices" of the "lower classes" in general, and more particularly, of the "marginal segments" of the Portuguese population, i.e. criminals, prostitutes, alcoholics and beggars.

Criteria of "racial order" played a decisive role in the international positioning of Portugal and in colonial relations. Without a shadow of a doubt, Portugal integrated the group of nations responsible for the construction and affirmation of "Western Civilization". However, the "quality of genetic heritage" of the population (or even of the elites) was interpreted differently. At best, the Portuguese were considered a specific type of "superior race", resulting from a mixture of several gene pools (i.e. from Southern and Central/Northern Europe, from pre and post-Roman times, from before and after the "Germanic invasions") and successive adaptations to a particular geographic context. Alternatively, it was considered a community of intermediate "racial quality", inferior to that of the "dominant populations" of Central and Northern Europe but equal or superior to that of all other populations, i.e. Southern Europe and the rest of the world.

Independently of the adopted perspective, both the role of Portugal as a colonising state and the legitimacy of this status were demonstrated by arguments of a historical and cultural nature, such as Portugal's pioneering past and the scale of the country's efforts since the 15th century to "discover new territories and peoples" and introduce millions of human beings to "Western Civilisation". In addition, genetic reasons were used, such as the European character of the "Portuguese race" and "undisputable leadership" of the "Old Continent", or that of "individuals of European origin" on a global scale. The preference for unilateral government modalities, or alternatively, multilateral modalities to govern unipolar, bipolar or multipolar international systems was associated to the "irrefutable truth" of the existence of a permanent struggle between "races" and states for world domination, or on the contrary, for "normal" cooperation between countries aiming to create a binding corps of international law. Portugal would have to choose between a preferential bilateral relation with the hegemonic power in the Atlantic and the membership in international organisations that guaranteed the fundamental rights of small nations.

Most foreign individuals who resided or visited Portugal explicitly interpreted the Portuguese situation and/or disseminated these readings, thus reinforcing the self--perception that we have tried to describe and interpret concisely. The said diplomats, military personnel, entrepreneurs or executives nearly always came from developed countries (especially Britain, France, Belgium, Germany, the USA) and saw the Portuguese as a "mixed race", the fruit of a "superior genetic heritage" mixed with "Mediterranean European", "North African" and "Negroid" traits. This resulted in the proximity of many Portuguese inhabitants to the populations of the colonial territories, protectorates or mandates and to Latin American states; to the unavoidable fact that Lisbon would be under the guardianship of a "Great Power"; to the advantages of the fact that the Government and state apparatus were led by members of the scarce "genetically and intellectually superior" elite – if necessary, by means of dictatorship.

Typically, mass-scale or high levels of violence were not reached. However, during the first half of the 20th century, it is important to note that there were several signs of "systemic Neo-Darwinism". Focusing on the "Metropolis" only, some of the concepts disseminated and options that materialised during the first stages of the Estado Novo (until the end of World War II) were: the Portuguese were divided into "elites", "intermediate groups" and "popular classes", all with differing features and roles; most individuals were considered to have a genetic heritage (i.e. cognitive, moral and physiological abilities) compatible with their responsibilities; the global architecture of the "Government system" and sectoral politics (such as education and culture, economics and taxation, "social welfare" and health) should strengthen (and not weaken) the "historic proof" and "scientific evidence" at stake.

Anti-Semitism, which took on several traits, is mentioned as well. In politico--ideological terms, Marxism was seen as a "Jewish world view" and/or part of the "Jewish conspiracy" for world domination. Liberalism, "plutocratic capitalism" and "Masonic agnosticism" were believed to be instruments of "international Judaism". In socio--cultural terms, the Jews were believed to be a non-assimilable race, and Judaism a "false religion". Condemnations of the "excessive presence of Jews" in certain strategic professional fields in other countries received Portuguese support. There was also hostility towards attempts to track down and rebuild "Crypto-Jewish" traditions and "Marrano" communities. On the diplomatic and military levels, the dissemination and agreement with "moderate anti-Semite positions and measures" from other states took place. There was practically no explicit criticism of radical racist ideas and practices, such as the Holocaust.

The present paper concludes by highlighting the scientific values of a more in--depth study of the presence of social Darwinian readings in Portugal, and of their influence on a wide range of world views and activities. Issues such as the importance of Neo-Darwinism in Portugal during the first half of the 20th century have been sufficiently discussed, as well as the central position of this form of scientism (rationalist or irrationalist, modernising, conservative or traditionalist) in multiple sectors of Portuguese life, and the similarities between Portuguese social Darwinism and its evolution both in most European countries and in other states of the world.

Documentation and bibliography

ALEXANDRE, Valentim, *Velho Brasil, novas Áfricas. Portugal e o Império (1808-1975)*, Porto, Edições Afrontamento, 2000.

AMEAL, João, *História de Portugal*, Porto, Livraria Tavares Martins, 1940.

BRAUDEL, Fernand, *Gramática das civilizações* (translation from French), Lisboa, Editorial Teorema, 1989.

CEREJEIRA, Manuel Gonçalves, *Obras pastorais*, 7 volumes, Lisboa, União Gráfica, 1936-1970.

Congresso Nacional das Ciências da População. Actas, memórias e comunicações, Lisboa, Comissão Executiva dos Centenários, 1940, vols. XVII e XVIII.

I Congresso da União Nacional. Discursos, teses e comunicações, 8 volumes, Lisboa, UN, 1935.

DURAND, Yves, *Le nouvel ordre européen nazi (1938-1945)*, Bruxelles, Éditions Complexe, 1990.

FERRO, António, *Salazar. O homem e a sua obra*, Lisboa, ENP, 1933.

GEARY, Patrick J., *O mito das Nações. A invenção do nacionalismo* (translation from English), Lisboa, Gradiva, 2008.

HAWKINS, Mike, *Social Darwinism in European and American thought (1860-1945)*, Cambridge, CUP, 1998.

Indústria Portuguesa [nº 1, March of 1928 – nº 250, Dezember of 1948].

JOLL, James, *A Europa desde 1870* (translation from English), Lisboa, Publicações Dom Quixote, 1982.

LEAL, João, *Antropologia em Portugal*, Lisboa, Livros Horizonte, 2006.

LIMA, Joaquim Alberto Pires de, *Mouros, judeus e negros na história de Portugal*, Porto, Livraria Civilização, 1940.

LOFF, Manuel, *As duas ditaduras ibéricas na nova ordem eurofascista (1936-1945)*, Florença, 2004, vol. 3 (multicopied).

Lumen [fasc. 1, January of 1937 – fasc. 12, December of 1947].

MEA, Elvira de Azevedo e STEINHARDT, Inácio, *Ben-Rosh. Biografia do Capitão Barros Basto, o apóstolo dos Marranos*, Porto, Edições Afrontamento, 1997.

MILZA, Pierre, *As relações internacionais de 1918 a 1939* (translation from French), Lisboa, Edições 70, 1998.

NUNES, João Paulo Avelãs e outros, *O CADC de Coimbra, a democracia cristã e os inícios do Estado Novo (1905-1934)*, Coimbra, FLUC, 1993.

NUNES, João Paulo Avelãs, *A história económica e social na FLUC (1911-1974)*, Lisboa, IIE, 1995.

NUNES, João Paulo Avelãs, *O Estado Novo e o volfrâmio (1933-1947)*, 2 volumes, Coimbra, 2005 (multicopied).

PEREIRA, Ana Leonor, *Darwin em Portugal: filosofia, história, engenharia social (1865-1914)*, Coimbra, Livraria Almedina, 2001.

RÉMOND, René, *Introdução à história do nosso tempo* (translation from French), Lisboa, Gradiva, 1994.

SALAZAR, António de Oliveira, *Discursos e notas políticas*, 6 volumes, Coimbra, Coimbra Editora, 1945-1967.

SEN, Amartya, *Identidade e violência. A ilusão do destino* (translation from French), Lisboa, Edições Tinta--da-China, 2007.

SÉRGIO, António, *Bosquejo da história de Portugal*, Lisboa, Publicações da Biblioteca Nacional, 1923.

STERNHELL, Zeev, *La droite révolutionnaire (1885-1914). Les origines françaises du fascisme*, Paris, Éditions du Seuil, 1978.

TELO, António José e TORRE GÓMEZ, Hipólito de la, *Portugal e a Espanha nos istemas internacionais contemporâneos*, Lisboa, Edições Cosmos, 2000.

WINOCK, Michel, *Nationalisme, antisémitisme et fascisme en France*, Paris, Éditions du Seuil, 1982.

Sérgio Neto

CEIS20-Centro de Estudos Interdisciplinares do Século XX, Universidade de Coimbra, Portugal

FROM THE ARIAN MYTH TO THE LUSO-TROPICALISM: ECHOES OF SOCIAL DARWINISM IN PORTUGUESE FOREIGN PRESS

In the beginning it was not the word anymore, but the long cosmic silence of the unpopulated Earth, followed by the painful screams of life breaking through. With the most diverse shapes. Without an all-powerful entity. Evolving and adapting. Without a final and metaphysical objective. Not necessarily culminating in the human being...

Revolutionary, mainly in biology, Charles Darwin's theory[1] became known within numerous scientific domains. Even art reflected this impact, and Gustav Mahler could, in 1895-1896, write a Third Symphony as a tribute to evolutionary hypotheses. On the other hand, human sciences, as well as common knowledge, saw themselves enriched by new concepts which redefined the way in which the Other overseas was perceived. Natural selection, influenced by Herbert Spencer's sociological formulations, Francis Galton's Eugenism, Ernst Haeckel's Monism and the so-called "Arian myth"[2], was maybe more than any other theory, a product of its time. In fact, if Darwin tried to answer the questions "where are we from?" and "who are we?", social Darwinism as a result of the thinking of those authors revealed itself to be more attached to "where are we going?", having debated with the beliefs and conceptions of those who defended the colonial imperialism solution as the path to follow through nineteenth-century Europe[3]. Certainly, social Darwinism set other questions regarding its application. First: who were the competing groups and what was the nature of the dispute? Was it at a socio-economic level? At a national level? Racial level? And extinction, was it a reality to consider?

The lecture hereby proposed aims to trace, in a comprehensive manner, the way social Darwinism was present in some Portuguese periodical publications of a colonial theme. This is, in what way these important sources of knowledge of overseas mentality accompanied, integrated or ignored the appeals from a theory that, at first sight, seemed to legitimate the occupation of inhabited territories of "races" considered less capable.

---

[1] See: Ana Leonor Pereira, *Darwin em Portugal. Filosofia. História. Engenharia Social.* Coimbra: Almedina, 2001.

[2] See: Léon Poliakov, *O Mito Ariano. Ensaio sobre as fontes do racismo e dos nacionalismos.* S. Paulo: Editora Perspectiva, 1985.

[3] See: Fernando Costa, "A Política Externa. Do Ultimatum à República", in *Diplomacia & Guerra. Política Externa e Política de Defesa de Portugal do Final da Monarquia ao Marcelismo.* Lisboa: Edições Colibri, 2001, pp. 45-67.

The periodicals consulted were *Revista Colonial Portuguesa e Marítima* (1897-1910), *Revista Colonial* (1913-1923) and *O Mundo Português* (1934-1947) – which include the chronology involving the last years of the Constitutional Monarchy, part of the First Republic and the initial period of the *Estado Novo* (New State).

Archaeology of racism and racism in Anthropology

The so-called "scramble for Africa" towards a "place in the sun", metaphor of nineteenth-century colonialism, was preceded and accompanied by various attempts of getting to know and cataloguing the Other found in those territories. Such coincidence should not be perceived as strange. The "Arian myth", which has the stamp of those times, came to intertwine with social Darwinism, being famous the *Essai sur l'inégalité des races humaines* (1853-5), of Arthur de Gobineau, almost an exact contemporary of *On the origin of species* (1859). On the other hand, Phrenology and the growing proliferation of taxonomies of different human groups encouraged the development of racism[4], having been recovered the stereotypes – already existing – on miscegenation and degeneracy. As so, science, pseudo-science, myth and tradition, hand in hand, tried to paint colonialism with more bright colours.

In Portugal, we know that the colonial ideology invoked indisputable historical rights consecrated by fifteenth and sixteenth-century discoveries. In the same way, this ideology claimed a special talent in the relations with the Other as a result of the many centuries of contact, which would compensate the lack of economical and demographic capital to occupy, "civilize" and explore the overseas territories[5]. Besides, these were the only arguments which Portugal, as a second class power, could use against the other colonizing nations, when the division of the African continent took place in the Berlin Conference of 1884-5.

Besides the reduced influence in the international political scene, to which accusations of continuing to maintain situations of dissimulated slavery were added, a third aspect weighed in the disdain given by the other nations. It consisted in the belief that the successive invasions of the Iberian Peninsula, during the Ancient days by African people and Semites, as well as the miscegenation of Portuguese people during the maritime expansion, had usurped the purity of their, supposedly, Arian blood.

Various Portuguese authors tried to develop these ideas but also valued the role of ethnic multiplicity in the construction of national identity. The writings of some members of the Geração de 70 (Generation of the 1870's) are remembered, such as Teófilo Braga and Oliveira Martins, who discussed the mingling among the invaders of the Peninsula[6]; or, two generations later, although in another perspective, the poet Teixeira de Pascoaes, considering the idiosyncratic "saudade"(longing/nostalgia)

---

[4] Léon Poliakov, *ob. cit.*, p. 137.

[5] Cf. Valentim Alexandre, "Prefácio" in Cláudia Castelo, "O Modo Português de estar no Mundo" – o luso-tropicalismo e a ideologia colonial portuguesa (1933-1961). Porto: Edições Afrontamento, pp. 5-6.

[6] Cf. Fernando Catroga, "História e Ciências Sociais em Oliveira Martins", in *História da História em Portugal*. Lisboa: Temas e Debates, 1998) 137-185.

as a product of the desire of the Arian people (Greeks, Romans, Goths, Celtics) and the hope of Semitics (Phoenicians, Jewish and Arabs)[7]. In fact, until today, History manuals of the first cycle of Primary education maintained the famous "list" which includes, among others, Celtics, Iberians, Lusitanian, Phoenicians, Carthaginian, Greeks, Romans, Alani, Vandals, Suevi, Visigoths, Jewish, Berbers and Arabs – proving, therefore, that at least at an ideological level, the "racial fusion" which operated on peninsular soil always had some credit. In any case, the testimonies of the time explain that miscegenation resulting from the overseas colonization continued to be faced as a sub-product and/or necessary evil of previous centuries. The end of the 19th century and the first decades of the 20th century did not mark great differences in the view of what regards the colonized. The assimilation measures were always timid and only the inhabitants of Cape Verde, India and Macau enjoyed full citizenship. The schooling was at an early stage and the establishments of teaching took time to arrive overseas: some primary schools, few high schools, no university. In the end, the idea was to stop the appearance of native cultured elites, more capable of fighting for their rights of equality and even a hypothetical decentred autonomy[8].There were actually authors who considered the schooling given to the colonized unnecessary, since the latter "is condemned to not advance beyond some certain limits"[9]. Due to this, it was not until the 1950's/1960's period, in which the international pressure to decolonize started to gain strength, accusing Portugal of not developing the colonies, the successive political regimes little invested in the overseas education. Furthermore, the concession of citizenship to all colonized peoples – S. Tomé and Príncipe and Timor (1953) and Guinea, Angola and Mozambique (1961) – did not go beyond a cosmetic operation, aimed to convince the international community of the supposedly benign and modernizing character of Portuguese colonialism[10].

In the same sense it should be understood as an apparent change in ideological paradigm: social Darwinism gave way to the luso-tropical theory of the sociologist Gilberto Freyre. This thesis defended that the "success" of the colonising action was due to the "plastic" character of the Portuguese, which stimulated the ethnic-cultural miscegenation and healthy racial interaction[11]. Inspired by the theories of mixed race population of the "Generation of the 1870's", the teachings of anthropologist Franz Boas and in many aspects Brazilian colonization, luso-tropicalism was a foundation of the Estado Novo when the anti-colonialist campaigns directed toward Portugal started during the decades of 1950-1970[12].

---

[7] Cf. Teixeira de Pascoais, *A arte de ser português*. Lisbon: Assírio & Alvim, 1998, pp. 56-57.

[8] Mário Pinto de Andrade, Origens do Nacionalismo Africano. Continuidade e ruptura nos movimentos unitários emergentes da luta contra a dominação colonial Portuguesa (1911-1961). Lisboa: Publicações Dom Quixote, 1997.

[9] *António Lourenço Farinha,* "A mentalidade do preto V", in *Revista Colonial*. Lisboa: Junho 1917, no 54, p. 132.

[10] Cf. Luís Reis Torgal, "'Muitas Raças, uma Nação' ou o mito do Portugal multirracial na 'Europa' do Estado Novo", in *Estudos do Século xx*. Coimbra: Quarteto, 2002, no 2, pp. 147-165.

[11] Cf. Gilberto Freyre, *Casa Grande e Senzala*. Lisboa: Edições Livros do Brasil, 1957, pp. 18-29.

[12] Cláudia Castelo, *ob. cit.*

Social Darwinism and the colonial issue

The *Revista Colonial Portugueza e Marítima* presented some impressions which were more relevant than the ones in the overseas themed periodicals regarding the end of the Constitutional Monarchy due to the exception made to the *Boletim da Sociedade de Geografia de Lisboa*. The *Revista Portugueza Colonial e Marítima* started publishing in 1897, "under the high protection of His Majesty the King D. Carlos" and practiced studying the overseas in a perspective related to the exploration of local potentialities, attributing, therefore, less importance to the ethnographic aspect. Even so, some articles did not avoid making some considerations about the evolution/education/civilization of the Africans.

For example, in "O Negro perante a Pedagogia" [The Black before Pedagogy], the author said that the fact that "Africans were lazy" made the European observer "think them incapable of superior inclinations"[13], because they "have received from Europe, centuries ago, more prejudicial than beneficial influxes". However, based on contemporary researchers, which affirmed that Black Africans were "susceptible to improving and even capable for intellectual culture", the author established that the multiplicity of schools could improve "some qualities of the race". However, to lead to that desire to the wanted point, it was necessary to "psychologically study [...] the different ethnic types of the colonies"[14].

Another number of the same magazine remembered that, despite the different "races" not having "the same ability to evolve", that in no way would compromise the colonial work. In his words, "the white race before reaching the degree of development that it has nowadays" would have been "much inferior to other races"[15]. Praising, mainly, the "perfect and elegant" type of the Cape-Verdean, but without referring to miscegenation as the possible origin of their "talent" and "knowledge", the author did not disdain the other Africans, guaranteeing that "the African of today is not the African of our predecessors [...] judged as an unconscious being and a despicable thing"[16]. It was important to, thus, "elevate the indigenous mentality [...] maintaining the sympathy that it always had for the Portuguese", in order to guarantee a better economic improvement of each colony[17]. More radical opinions could be found in *Revista Colonial*, published during the First Republic. If most of the articles directed appeals to colonists and potential colonists, indicating the conditions and impediments they found and would find, the fact is that the "indigenous" was also studied. In general, the tone was similar to that followed by the *Revista Colonial Portugueza e Marítima*, which did not impede one or other opposing voice, which was the case of primary teacher António Lourenço Farinha. Farinha, in a series of five articles, resorted to a generalisation, describing the "character" of all Africans based on the inhabitants of the south of Mozambique. Attributing to them various flaws and vices,

---

[13] Ferreira Desusado, "O Negro perante a Pedagogia", in *Revista Portugueza Colonial e Marítima*. Lisboa: 1897, p. 583.

[14] Idem, ibidem, p. 585.

[15] José de Macedo, "A Educação do Negro", in *Revista Portugueza Colonial e Marítima*. Lisboa: 1901, p. 239

[16] Idem, ibidem, p. 297.

[17] Idem, ibidem, p. 288.

with a harsh language, full of improper words, Farinha affirmed that "anthropologically the black is of an extreme inferiority" and that, due to the new diseases which arrived with the colonizers, actual "civilization annihilates them". Quoting Darwin, he concludes that the assimilation would take a long time, if it wasn't impossible, announcing that "the inferior species in the vegetal and animal kingdom, tend to disappear, to give way to other superior species selected by nature"[18].

The end of the 1920's and beginning of the 1930's, coincided with the agony of the First Republic and the affirmation of the Estado Novo, after the "interval" of the Military Dictatorship, and were marked by the development of the periodical editorial activity with the overseas theme. *O Mundo Português* was published for the first time in 1934 by the Secretary of National Propaganda (SPN) and by the General-Agency of the Colonies (AGC); this magazine embodied the so-called "imperial mystique" sustained by Salazar's regime during the 1930's and 1940's.

The magazine published apologetic articles of colonization, stories and "exemplary" poems, photographs of "indigenous" and of "virgin" landscapes, small ethnographic essays and idealized "portraits" of each of the colonies. To preserve are the narratives versing the "indigenous" and their idiosyncrasies. Presented with the usual mottos – indolence, brutality, lack of knowledge of the colonizing language –, the "indigenous" continued to be seen as a big child.

However, certain tales explored a less depreciative aspect, looking to insert them in their "natural" environment without the presence of the white man. Usually, a moralist conclusion ended these texts, being as a sort of literary version of those essays which recovered the myth of the "good savage". Also normal was the collecting of "indigenous" proverbs and thoughts, not contradicting the value of the popular knowledge there manifested.

Despite the omnipresent paternalism and disdain for the colonized, *O Mundo Português* started to insert some apologetic articles of miscegenation. In general, the articles were ambiguous: they did not censor it openly, but did hesitate in recognizing any usefulness. However, one of the first Portuguese followers of Gilberto Freyre, the writer José Osório de Oliveira, gave the name for the future adoption of the luso--tropical theory by the Estado Novo, not inhibiting to demonstrate great interest in the human reality in Cape Verde. It was, however, an exception.

Conclusion

Social Darwinism marked the Portuguese overseas ideology until the 1950's of the 20th century. Despite Darwin, Spencer and Haeckel scarcely being quoted, their teachings gained followers among doctors, publicists and colonists. The inability of the colonised peoples to acquire the beginnings of the industrial civilization was believed. This fact cannot be viewed as strange since science started the dialogue with the "Arian myth", with ancestral beliefs about the Africans as crystallized in the Middle Ages and during the maritime expansion. Thus, the referred periodicals limited themselves to developing and advertising, according to the dominant thought at the time, a racist ideology fixed on stereotypes.

---

[18] *António Farinha*, "A mentalidade do preto V", in *Revista Colonial*. Lisboa, June 1917, no 54, p. 132.

Conceição Tavares

Faculdade de Ciências, Universidade de Lisboa; CIUHCT- Centro Interuniversitário de História das Ciências e da Tecnologia

DYNAMICS AND SINGULARITIES OF SCIENTIFIC APPROPRIATION:
DARWINISM IN THE AZORES

When dealing with the reception of a new scientific theory in Portugal, usually it means the allusion to resistances and difficulties of participants to integrate new concepts and practices. To start with I would like to introduce a different point of view.

Firstly, by assuming that science is a slow, vast and collective construction of facts and practices, some associated with well-known people. The practice of scientists is the living proof of this argument. Historians have arrived at a similar understanding through the identification of the circulation and production of knowledge in courts, universities, scientific societies, and other intellectual circles. It is from the continuous dynamics of these mechanisms of anonymous contributions that, occasionally, and in articulation with a set of external factors to science itself, episodes which come to be seen as crucial, and the great personalities which are often associated with grand scientific narratives, emerge. Although not always evident, the Portuguese are also part of such history because they have always belonged to the pathways of a primeval Republic of Letters which was the structural cradle at the origin of modern scientific networks.[1]

Secondly, underlining the active participation of the Portuguese in scientific works, I would like to introduce the concept of *appropriation*. A very common idea prevails that well-equipped centres, with infrastructures, means and critical mass, produce the major scientific innovations which are later diffused and received in the so-called peripheries, less gifted with people and means. This perspective, based on the *separation* between production and distribution,[2] treats scientific knowledge as if it were a material asset, something that is produced there and used here. This conception, which, furthermore, takes for granted the implicit weakness of the peripheries, ignores an important aspect of the transmission of knowledge: "that ideas and techniques are, more often than not, transformed in unexpected and sometimes starling ways when introduced in a different social and educational context."[3] Peripheries are epistemologically active

---

[1] Ana Simões, Ana Carneiro, Maria Paula Diogo (eds.), *Travels of Learning. Towards a Geography of Science in Europe*, Dordrecht: Kluwer Academic Publishers, 2003; Maria Paula Diogo, Ana Carneiro, Ana Simões, "The Portuguese naturalist Correia da Serra (1751-1823) and his impact on early nineteenth--century botany", *Journal of the History of Biology*, 34 (2001) 353-393.

[2] Kostas Gavroglu, Manolis Patiniotis, Faidra Papanelopoulou, Ana Simões, Ana Carneiro, Maria Paula Diogo, José Ramón B. Sánchez, Antonio Garcia Belmar e Agustí Nieto-Galan, "Science and Technology in the European Periphery: Some historiographical reflections", *History of Science*, 46 (2008) 159.

[3] Idem, *ibidem*, 159.

regardless of their constraints. Peripheries appropriate new theories, new techniques, and new models and become part and parcel of the history of these new practices. Appropriation is, by itself, a process of production of knowledge[4], which includes cultural diversity and intellectual creativity of its recipients, and the different directions taken by scientific interactions. Furthermore, appropriation integrates cultural dialogues stretching beyond the laboratory space over society as is so well illustrated by the case of Darwinist evolutionism.

These considerations were essential to trace the conceptual framework for my interpretation of the reception of Darwinism in the Azores. However, to look at the Azores, it is mandatory to introduce in our narrative Júlio Henriques, a central figure of Darwinism in Portugal, for two reasons: firstly, to identify him as a case of scientific appropriation in a country of the European periphery; secondly, because he was a mediator, that is, one of the agents of the reception of Darwinist evolutionism in the Azores. As it is often the case, this process was neither linear nor single voiced, but it occurred through national and international dialogues of a more or less scientific character, as well as through local controversy and cultural appropriation.

As it is well known, Henriques played a founding role in the reception of evolutionism by natural selection in Portugal. As an answer to the question *Are species changeable?* (1865) Henriques summarises very well the basis of Darwinism and does it to the point of even sharing Darwin's doubts.[5] Although the articulation of the four stages of Cuvier's animal organization with the prototypes presented by Darwin was already an imaginative solution for the compatibilization of different scientific models[6], Henriques' appropriation of Darwin's theory reached a higher level of creativity. In the last chapter of his thesis, "Henriques did not avoid to consider man a product of the same evolution as other animals"[7]— a development only stated by Darwin in 1871, while Henriques phrased it in 1866, in *Antiguidade do Homem* (*The Antiquity of Man*). This is a case in which someone who was not involved in the seminal work of Darwinism appropriated its ideas and arguments to contribute to its development and consolidation.

The construction of a new paradigm is not the work of a single person, as Darwin knew so well. He had always the intellectual honesty to make it clear. The construction of a paradigm does not dispense the scientific creativity of its recipients. In Portugal, many other recipients of Darwin's evolutionism published works which illustrate precisely the plural dynamics of scientific appropriation and are a testimony to Portuguese participation in the construction of evolutionism by natural selection.[8]

The evidence of diversity in the appropriation of a theory can also be captured by the ways a theory permeates into a certain community. In Portugal, the introduction

---

[4] Idem, *ibidem*, 161.

[5] Carlos Almaça, *O Darwinismo na Universidade Portuguesa (1865-1890)*, Lisboa: Museu Bocage, Museu Nacional de História Natural, 1999, pp. 34 and 37.

[6] Idem, *ibidem*, 38.

[7] Idem, *ibidem*, p. 39.

[8] Ana Leonor Pereira, "A recepção do Darwinismo em Portugal", in Ana Leonor Pereira *et al.*, *A Natureza, as suas Histórias e os seus Caminhos*, Coimbra: Imprensa da Universidade de Coimbra, 2006, pp. 14-19.

of Darwinism through French translations of *The Origin of Species* is taken as part and parcel of the received view.[9]

As the writer Eça de Queirós beautifully expressed "By Railways, which crossed the Peninsula, torrents of new things, ideas, systems, aesthetics, forms, feelings, humanitarian interests broke down daily from France and Germany (through France) (...) Michelet, Hegel, Vico, Proudhon, Victor Hugo and Balzac, Goëthe as vast as the Universe; and Poë, and Heine and, I believe, Darwin as well, and many others!"[10] However, that new world "which the North sent us in packages"[11], did not always come by train and did not always speak French, as I will argue concerning Darwinism in the Azores.

The memoirs of Eça de Queirós reporting the intellectual turmoil of Coimbra from 1862 or 1863, take us, precisely, to the years in which Henriques was a university student; a student who loved botany more than the rebellious gatherings of Coimbra, since he was a regular collaborator of an Azorean, graduate of medicine, high school teacher, and assistant of the Botanical Garden, named Carlos Maria Gomes Machado. Machado was in charge of the phytological survey of the country,[12] and one of his collaborators, who collected and drew specimens for the *herbarium*, was precisely Henriques. Most probably this partnership gave way to interesting conversations on scientific novelties, and namely on Darwin's theory of evolution, which Henriques was to advocate in his dissertation thesis.

When, in 1870, Machado decided to go back to the island of S. Miguel, he took with him the naturalist experience and those new ideas. In Ponta Delgada, he became a high school teacher and there he reorganised the natural history cabinet. In this process, which exceeded didactical aims, Machado found new collaborators. One of them was a young autodidact in his twenties called Francisco de Arruda Furtado. The natural history cabinet gradually led to the installation of the Natural History Museum and Arruda Furtado, at first an immature young man eager to learn, became an experienced naturalist with well defined scientific objectives, owing to Machado's guidance.[13]

The network of personal relationships which connected Coimbra to Ponta Delgada was one of the paths through which Darwinism entered the Azores.[14] A good working hypothesis is that Furtado came to its acquaintance through Machado, but not by reading a French translation of *The Origin of Species*. Furtado not only read the book outside the usual academic context but he read it in the English version of 1878. This fact can be verified in the very same book that belonged to him, which is held at the Library of the Museum of Science of the University of Lisbon.

---

[9] The date of the first French translation is 1862. See: Ana Leonor Pereira, *op. cit.*, p. 11.

[10] Eça de Queirós, "Um génio que era um santo", in AA. VV., *Anthero de Quental. In Memoriam*, Edição fac-simile, Lisboa: Ed. Presença e Casa dos Açores, 1993, pp. 484-485.

[11] Idem, *ibidem*, p. 485.

[12] Carlos Machado published the "Catalogo methodico das plantas observadas em Portugal" in the *Jornal de Sciencias Mathematicas, Physicas e Naturaes*, between 1866 and 1869. While incomplete, this Catalogue was one of the sources of *Pharmacopêa Portugueza* edited in 1876.

[13] See autobiographical article of Arruda Furtado, "Sciencia e Natureza", *Era Nova*, 1 (1880-1881) 83-88.

[14] Besides Machado, Henriques influenced many others Azorean students, namely Bruno Tavares Carreiro, a graduate of medicine who returning to the Azores brought with him the passion for botany and the friendship of the botanical garden's director.

In what follows, let us find out who Furtado really was. But before proceeding I want to stress that during 2009, after a century of silence, suddenly, Furtado became a public figure, and a prominent reference in the context of the Darwinian celebrations. But in my opinion, his name was invoked for equivocal reasons: the Azorean naturalist is presented as an almanac curiosity whose importance is reduced to the circumstance of having been the single Portuguese person to have corresponded with Darwin. And people assess his brief exchange of letters with Darwin completely out of context, ignoring the scientific correspondence that Furtado maintained, during almost seven years, with more than 70 correspondents.[15] The idea conveyed to the public is, wrongly, that Furtado's scientific research was originated through the Master's recommendations. Finally, nothing is said about Arruda's scientific work, which is completely ignored. The recent publication of his scientific publications calls for a thorough analysis of his scientific contribution using the standards of international historical scholarship.[16]

Actually, Darwin was not Furtado's first correspondent. In his first letter to Darwin of June of 1881, Furtado already had very clear ideas of his scientific objectives. For instance, in 1880, when he wrote to the arachnologist Eugène Simon, explaining his option to study terrestrial molluscs, he states: "... and since I was very interested in the question of the origin of species, I threw myself into the study (mainly of internal anatomy) which is the most adequate to my taste and, regarding endemic species, completely new."[17] Furtado wanted to produce new knowledge within the theoretical framework of Darwinian evolutionism. He knew the importance of the insular environment to study evolutionary speciation and very early he identified some endemic species. Therefore, he plunged into dissection, description, anatomic illustrations, and systematic comparison with other malacological studies, with special attention to those referring to other Atlantic archipelagos. Simultaneously, he sought for support and scientific guidance from reputed researchers. Furtado not only received positive answers, offers, and requests for sample exchanges, but also providential material and scientific support from two researchers of Yorkshire College in Leeds: the chemist T. E. Thorpe who briefly stopped in S. Miguel and made his acquaintance, and the biologist L. C. Miall. In fact, the latter turned into a tutor for Furtado, sending him not only books, a microscope and drawing material, but also translating into English Furtado's article "*On Viquesnelia atlantica*, Morelet&Drouet" and publishing it in the *Annals and Magazine of Natural History* (1881). This small work described, for the first time, the internal anatomy of a rare species collected in S. Miguel of a *genera* which at the time was only known alive in India and as a fossil in France. The following year it was published in Portugal, in the *Jornal de Sciencias Mathematicas, Physicas e Naturaes*, under the auspices of the Academy of Sciences.[18] Thus, this article stood as

[15] *Correspondência Científica de Francisco de Arruda Furtado*, Introdução, levantamento e notas de Luís M. Arruda, Ponta Delgada: Instituto Cultural, 2002.

[16] *Obra Científica de Francisco de Arruda Furtado*, Introdução, levantamento e estudo de Luís M. Arruda, Ponta Delgada: Instituto Cultural de Ponta Delgada e Instituto Açoriano de Cultura, 2008.

[17] Correspondência científica de Francisco de Arruda Furtado, doc. M.C. 5 [7], p. 29.

[18] Arruda Furtado, "*Viquesnelia atlantica*, Morelet et Drouet", *Jornal de Sciencias Mathematicas, Physicas e Naturaes*, 32 (1882).

the recognition by his peers of Furtado's work, first in England and then in Portugal. Meanwhile, Miall provided Darwin's contact to the young Azorean.

Darwin was already 72 years old while Furtado was a strong-willed 27 year old man. However, there was a deep understanding between them. As usual when speaking to a well-known scientist, Furtado asked Darwin for practical and scientific advice. Nevertheless, he clearly stated his will: "My purpose is to establish comparisons with the continental American and European fauna, in order to throw some light on *the origin of Azorean species.*" To which he added: "I try not to discard any single fact which may bring about proof, as weak as it may be, to your theory."[19] This sentence bears witness to a pro-active attitude of appropriation of a new theory, and is far from translating uncritical adulation of the disciple towards the master. Thus, Furtado expressed his will to participate in the process of scientific construction of evolutionism by natural selection. It is obvious that the methodological advice he received from Darwin held great scientific significance and a particular personal meaning, but let us not mix scientific admiration and lack of intellectual autonomy. The critical and historical analysis of Furtado's work will show, in due course, Furtado's strong personal identity.

Before concluding, I want to argue the case for the phenomenon of appropriation of Darwinism in the Azores via British agents, not via French, as usually assumed. I have already mentioned the English edition of *The Origin of Species* (1878) held in Furtado's library; but I want to add that long before the young malacologist enrolled in the process of scientific appropriation of Darwinism, the islanders of S. Miguel had already begun their own socio-cultural appropriation. The local intellectual elites, who kept in close touch with the literary, philosophical, and scientific novelties, brought them back home from their travels abroad or ordered them from their usual book shops. Thus, from a search at the Public Library of Ponta Delgada, I found nine copies of *The Origin of Species* (editions between 1866 and 1906): of those only three were French, one belonging to Teófilo Braga, and the others were all English. The oldest edition dates from 1866, is in English, and belonged to José do Canto, an important and notorious land owner. Another remarkable fact relates to the Darwinian collection of books in José Bensaúde's library: they add up to eight books by Darwin, all in English, except for one. These books were gathered by a curious businessman, in the past a young close friend of Antero de Quental, who dreamed of being a poet, but owing to lack of resources never managed to get a university degree. His Darwinian library tells us something about the social appropriation of Darwin's work in S. Miguel.[20]

We have to find explanations for the English path to Darwinism's appropriation in the Azores. Besides the cosmopolitism of social elites, one was, no doubt, the direct commercial flux connecting for over a century the English ports to the Azores.[21] Other

---

[19] *Correspondência Científica de Francisco de Arruda Furtado*, Letter from A. Furtado to C. Darwin, June 13, 1881, doc. M.C. 32 [43], p. 107.

[20] Some of these books belonged to other members of the family, namely Alfredo Bensaúde, the founder of the Instituto Superior Técnico, who returned to S. Miguel to succeed his father in the family business administration. The so-called José Bensaúde's library is housed at Public Library of Ponta Delgada (BPARPD).

[21] From the last quarter of the 18th century until the 1870's, there was a regular flux of orange exportation from Azores to England. See Sacuntala de Miranda, *O ciclo da laranja e os "gentlemen farmers" da Ilha de S. Miguel: 1780-1880*, Ponta Delgada: Instituto Cultural, 1989 and Fátima Sequeira Dias,

factors to be explored are the impact of regular cargo ships and passengers' ships connecting Europe to America and stopping at the Azores, and the impact of the ships of the English Royal Navy surveying the Atlantic and frequently scaling the islands. The naval crews had a high level of technical and scientific training and, while on land, they looked for intercourse with similar social circles; in turn, they were sought for by naturalists and occasional explorers arriving there. Finally, I refer to two cases of travellers who did not reach S. Miguel neither by railway, nor speaking French – the chemist Edward Thorpe who was the mediator of Miall's scientific protection to Furtado, and the *Challenger* expedition, well documented for its stops in the Azores.

Although this work is the result of an on-going research, it already brings forward a fresh stand-point to be taken into account by the new historiography of appropriation of Darwinism in Portugal. [22]

"A importância da 'economia da laranja' no arquipélago dos Açores durante o século XIX", *Arquipélago – História*, 1 (2) (1995) 189-240.

[22] The author wishes to thank the collaboration of her FCUL and CIUHCT colleague Júlia Gaspar in the translation of the text into English

José Fonfría Díaz
Departamento de Biologia Celular, Facultad de Biologia, Universidad Complutense, Madrid, España
Alfredo Baratas Díaz
Departamento de Biologia Celular, Facultad de Biologia Universidad Complutense, Madrid, España

DARWINISM IN *LA REVISTA EUROPEA*

Even though in Spain there had been references to Darwin's ideas before the Glorious Revolution of 1868, mainly critical references, the public debate did not appear until the Republican stage, coinciding with a period of scientific recovery (López-Ocón, 2003) in which censorship was abolished and freedom of speech and academic freedom prevailed (Núñez, 1977; Sala Catalá, 1987). The penetration of Darwinist ideas was so important during the Six-Year Revolution (1868-1874) that, apart from the exclusion that many of his divulgers faced during the Restoration (1874-1924), it was impossible to avoid its continuity (López-Ocón, 2003).

However, the appearance of Darwinism in Spain was characterised by strong controversy whose virulence was due to, as Núñez (1977) has said, the inmeasurable degree of illiteracy in Spanish society, the strong economic and political division, a powerful Church allied with conservative powers, reluctant to any idea which could contradict the Biblical text, and the precarious situation of Spanish society.

Taking into account the appearance of Darwinist evolutionism in Spain, it is important to mention the important role played by the intellectual Krausists who accepted and adapted evolutionism to their ideological assumptions (Blázquez Paniagua, 2007). The Krausists had a crucial importance in Spanish thought, culture and science in the second half of the 19th century and the first third of the 20th century, both directly and indirectly. In a direct way, inspiring the political reforms of the Six-Year Revolution; indirectly, through the investigation and education institutions which were created or promoted, such as the Institución Libre de Enseñanza or the Junta para Ampliación de Estudios e Investigaciones Científicas (Baratas, 1997).

On the other hand, the divulging of Darwin's ideas was especially carried out through Ernst Haeckel's (1834-1919) works and articles. Haeckel's ideas rooted among the Krausists, through the discovery of a form of relating positivism with the idealistic philosophy in his Monism as a complete response to the mysteries of the Universe. If the Krausists had defended an idealistic Monism, it was now a positivist, scientific Monism; but the Monist philosophy and the anticlericalism fully clashed with the Orthodoxist Catholicism (Núñez, 1996).

These facts have determined that the line that separated creationists and Darwinists was the same that separated clericals from anticlericals and conservatives from liberals. Darwin became, for some, the archetype of progress, modernity and science, and for others, the representative of anticlericalism, materialism and atheism.

A proof of those debates can be observed in the short life of the *Revista Europea*, published weekly from its first number on March 1st, 1874, to January 1880, included, when it then passed on to be published twice a month, appearing during its last five months, on the 5th and 20th day of each month.

The *Revista Europea* represented one of the pillars of the philosophical reform of the Spanish language created during the last decades of the 19ᵗʰ century. In it, the predominate idea was the interest for positivism and evolutionism and the translations of abundant texts belonging to E. Haeckel, Herbert Spencer (1820-1903), Thomas Henry Huxley (1825-1895), John Tyndall (1829-1893), Karl Vogt (1817-1895), Geroge John Romanes (1848-1894), etc. even though some written texts were published from different perspectives such as those following Neokantianism, Neohegelians, Krausists, etc..

The first reference to Darwin that appears in this magazine is a review of a meeting of the Société de Géográphie of Paris, in which M. Simonin, in an obvious demonstration of social Darwinism, justified the control of the indigenous peoples of North America in reserves as a consequence of the *"fight for existence, in which the inferior races yield with the simple contact of the civilised races"* (nbr. 11, pg.350).

In number 55 (March 14th, 1875), Herbert Spencer signed an article, *La creación y la Evolución* (Creation and Evolution), in which, after proving the inconsistency of the hypothesis of special creations and pointing out a series of facts in favour of evolution, considers that *"under all those points of view the hypothesis of Evolution contrasts in a favourable way with the hypothesis of Special creations"* (nbr. 55, pg. 72).

On the other hand, number 114 (April 30th, 1876) included an article signed by Carlos Martins, which had been published in the French magazine *Revue des Deux Mondes*, in which much evidence was presented in favour of evolution, defending Lamarck's approaches, without citing Darwin at any moment.

Number 136 (October 1st, 1876) includes a study belonging to T. H. Huxley centred on the Protists *(On the Border Territory between the Animal and the Vegetable Kingdoms)* which helps us detect the evolutionist thoughts of its author, the same as *On the Study of Biology* published in number 231 (July 28th, 1878), even though they are not articles especially dedicated to the defense of evolutionist positions.

This defense does appear in Karl Vogt's article on *El origen del hombre*, (The origin of man), published in sequences in numbers 193, 194 and 195 (November 4th, 11th and 18th, 1878), in which he defended the phylogenetic relation between man and monkey through an extensive study of comparative anatomy.

Even clearer in its support of the Evolutionist ideas is the article of the French Physiologist and Anthropologist, Nicolás Joly (1812-1885), *La especie orgánica considerada bajo el punto de vista de la taxonomía*, (The organic species seen under de taxonomical point of view) published in number 217 (April 21st, 1878) and, most of all, in a subsequent article, *Las formas transitorias de las especies* (The temporary forms of the species) in numbers 226 and 227 of June 23rd and 30th, 1878, in which he confirms the existence of intermediate species between the actual ones and the analogous of the fossil record, opposing Cuvier's ideas. Taking into account the origin of these forms, he asks *"were they virtually found included in the organogenic laws? What was carried out when the fixed moment for its emergence came? Or finally, were they produced under the triple and powerful influence of natural selection, of succession* and of the surrounding environment?", answering that *"This last alternative seems more probable to us though we still do not see ourselves authorised to say the most genuine one".*

According to the main line of the magazine, the most important contribution in support of the Darwinist theory is due to the German Naturalist Ernst Haeckel. It starts with an article named *La teoría de la evolución en sus relaciones con la filosofía natural,* (The Theory of Evolution in its relation with Natural Philosophy) published in two sequences, (nbr. 204 and 205, of January 20th and 27th, 1978), without mentioning the translator. In it, besides defending the theory of natural selection and its application to the human species, and of expressing the victory of scientific Monism over Dualism, it presents the necessity of introducing *"the main principles of the doctrine of evolution"* in schools.

In this same year, 1878, another seventeen of Haeckel's articles were published; all translated by the naturalist Claudio Cuveiro. The series started with *Sentido y significación del sistema genealógico ó teoría de la descendencia* (Sense and meaning of the geonological system or theory of descent) (number 228, July 7th) and is continued with revisions of the creationist assumptions of Linneo, Cuvier and Agassiz (numbers 229 and 230, 7th and 14th of July, respectively). Following that, we can observe a revision of all the Evolutionist theories (numbers 231 to 233), dedicating special attention to all questions related to the Darwinist theory (numbers 234 to 242). In the last one *Leyes del desarrollo de los grupos orgánicos y de los individuos. Filogenia y ontogenia,* (Laws on the development of organic groups and individuals. Phylogeny and ontogeny) considered the importance of deepening the establishment of the correct genealogy of the different groups of living beings.

This issue was developed in six extensive articles, also translated by Claudio Cuveiro, that appeared in sequences in different numbers of this magazine. The series started with *Árbol genealógico é historia del reino de los protistas* (Genealogical tree and history of the Protists' Kingdom) (numbers 254 and 255) and continued with *Árbol genealógico ó historia del reino vegetal* (Genealogical tree or history of the Vegetable Kingdom) (numbers 257 and 258), *Árbol genealógico é historia del reino animal* (Genealogical tree and history of the Animal Kingdom) (numbers 259 to 266) and *Origen y árbol genealógico del hombre* (Origin and genealogical tree of man) (numbers 267 and 268). Shortly after, an article dedicated to the *Emigraciones y distribuciones del género humano. Especies y razas humanas* (Emigration and distribution of the human gender. Species and human races) appeared in numbers 269, 270 and 272, including a taxonomic scale with twelve human species. The series finishes with *Objeciones contra la verdad de la doctrina genealógica y pruebas de esta teoría* (Objections to the truth of the genealogical doctrine and evidence of this theory) (number 273) in which he defended the application of the Darwinist theory in order to establish the genealogy of man for *"The evolutionist doctrine gives a purely natural explanation of the origin of man and of the course of his historical evolution and, in my idea the progressive elevation of man through the inferior vertebrates is the greatest success that human nature has obtained over all of its nature"* (nbr. 273, pg. 626).

In number 267 (April 6th, 1879) Oscar Schmidt exposes *Una controversia transformista* (A transformist controversy) between Virchow and Haeckel on the *"theory of descent"*, centred specially in the origin of man, supporting Haeckel's position.

In number 175 (July 1st, 1877) an article signed by G. Gueroult reviews the French translation of the text corresponding to the Philosopher E. Hartmann (1842-1906) with the title *Le darwinisme. Ce qu'il y a de vrai et de faux dans cette théorie*. In his analysis, Gueroult considers that *"natural selection plays a role, but a relatively secondary role; it is, in a certain way, the moderator of the liveliness of evolution"* (pg. 22).

Number 6 (April 5th, 1874) included an article of the Belgian Geologist J. B. J. d'Omalius d'Halloy (1783-1875) in which he defended the possibility that organisms may modify themselves according to the circumstances, but due to a type of divine design.

Even though it only has an indirect relation with Evolutionism, it is interesting to highlight the publication in number 184 (September 2nd, 1877), of an article signed by Darwin with the title *Los preludios de la inteligencia. Bosquejo biográfico de un niño*. [The preamble of intelligence. A biographical sketch of an infant]. It is a translation of an article published in Number 7, Volume 2 of the magazine *Mind* in 1877, with the title *A Biographical Sketch of an Infant*. In this article, Darwin describes a series of observations on the initial processes of the cognitive development of one of his sons. Since Darwin mentions that these observations had been carried out 37 years ago, it is unquestionably his son William Erasmus, born in 1839.

Among the articles contrary to evolutionist ideas we can differentiate two groups: those signed by naturalists, who try to justify their position with more or less scientific reasonings and those who come from the Philosophical field who, generally, show clearly idealistic positions.

Among the first we can find in number 10 (May 3rd, 1874), an article of Louis Agassiz (1807-1873), *El tipo específico*, (The specific type) in which he denied the validity of the evolutionist theory by natural selection insisting mainly in the non--existence of temporary forms in the fossil record, for which *"in the geological succession of animals there is no proof that the relatively modern species come directly from those of remote antiquity"* (pg. 309).

The Spanish Geologist and Paleontologist Juan de Vilanova (1821-1893) published, between number 40 (November 29th, 1874) and number 116 (May 14th, 1876), a series of articles on Paleonthology with the title *Ciencia prehistórica* (Prehistoric Science) based on his lectures as professor, in which you can clearly observe his membership to the field of the Catastrophics. The second to last of these articles, published in number 114 (April 30th, 1876) was dedicated to *La doctrina de Darwin* (Darwin's Doctrine). In it, he shows his resistance to the thought of Darwin's followers because *"Starting from the most genuine representatives of this doctrine of the hypothesis of the eternity of the material, who think, without proving enough evidence in its favour, that this is enough to produce on its own the life represented by vegetables and animals, starting from the most simple organism or Protists, which, obeying certain laws, named of selection and competition for life, are supposed to have been improving and transforming one another/.../But it is the case that, arriving to the actual moment, we observe that each species only produces beings similar to them, without any intermediate ancestor to which the theory appeals in order to explain the origin of the diverse organisms"* (pg. 357), and affirmed a catastrophic criteria based on the lack of intermediate forms.

In the same line we can also take into account an article of the Botanic E. P. Fournier (1834-1884), *Los centros de creación y la aparición sucesiva de los vegetales* (The centres of creation and the successive emergence of vegetables) (nbr. 104, February 20th, 1876), in which he criticises the theory of the centres of creation exposed by A. Grisebach (1814-1879) and substituted it with the successive creations.

From the philosophical field, the Hegelian Philosopher *A. M. Fabié* (1832-1899) published a series of 10 articles, with the title *Examen del materialismo moderno*, (Examination of modern materialism) which was distributed between numbers 40 (November 29th, 1874) and 53 (February 28th, 1875), all marked with an idealistic character. The article on number 43 (20th of December) was dedicated to Darwinism. He presented himself as an evolutionist but accepting Lamarck's approaches against the "struggle for existence" and "natural selection", among other reasons because *"if there were a natural selection, this would show each individual passing on to its offspring those organic modifications which make them more suitable to accommodate themselves to the environment and not those that give them advantage in their fight over its similar or with other organised beings"* (pg. 229). Consistently, the following number (January 3rd, 1875) was dedicated to criticize all of Haeckel's work.

In number 257 (January 26th, 1879) an article was initiated, continuing with numbers 259 (9th of February), 263 (9th of March) and 264 (16th of March), signed by L. Carrau with the title *El darwinismo y la moral*, (Darwinism and morality) in which he accepted the evolutionist character of animals' social instinct but denied that moral sense could have been achieved by man through a progressive process during his history.

On the other side, M. Guyan signed, in number 272 (May 11th, 1879), the article, *La moral del darwinismo*, (The morality of Darwinism) in which he accepted, with certain precision, the evolutive origin of morality, for he considered that, with Darwin's work, *"the empirical genesis of the moral conscience would have never been carried out in such a remarkable way. The theory of natural selection offers a serious confirmation of the inductive morality. This production of the conscience through instinct appears in the mental chemistry as a sign of progress similar to that which has recently carried out the physical chemistry forming with inorganic and organised bodies, producing vegetable substances with minerals, almost creating the plant with the rock".*

Bibliography

BARATAS DÍAZ, L. A. (1997). *Introducción y desarrollo de la biología experimental en España entre 1868 y 1936*. Madrid, Consejo Superior de Investigaciones Científicas.

BLÁZQUEZ PANIAGUA, F. (2007). Notas sobre el debate evolucionista en España (1900-1936). *Revista de Hispanismo Filosófico*, **12**; 1-19.

LÓPEZ-OCÓN, L. (2003). *Breve historia de la ciencia española*. Madrid: Alianza Editorial.

NÚÑEZ, D. (1977). *El darwinismo en España*. Madrid, Castalia.

NÚÑEZ, D. (1996). La religión y la ciencia. *Mundo científico*, **166**, 247-263.

SALA CATALÁ, J. (1987). *Ideología y ciencia biológica en España entre 1860 y 1881: la difusión de un paradigma*. Madrid, Consejo Superior de Investigaciones Científicas.

José Morgado Pereira
CEIS 20, Universidade de Coimbra, Portugal

THE INFLUENCES OF DARWIN'S THOUGHT AND DARWINISM
IN PORTUGUESE PSYCHIATRY

The publication of *The Origin of Species* by Charles Darwin in 1859 triggered a profound scientific and cultural revolution. The image of man and his place in nature became different to that which had been established by the Sacred Texts. Man stopped considering himself as a being separate from the rest of nature, to start considering himself as simply a species among others, from the order of primates and the class of mammals, influenced by the same natural causes which determine them. Thus, a line of thought, still present today, was initiated, explaining man and nature not by religious or metaphysical means, but resorting solely to one science: Biology.

Its influence on the most diverse domains and subjects was great, frequently questioning Theology and Religion, making it possible for "Man to enter the scope of Zoology" and enabling the "disassembling of Theology". Darwin's influence upon Herbert Spencer and Karl Marx was great and Biology became a key discipline. Physicians like Bombarda frequently defined themselves as biologists and physiologists and it is evident now that a retrospective analysis reveals a frequent "biologization" of social facts.

The first evolutionary psychologists understood that individual evolution should situate itself in a broader process of phylogenetic evolution. The German naturalist Ernst Haeckel popularized the fundamental biogenetic law, according to which *ontogeny recapitulates phylogeny*. Also, the onto-phylogenetic parallelism was transferred to the stages of psychological development. We know today that these hypothetical parallelisms taught us little about the more important processes which are produced in psychological development. However, despite the mistakes, these positions were considered progressive at the time because they introduced psychological evolution within a naturalistic framework – until then the reference points had been philosophical or religious ideas.

It did not take long for Darwinism to extend itself into an ideology – social Darwinism – which abusively applied to human society the concepts of "Struggle for life" and "Natural selection", aiming at the rationalisation of violence, misery and injustice, in an attempt to justify the social conditions which characterized the industrial society of the 19th century.

Colonialism also tried to support itself on social Darwinism, through an ordinary usurpation of a scientific theory. Lombroso's publication of *The Delinquent Man*, in 1876, is significant: the Italian criminologist presented a personal interpretation of the Theory of Darwinian Evolution to prove the inferiority of criminals in relation to "honest people", women in relation to men, coloured people in relation to Caucasians, reinforcing the prevailing policies of sexual and racial hierarchy.

The immediate repercussion of Darwin's theory in Psychology and Psychiatry varied. There were clear influences upon William James and James Marc Baldwin and upon the philosopher and teacher John Dewey as well. In the scope of neurology it is the work of Hughlings Jackson which most reflects the influence of evolutionary theories. His interpretive model of neurological symptoms as a phylogenetic hierarchy of disintegration of the Nervous System was a very advanced global concept for the time and had further repercussions on psychiatric thought, mainly upon Henri Ey. Another less direct influence, but also evident, was Sigmund Freud's work based on his theoretical model of Mind in the Theory of Instincts, considering survival instincts, on the one hand, and sexual instincts, on the other.

However, it was the English philosopher Herbert Spencer who, in the 19th century, most strived to erect an evolutionary Psychology, popularising the term "survival of the fittest" and introducing evolutionary matters into sociologic and philosophic theories.

Indeed, social Darwinism is far from Darwin's positions and, according to some authors, should be called "social Lamarckism", because it is centered on the hypothesis of the transmission of acquired characters.

These theories ended up wearing down Darwinist theories among sociologists and the practitioners of human sciences, a reality that extended itself almost until the present.

The influences and the testimonies of the influence of Darwin's work have been the subject of various studies. In this essay, and regarding Portuguese Psychiatry, we mention the importance of the notion of Degeneration, in line with the French psychiatrists Morel and Magnan, which would have a great influence throughout many countries, including Portugal.

The so-called Criminal Anthropology also had an enormous importance in Law, Psychiatry, Criminology, and Legal Medicine.

If we check Patrick Tort's monumental dictionary of Darwinism and evolution, we find the names of Morel and Magnan in France, Maudsley in England, Kraft-Ebing in Germany, Lombroso in Italy, who powerfully influenced our alienists of the end of the 19th century and the beginning of the 20th century. The idea of Degeneration became a broadened basic concept, but it needs to be disclosed, because its meaning changed from the 18th century to the 19th century, only gaining an almost derogatory meaning towards the end of the 19th century.

The problem is that it is not easy to rigorously limit the Darwin/Darwinism or Science/Ideology dichotomy. The physician and politician Brito Camacho writes that "the principle of the *struggle for life* collected from Darwin's observation and applied by him to all biological beings extends to social aggregates and dominates the very complex phenomenability of the world of ideas and emotions".

In 1878, Júlio de Matos, in a letter to Teófilo Braga, mentions that he is writing an essay on the Evolution of Biology in which "I aim to demonstrate that this hypothesis, despite the opposing resistance at first by Auguste Comte, should be embraced by Positive Philosophy". He further adds that he also attempts to justify the criticism which Comte opposed to Lamarck, because for the latter "there was an intrinsic force, predetermined and pre-established, an initial impulse viewed as the most important factor in the explanation of species transformism". And concludes by stating, "this is

176

pure Metaphysics". The question changed form, adds Júlio de Matos, "after the Works of Darwin, Wallace and Haeckel, and I believe that it is impossible today for a positivist not to accept transformism as a legitimate hypothesis. This is the basis of my work". The essay "Ensaio sobre a evolução em Biologia" (Essay on evolution in Biology) appears published in the journal "O Positivismo" in three parts. In it he emphasizes how illegitimate it would be for a contemporary positivist to, despising the achievements of modern science, which are entirely favourable to transformism, insisted in opposing this fertile biological conception; and, in the second part writes: "natural selection is an unconscious fact, the blind product, nothing else, of physical-biological conditions of our planet. The principle does not represent anything more, and it is with the condition that it does not exceed these limits in which Science accepts it and thus, Positive Philosophy".

In volume 4 of "O Positivismo" it was also Júlio de Matos who signed Darwin's obituary, giving public testimony "of the sadness that the loss of that beautiful spirit for which despite the disagreements in many of his philosophical views, attracted our profound sympathy". In 1880, Júlio de Matos publishes his first volume of "Historia Natural Ilustrada" (Illustrated Natural History), which will have a total of 6 volumes. The volume seems written by a naturalist and, as the author indicates in the preface, consists of a rational compilation of everything which has been written on the subject by sages like Brehm, Buffon, Figuier, Milne Edwards and is destined to fill an urgent need: the teaching of natural matters. The author further adds: "from the new works of the transformist school appear principles and thesis which are as of now, undeniable acquisitions of science. We will give them the exposure they deserve as positive and confirmed doctrines. In this case, these principles of struggle for life and natural selection are justly considered the safest and richest of modern natural history". Further ahead, and regarding the question of the origin of man, he explains that the evolutionary school invoked the principles of the struggle for existence, of natural selection, of adaptation, of heredity, quoting Haeckel, Quatrefages, Darwin and Spencer.

Júlio de Matos will remain faithful to his program, especially to the defense of the integration of Darwinian evolutionary principles within Positive Philosophy. Gil Cremades highlights the relationship of Positivism with Republicanism in Spain and Portugal, considering that to support that political project, the reception of Positivism will adapt Comte, admit Darwin's dynamic and reiterate the organicism of Herbert Spencer and adding, curiously, that this process was more conscientious in Portugal, quoting the journal "O Positivismo" and the works of Teófilo Braga and Manuel Emídio Garcia.

The positions of Miguel Bombarda are different. In 1891, in "Traços de Fisiologia Geral e de Anatomia dos Tecidos" he considers that "Darwin's hypothesis is the one that best agrees with the great generality of phenomenons of heredity and its numerous particular laws", but also believes that "the heritage of acquired qualities, which are undeniable, is entirely understandable in the Darwinian hypothesis.". Although valuing the work of Darwin, Bombarda criticizes natural selection, stating that "Lamarckian ideas dominate Science in all of the transformist doctrine" in 1909.

In 1908, Bombarda wrote in the preface of Ladislau Batalha's book "O Negativismo" (The Negativism) that he disagreed with the author when he tried to demonstrate that the supreme lie is altruism and that the fight of egoisms is the condition itself of progress and civilization. For Bombarda, on the contrary, "in all of nature, the cooperation factor has been the superior source of adaptation and evolution" and adds "Darwinian selection, with its heartbreaking and impotent struggle for existence, has had its time" and yet "with prince Kropotkin I would even say, for man's moral progress, more precisely, in a larger extent of mutual help resides the best guaranty of a more upright evolution of our species". We know that the anarquist Kropotkine, regarding the mechanism of organism transformation, supported the decisive importance of the direct influence of the environment over the living being. In his memoirs, he criticizes the conclusions to which the formula "struggle for life" dragged most of Darwin's disciples, adding that "nowadays infamy is not practiced in civilised society or in the relationships of white people with so-called "inferior" races, or the strong and the weak, that do not find in that formula an excuse". For him, "mutual help" (the expression Bombarda also uses) is as much a law of nature as "reciprocal struggle", but for the progressive evolution of a species, the first is more important than the second.

In an essay on *Loucura Penitenciaria* (Penitentiary Insanity), in 1897, Bombarda tries to show the pernicious action of the cellular comfinement on the psychic life of prisoners and accepts the existence of a penitentiary psychosis, establishing a small controversy with Júlio de Matos. Despite his biologist orientation, Bombarda valued the social environment, while Júlio de Matos "tended to view the social question as of bio-anthropological nature" (A.L.Pereira). The differences in political orientation occurring from that divergence of opinion are noticeable: a democracy with socializing tendencies and the primacy of the environment for Bombarda; and the anti-socialist republicanism of Julio de Matos, which appears linked to his defense of Darwinism and evolutionism, and their integration within Positive Philosophy.

Overcoming these conceptions brings us closer to contemporary Psychiatry, implying a distancing from Biologism, understood by the overwhelming weight of Biology and heredity, perceived as an almost absolute determinism.

The interest in psychological life, after important psychoanalytical, phenomenological and human and social sciences contributions, will lead to a distancing, in some cases, of the biological bases of behaviour, which only returned decades later, based on new and distinct scientific principles.

Bibliography

BATALHA, Ladislau – *O Negativismo*, Lisboa, Parceria António Maria Pereira, 1908

BOMBARDA, Miguel – *Traços de Fisiologia Geral e de Anatomia dos Tecidos*, Lisboa, Letterpress of the General Academy of Sciences, 1891

BOMBARDA, Miguel – *La Folie Penitentiaire* in "Revista Portuguesa de Medicina e Cirurgia Práticas" nº14, 1897

BOMBARDA, Miguel – *Estudos Biológicos. A Consciência e o Livre Arbítrio.*, Lisboa, Parceria António Maria Pereira, 1898

CAMACHO, Brito – *A reacção*, Lisboa, Editora Luz Lda, 1932

CONRY, Yvette (Ed.) – *De Darwin au Darwinisme: Science et Idéologie*, Paris, Vrin, 1983

CREMADES, Gil – *La Dimension Politica del Positivismo en España y Portugal* in *Actas II Congreso de la Sociedad Española de Historia de las Ciencias* by Hormigón, Mariano (Ed.), 1984

FERRÃO, António – *Teófilo Braga e o Positivismo em Portugal*, Lisboa, Offprint of the Second Grade Bulletin of the Academy of Sciences of Lisboa, 1935

KROPOTKINE, Pedro – *Em volta duma vida. Memórias*, Lisboa, Tipografia do Comércio, 1907

MATOS, Júlio de – *Ensaio sobre a Evolução em Biologia*, in "O Positivismo" vol. 1, Porto, 1878-1879

MATOS, Júlio de – *História Natural Ilustrada*, Porto, Livraria Universal, 6 volumes, 1880-1882

MATOS, Júlio de – *Carlos Darwin*, in "O Positivismo" vol. 4, Porto, 1882

PEREIRA, Ana Leonor – *Darwin em Portugal (1865-1914)*, Coimbra, Almedina, 2001

TORT, Patrick – *Dictionnaire du Darwinisme et de l'evolution*, 3 volumes, Paris, Presses Universitaires de France (P.U.F.), 1996

TÍTULOS PUBLICADOS

1 - Ana Leonor Pereira; João Rui Pita [Coordenadores]
   — *Miguel Bombarda (1851-1910) e as singularidades de uma época* (2006)

2 - João Rui Pita; Ana Leonor Pereira [Coordenadores]
   — *Rotas da Natureza. Cientistas, Viagens, Expedições e Instituições* (2006)

3 - Ana Leonor Pereira; Heloísa Bertol Domingues; João Rui Pita; Oswaldo Salaverry Garcia
   — *A natureza, as suas histórias e os seus caminhos* (2006)

4 - Philip Rieder; Ana Leonor Pereira; João Rui Pita
   — *História Ecológico-Institucional do Corpo* (2006)

5 - Sebastião Formosinho
   — *Nos Bastidores da Ciência - 20 anos depois* (2007)

6 - Helena Nogueira
   — *Os Lugares e a Saúde* (2008)

7 - Marco Steinert Santos
   — *Virchow: medicina, ciência e sociedade no seu tempo* (2008)

8 - Ana Isabel Silva
   — *A Arte de Enfermeiro. Escola de Enfermagem Dr. Ângelo da Fonseca* (2008)

9 - Sara Repolho
   — *Sousa Martins: ciência e espiritualismo* (2008)

10 - Aliete Cunha-Oliveira
   — *Preservativo, Sida e Saúde Pública* (2008)

11 - Jorge André
   — *Ensinar a estudar Matemática em Engenharia* (2008)

12 - Bráulio de Almeida e Sousa
   — *Psicoterapia Institucional: memória e actualidade* (2008)

13 - Alírio Queirós
   — *A Recepção de Freud em Portugal* (2009)

14 - Augusto Moutinho Borges
   — *Reais Hospitais Militares em Portugal* (2009)

15 - João Rui Pita
   — *Escola de Farmácia de Coimbra* (2009)

16 - António Amorim da Costa
   — *Ciência e Mito* (2010)

17 - António Piedade
   — *Caminhos da Ciência* (2011)